POKOT PASTORALISM

FUTURE RURAL AFRICA

Series Editors
Michael Bollig and Detlef Müller-Mahn

In recent years, there has been a social-ecological transformation in land use in Africa, brought about by climate change and the globalisation of natural resource management and rural landscapes, such that rural Africa has become a laboratory of global future-making. This new series offers a rich and valuable perspective on the processes and practices that produce and critically reflect upon visions of the future on the continent. Volumes within the series will address social-ecological, cultural and economic development in sub-Saharan Africa, and their relation to climate change, sustainability and migration. Showcasing cutting-edge research into societal change and the reverberations of global dynamics playing out in sub-Saharan Africa, the series will provide an essential resource for an interdisciplinary scholarly audience in areas such as geography, anthropology, history, political science, natural science and African studies as well as political planners, governmental and non-governmental organisations.

Published in association with the University of Bonn and Cologne's Collaborative Research Centre 'Future Rural Africa', funded by the German Research Council (DFG), the series will be mainly monographs, but we also welcome occasional edited volumes that enable a continent-wide, multi-disciplinary approach – see https://boydellandbrewer.com/future-rural-africa.

Please contact the Series Editors with an outline or download the proposal form at www.jamescurrey.com.

Prof. Dr Michael Bollig, University of Cologne, University of Cologne: michael.bollig@uni-koeln.de

Prof. Dr Detlef Müller-Mahn, University of Bonn: mueller-mahn@uni-bonn.de

Previously published titles in the series are listed at the back of this volume.

Pokot Pastoralism

Environmental Change and Socio-Economic Transformation in North-West Kenya

Hauke-Peter Vehrs

JC JAMES CURREY

Published in association with
Future Rural Africa

First published 2022
Paperback edition 2024
James Currey

ISBN 978 1 84701 296 8 hardback
ISBN 978 1 84701 376 7 paperback

James Currey is an imprint of Boydell & Brewer Ltd
PO Box 9, Woodbridge, Suffolk IP12 3DF, UK
and of Boydell & Brewer Inc.
668 Mt Hope Avenue, Rochester, NY 14620–2731, USA
website: www.boydellandbrewer.com

A CIP catalogue record for this book is available
from the British Library

The publisher has no responsibility for the continued existence or accuracy
of URLs for external or third-party internet websites referred to in this book,
and does not guarantee that any content on such websites is, or will remain,
accurate or appropriate

To
Kudee Losiwanyang ngisapan ntanyan Kormesek,
Papoyan Chesumkat, ngo yotinechan Chemarkyau ngo Cheptoyö,
Apoitanyan Tepakiang nyo kikonu epogh sapan,
ngo Pokot chopo Tiaty chomoghoi rongo Paka.

and to

Fredrick Kibet Cheretei
(† 17 February 2017)
and
Symon Pepee Kitambaa
(† 17 February 2017)

CONTENTS

ILLUSTRATIONS

Maps

Figures

Photographs

Tables

Full credit details are provided in the captions to the illustrations in the text. The author and publisher are grateful to all the institutions and individuals for permission to reproduce the materials to which they hold copyright. Every effort has been made to trace the copyright holders; apologies are offered for any omission, and the publisher will be pleased to add any necessary acknowledgement in subsequent editions.

PREFACE AND ACKNOWLEDGEMENTS

In 2013, I started work in the interdisciplinary research group at the University of Cologne 'Resilience, Collapse and Reorganisation in Social-Ecological Systems of East and South Africa's Savannahs'. My main interest during fieldwork in 2014 and 2015 was in the relations between pastoral livelihoods and their environments. Anyone who knows East Pokot will be aware that it has an image characterised by pastoral livelihoods, remoteness and the repeated occurrence of violent conflicts between neighbouring ethnic groups. Obviously, this generalising image does not do justice to the pastoral Pokot I came to know. But how can one adequately do justice to the people, the region and their everyday life? This book is an attempt to show the socio-ecological transformations in East Pokot over the last 250 years by illustrating the extent of changes the Pokot have experienced and the ways they have responded to them. This also includes the interaction between changes in the environment and transformations in the social context.

I also want to deliver an insight into a society that is often discredited and at times feared in the broader Kenyan context. In my opinion, this is an extension of the pre-colonial and colonial perspective emphasising the 'ferocious and barbarous character' of Pokot people (Johnston, 1884, p. 295) – a view that is projected onto the group from an external position with little understanding of its internal dynamics. There is a lot that strikes the distanced observer as strange and sometimes even incomprehensible. However, whether we want to particularly emphasise our etic perspective or try to understand and gain a representation of an emic perspective is entirely our decision. Here I want to contribute to an understanding of the pastoral Pokot not just in terms of the inconsistencies that provoke attention, but by delivering an appropriate description of life in the pastoral context. Hence, this book presents two main streams that often reveal the same story and at times even converge: the etic scientific perspective on the socio-ecological transformations and the Pokot perception of these.

Before starting my detailed description of East Pokot livelihoods, I would like to thank the people involved in this research. I am much obliged to Michael Bollig and Georg Klute who facilitated my work in many ways, and to the German Research Foundation (DFG) for the opportunity to have been part of two research groups – the FOR1501 'Resilience, Collapse and

Reorganisation' and the Collaborative Research Centre (CRC) 228 'Future Rural Africa'. I wish to express my utmost gratitude to the members of the CRC228 for their enormous support, and enabling this project to be accomplished in spite of many other commitments. Chapter 9, in particular, with its focus on the evaluation of current developments and pastoralists' aspirations towards the future, is inspired by the work in the CRC228 and by continual engagement with colleagues who have been conducting research in the region north of Lake Baringo since 2018. In addition to extending gratitude to Detlef Müller-Mahn and my CRC colleagues in Kenya and Germany for their great assistance, I sincerely thank Michael Bollig for his invaluable contributions. He enriched this work with his ready guidance, many lively discussions and his extensive engagement in the final formation of this book.

Many thanks also to my friends and colleagues at the Department of Social and Cultural Anthropology at the University of Cologne and my fellows from the research project – especially Gerda Kuiper, Andreas Gemählich, Gereon Heller, Miguel Alvarez, Clemens Greiner, Mathias Becker, Monika Böck, Astrid Hegemann and David Greven – for their support during and after fieldwork. Special thanks go to my dear family and friends, my parents Ina and Peter and my siblings Nadja and Markus, and particularly to Mirijam Zickel, Thomas Wolter, Marius Linnartz, Vera Krieger, Martin Bosak, Meryem Choukri, Georg Bosak, Ruppert Franz and Nina Haberland for adding their perspectives to mine and constantly challenging my worldview. In particular, I thank Michael Casimir, my fellow scholar at the University of Cologne during recent years, for his interest in discussing my results and comparing them to other cases. I greatly benefited from his critical mind and supportive friendship.

Research in Kenya was supported by several cooperation partners at the British Institute in Eastern Africa (BIEA), the National Museum of Kenya (NMK), the Kenya Agriculture Research Institute (KARI)[1] and the Kenya Forestry Research Institute (KEFRI). Many thanks to my colleagues at these institutions, especially Ambreena Manji, Joost Fontein, Helida Oyieke, Humphrey Mathenge, Fabian Ongaya, Janet Njoroge, Teresia Ngandi and Nicolas Gakuu. My thanks to the Kenyan authorities: the Ministry of Immigration, the National Commission for Science and Innovation and the Kenya National Archive, especially the Nakuru office. The fieldwork was conducted in compliance with the Kenyan authorities under the research permit NACOSTI/P/14/9991/2183.

Most of all, I want to express my gratitude towards the people at Mt Paka and my host family in Chepungus. My host father Chesumkat, my host mothers Chemarkyau and Cheptoyö, and their children welcomed me in Chepungus and patiently supported me in my daily struggles. I feel much honoured to

---

[1]   The predecessor of the present Kenya Agricultural and Livestock Research Organization (KALRO).

have been able to share life with you in your homestead, to have joined all Paka people in the community meetings, or simply waited at the water places and been part of the Paka community. Furthermore, I want to express my gratitude to the Paka elders Limatiang, who belonged to the Sowö generation set, and Lomonguria, Tinyanga, Tireng and Nakan, members of the Koronkoro generation set. It is impossible, of course, to thank individually everyone I met during my research, but I would like to express my gratitude towards the many who contributed in one way or another to the success of this project by working with us, spending time in the *kokwö* (assembly of initiated men) together, or simply by letting us spend a night at their homestead. Finally, yet importantly, I want to thank the Chief of the region Amos Losute, the Assistant Chief Wilfred Namuret, the Chief of Nginyang Robert Kanyakera, and Yusuf and Susan Losute for their warm welcome and constant care.

This work is dedicated to all the people of Mt Paka in general and especially to three of my companions. The first is Kudee Losiwanyang, initially my research assistant and later my Kormesek age-set brother. He has contributed to this book more than any other person, and I am grateful that we were able to undertake this fieldwork together. *Soror nyoman!* The other two are the politicians Fredrick Kibet Cheretei and Symon Pepee Kitambaa, who often spent several days and nights at Mt Paka discussing political issues with members of the community. They have been influential in changing my opinion about local politicians, showing how they care about the Paka people in many ways. On 17 February 2017, they were assassinated in Marigat at Lake Baringo. Kibet was the Member of the County Assembly (MCA) for the Loyamoruk Ward (including Mt Paka) and Pepee was a promising candidate running for the seat of Member of Parliament of the Tiaty constituency. Both were charismatic leaders and aimed to connect the hitherto marginalised East Pokot region to national politics. They had captivating ideas about the future of East Pokot, and Kibet's ideas about the prospects of pastoralism are illustrated in Chapter 9. In commemoration of Kibet and Pepee, this book is inspired by their visions for the future of East Pokot.

ABBREVIATIONS

ACK	Anglican Church of Kenya
AIC	African Inland Church
GIS	Geographic information system
FFFM	Finnish Free Foreign Mission
FGCK	Full Gospel Churches of Kenya
GDC	Geothermal Development Company Limited
LAPSSET	Lamu Port, South Sudan, Ethiopia Transport Corridor
PAG	Pentecostal Assemblies of God
SDA	Seventh-day Adventist church
TLU	Tropical livestock unit
UNICEF	United Nations International Children's Emergency Fund

1

Introduction

Much has been written about pastoralism in East Africa, the challenges faced by today's pastoralists and how these groups are transforming their livelihoods and environments in order to adapt to the ever more rapid changes. Kenya is home to many pastoral groups, most of which are in a state of change or have been exploring new forms of livelihood and income strategies off the beaten track of pastoral subsistence in recent decades. The most prominent example is the Maasai who live in both Kenya and Tanzania, and the changing lives of various Maasai groups are well documented (see for instance Hodgson, 2011; Homewood, 2008; Jandreau & Berkes, 2016; McCabe et al., 2014; Spear & Waller, 1993). The consequences of these changes for the groups themselves, as well as the environment in which they live, are not easy to assess. Besides the ecological changes and the resulting impacts on the pastoral economy, it is especially the social organisation of these groups that is transforming, either out of the necessity to respond to the environmental changes or due to emerging possibilities of generating cash income. What all these groups in East Africa, perhaps even worldwide, have in common is the increasing external influences on their livelihood systems.

On the one hand, they face the major challenge of having to deal with environmental change, especially against the background of climate change and in light of the novel character of rapid changes, such as ecological invasions, that occur over a relatively short period of time. The questions arise as to how these often marginalised groups can respond to such changes and also be integrated into the national context both politically and economically, but also how this process of integration of pastoral regions takes place and how this, in turn, affects pastoral livelihoods.

I seek to contribute to answering these questions by describing the history of human–environment relations in a specific group of pastoral people, and thereby going beyond the accounts of the prominent pastoral groups and the stereotyped representation of these in the media. Apart from the famous Maasai and Samburu pastoralists in Kenya and Tanzania, there are many other pastoral groups in East Africa that are facing tremendous changes on different temporal and spatial scales. One such group are the pastoral Pokot people who live in the north-west of Kenya, more precisely in the north of Baringo County that is also known more commonly as East Pokot.

Despite this relative proximity to Kenya's capital (just 300 kilometres north-west of Nairobi), up to the 2010s the region has received little attention as far as national and regional development efforts are concerned and remains dominated by the pastoral livelihoods. On the way from Nairobi to East Pokot, one passes through towns like Naivasha and Nakuru that have become regional centres and developed a great attraction for rural populations, as can be seen in the example of Naivasha with its flourishing cut-flower industry (Kuiper, 2019). But as soon as Marigat and Lake Baringo are passed, it becomes noticeable that this progressive character of these rapidly growing cities has not yet spread northward to East Pokot and how strongly the northern Baringo landscapes remain dominated by pastoral ways of life. These livelihoods are the focus of my descriptions and provide insights into a Kenyan pastoral group that has received only limited attention and is often ostracised in the Kenyan media and political debates.

In recent decades, major social transformation processes gained traction. On the one hand, this is the transformation of pastoral livelihoods in the highland regions of East Pokot towards an agro-pastoral lifestyle with a strong focus on agriculture. Moreover, since 2014, the Geothermal Development Company (GDC) is exploring the previously marginal and rural region, building a road and industrial infrastructure for the exploitation of geothermal energy and opening up inaccessible parts of the region and stimulating social and economic changes. Nevertheless, the pastoralists have so far maintained their focus on livestock husbandry. The social organisation of their communities continues to be constituted by generational and age sets, as does the pastoral economy, which is based on cattle, goat, camel and sheep husbandry. The livestock husbandry of the pastoral Pokot is not static and invariable, but as dynamic and changeable as the pastoral landscape of East Pokot.

In this book, I describe the interaction and history of landscape change and social transformation in a pastoral group that always experienced and to some extent also influenced these transformation processes. I outline the historical ecology of East Pokot, the transformations of the pastoral landscapes over the last 200 years and the continuing changes in Pokot pastoral livelihoods. It highlights three elements of change: the massive reduction in wildlife populations to the point of disappearance, the ecological processes of landscape change (both incremental bush encroachment and rapid ecological invasions), and the social transformations that have occurred in response to environmental changes. Over the last two centuries, the Pokot pastoral landscape and the pastoralists themselves have undergone major socio-ecological transformations. On the one hand, one fundamental component for successful cattle husbandry – the grasses – has disappeared. These have vanished through a long process of transformation that, contrary to earlier assumptions, is not due exclusively to the pastoralists' pasture management, but also to other factors such as the extinction of the wildlife populations in the region that were hunted heavily in colonial times. Over time, the acacia species have taken over large areas of formerly open savannah. The previously specialised pastoralists (with a strong preference for cattle) have had to deal with the landscape changes, and they have responded in different ways by adapting their herd management and partly transforming their livelihoods. Pokot pastoralists, in addition to the continued rearing of cattle, are increasingly raising goats and, in recent years, also camels that do not depend on the availability of grass forage but use the spreading bush vegetation as feed.

Beside the slow bush encroachment of the savannah, recent, rapid ecological processes confront the pastoralists with new challenges. Ecological invasion processes are associated with distinct plant species that are expanding rapidly in northern Baringo County. In the Pokot case, these especially include *Dodonaea viscosa*, *Prosopis juliflora* and *Opuntia stricta*. In contrast to the long-term transformation of the grass plains into a bush savannah, the new processes of rapid ecological invasions leave pastoralists with little room for similarly rapid responses to the changing environment. Moreover, it is not easy for pastoralists to expand their territory or migration range beyond their own region. In the past, attempts to move beyond the Pokot territory have often been accompanied by violent conflicts. Migrations south to the regions west of Lake Baringo and to the hard-fought Laikipia Plateau claim many lives almost every year and provoke the reaction of the Kenyan state that responds in the form of military interventions.

It is therefore important for many members of the younger Pokot generations to develop new sources of income and no longer rely exclusively on their livestock. This reorientation towards different income strategies that diversify their own livelihoods is reflected in, for example, the spread of agricultural activities in the region, the increasing production and sale of alcohol in the local context and the new job opportunities created by state agents involved in geothermal energy production. These social transformations and the different kinds of changes in the environment go hand in hand, and they intensify against the background of current developments. Some pastoralist households in specific regions are focusing on agro-pastoral lifestyles. In addition, the increased presence of the Geothermal Development Company is reinforcing the need for pastoral people to continually integrate external influences into their lives.

This book aims to make a contribution addressing the diversity of socio-ecological transformation processes among pastoral Pokot and also cover current rapid ecological and economic changes. It commences with a review of the pastoral history of the Pokot that began about 250 years ago. This excursion into the pre-colonial history and the further transition through colonial and post-colonial times aims to illustrate how strongly the pastoral economy and the pastoral landscapes were – and still are – subject to a variety of changes. These include not only the intra- and inter-annual changes in the environment but also far-reaching episodes on a socio-political level such as the exploration and hunting activities of European occupiers during the colonial period and the inter-ethnic conflicts with neighbouring groups. On the one hand, these led to strong fluctuations in their territorial spread; but, on the other hand, they were also part of a long-lasting practice of raiding in order to acquire livestock.

In this first chapter, I introduce the framework of historical ecology that guides the analysis and discussion of environmental changes in East Pokot throughout this work. This framework makes it possible to include not only diverse scientific approaches from the natural sciences and the humanities but also local perspectives on the transformation processes. In Chapter 2, I present an introduction to the fieldwork in East Pokot. This chapter briefly describes the methods applied and the challenges I faced.

The following chapter describes pastoral livelihoods and focuses on the formation of the pastoral Pokot in the eighteenth century and their transformation from a specialised cattle husbandry towards a diversified pastoral livelihood system in recent times. The historical analysis of the Pokot settlement in what is now northern Baringo County can be traced back to a time when Lake Baringo, at the southern end of today's Pokot territory, was dried up. This event is still very much present in the oral traditions of the pastoral Pokot. Over the course of generations, the region has changed, and it has been shaped by the explorations of conquerors and colonial powers as well as the ongoing confrontations with neighbouring groups.

After the historical review, Chapter 4 describes the current situation of the pastoralists on the basis of a case study of the pastoral Pokot at Mt Paka. This description of today's conditions not only provides a better understanding of the pastoral livelihoods per se but also serves as a basis for later comparisons when I go on to describe the transformation of pastoral to agro-pastoral ways of life in the escarpment regions towards the Laikipia Plateau.

Chapter 5 then deals with the environmental changes that have occurred in East Pokot over the past 200 years. First, the former pastoral landscape is described and contrasted with the current bush-encroached landscape. Along with results from analysing archival data, two entirely different types of data – local views of forage qualities and satellite images – are analysed and discussed to complement the archive material and illustrate the quantity and quality of land-cover changes in East Pokot and their implications for local livelihoods. It is particularly the combination of different types of data that makes these analyses and their results so rewarding. The archive material allows me to look at the past and examine the pastoral Pokot's accounts of life in past generations and the descriptions of the environment at that time while, at the same time, assessing the extent of the changes. Furthermore, analyses of aerial photographs and time-series analyses allow a concrete quantification of environmental changes over a comparatively short period of 30 years. The results of these analyses, in turn, serve as comparative material for evaluating the emic perspectives that report a rapid change in the environment within only a few decades. The triangulation of these methods and the complementary comparison of the results vividly shows how strongly the environment in northern Baringo County has been transformed not only in the long term but also over the past few decades.

In Chapter 6, I turn towards the agro-pastoral livelihoods in the Pokot highlands and compare their livelihoods with pastoral livelihoods in the lowlands of East Pokot. The application of agricultural practices in this relatively fertile region is also having far-reaching effects on local livelihood systems and changing them from pastoral subsistence to a focus on maize cultivation. However, this change did not take place without external influence. Development programmes introduced maize cultivation in the 1960s and, over time, once-mobile pastoralists have settled permanently. In addition, churches and schools have established themselves in the region and have influenced people's lives through the expansion of education and the introduction of new ideas. I furthermore describe the differences between lifestyles in the agro-pastoral and pastoral contexts in order to explain how socio-economic changes in the pastoral context are also related to specific local conditions. I use this example to show how the transformation of livelihoods has affected the environment in return. This is shown by the ecological invasion of *Dodonaea viscosa* that is rapidly spreading to fallow land and benefiting from land management and cultivation.

After describing different land-use and land-cover changes in the pastoral and agro-pastoral setting, Chapter 7 uses etic and emic explanatory models to discuss the causes of these changes. In this chapter, I first discuss the scientific contributions to environmental change in pastoral landscapes that highlight two factors: the first is the absence of the influence of wild herbivores such as elephants, giraffes and ungulates that were exterminated in the region in the first half of the twentieth century. The second is the pasture management of pastoralists who used fire to regenerate the pasture land. With the bush encroachment in the region and the availability of less grass vegetation below the bush vegetation, it became increasingly difficult to find combustible material for fires that would generate sufficient heat to burn large areas. This land-management practice became even more problematic during the course of population growth and the establishment of new settlements in larger parts of the region. However, the scientific insights into the debate are only part of the explanation. These are complemented by the accounts of pastoral Pokot elders who also relate environmental change to internal factors and the social organisation of the pastoral Pokot. In their opinion, the mistakes of the younger generation sets are particularly to blame for the current situation. The scientific and the local perspectives also differ strongly from each other in how they approach the situation. Whereas science refers to pasture management and restoration, the pastoral Pokot assume that, with the initiation of a new generation set, the internal social problems can also be approached, and this, in turn, will have a positive effect on their environment.

Chapter 8 takes up the different kinds of bush encroachment and discusses the three cases of *Prosopis juliflora*, *Opuntia spec.* and *Dodonaea viscosa* expansions against the background of ecological invasions. These species are common in different regions of East Pokot and they pose very different challenges to the population. Against the background of the different expansion processes of these three plant species, I discuss the concept of ecological invasion, its significance for the Pokot pastoralists and agro-pastoralists and the link between the invasion processes and the impact of changing human land use on the environment. I also consider including inverse processes, which could be seen as a kind of 'evasion', in the analyses of human–environment relations. The extermination of wildlife and the effects this has had on the pastoral landscape over time serve as an example of this.

The final chapter goes back to the notion of continually changing pastoral landscapes. It compares East Pokot to other cases in the broader region and offers an outlook on the future of pastoral landscapes in East Africa. It focuses particularly on various aspects of the possible future of pastoral landscapes and explores the various differences and contradictions between the local and etic perspectives. Whereas the scientific approaches emphasise pasture management and measures to restore the landscape, pastoral explanations rely particularly on anticipating the renewal of pastoralism. Finally, I describe the possibilities and limitations faced by pastoral groups when dealing with rapid environmental changes, and I use the Pokot situation described here to discuss future options of pastoral groups and how they can position themselves in the face of the great challenges of our time.

The historical ecology framework

Pastoral livelihoods, their demise and their revival have been a topic of controversial debate over the past decades, and there have been many monographs and edited volumes on the characteristics, dynamics and conceptual boundaries of African pastoral livelihoods (e.g. Anderson & Broch-Due, 1999; Bollig, 2006; Bollig et al., 2013; Catley et al., 2013; Dietz, 1987; Fratkin et al., 1994; Fratkin & Roth, 2005; Galaty, 1990; Galaty & Bonte, 1991; Galvin et al., 2008; Hodgson, 2000; Homewood, 2008; Homewood & Rodgers, 1991; Homewood et al., 2009; Lind et al., 2020a; McPeak et al., 2012; Reid, 2012; Roth et al., 1994; Scoones, 1994; Spencer, 1997; Westley, 1977). The 'pure pastoralists' paradigm of the pre-1980s has moved towards an emphasis on change and adaptation (Fratkin, 2013; McCabe et al., 2010), more recently emphasising the processes of diversification and state inclusion in pastoral communities (Bollig, 2016; Leslie & McCabe, 2013; Little et al., 2001). Numerous challenges and transformations in pastoral livelihoods in East Africa have come to the fore in recent scientific observations. The many issues that indicate the dynamics of pastoral societies include land loss (Galaty, 2013), bush encroachment (Homewood, 2008; Roques et al., 2001; Vehrs & Heller, 2017), crop cultivation coupled with increased sedentariness (Fratkin & Roth, 2005; Greiner et al., 2013; McCabe et al., 2010), rangeland fragmentation and livelihood transition (Galvin, 2009), commodification of livestock husbandry (Catley & Aklilu, 2013), violence (Bollig & Oesterle, 2008), wage labour (Fratkin, 2013) and development projects and conflicts (Drew, 2018; Lind, 2018).

Degradation is often central to the discussion of changing pastoral landscapes, but it is also frequently presented in the form of a general description of dominant degradation narratives such as soil erosion or biodiversity loss. In the humanities, the disadvantageous changes in vegetation are more or less assumed to prevail, and are therefore described only briefly. As a result, studies often lack detailed accounts of vegetation changes. One might even suppose that the generality of the descriptions has increased with the dominant omnipresence of climate-change and Anthropocene debates. Social and cultural scientists often turn quickly from the examination of environmental dynamics to the supposedly more significant processes of progressive market integration of pastoral groups, the differentiation of rural income opportunities or the increasing social stratification in rural areas.

In this work, I want to take a different approach to environmental changes. A central focus of this work is to examine the transformation of pastoral landscapes with particular attention to the notions of 'invasive species' and 'defaunation' (the local extinction of wildlife species) and discuss different perspectives on several types of environmental change. From a pastoral Pokot point of view, the formerly dominant grass savannah has changed almost everywhere due to encroachment and invasive processes. Over the past centuries, various acacia species have spread aggressively and quickly, initially forming dense stands and then populating entire regions. Grasses can hardly thrive in areas covered with thick populations of thorn bushes. Pokot pastoralists can also specify the species that drove this encroachment: *Vachellia reficiens*, *Vachellia nubica* and *Senegalia mellifera* are identified as the main perpetrators. This extensive and near-ubiquitous land-cover change is contrasted with recent, locally limited invasions. *Prosopis juliflora*, a plant introduced from Latin America for use in anti-erosion projects in the 1980s, has expanded quickly around Lake Baringo. *Dodonaea viscosa* is another invasive species that has expanded rapidly over the past 30 years from the Baringo–Laikipia border area to the west. In contrast to *Prosopis juliflora*, it is not a species introduced into a region from the outside, but a native plant that has penetrated more or less suddenly into new neighbouring habitats, mainly displacing grasses and other bush species. Today, *Dodonaea viscosa* also occupies large areas and makes them unusable as grazing areas.

These descriptions serve as a basis for understanding the agency of invasive plants before addressing the following questions throughout this work: how could such a comprehensive and rapid change of landscape vegetation take place? What are its consequences? And how do local people interpret and evaluate these changes? To understand these changes from a scientific view, which is also informed by local perspectives on the topic, I chose the historical ecology framework in order to gain a better understanding of the processes described and to consider both the surface changes of the landscape and the social transformations as one process whose components interact and influence each other.

Historical ecology, as Crumley (1994, 2018) outlines, is an approach with both ecological (including humans) and historical relevance. Gaining momentum in the 1990s, it is based on the premise that different disciplinary insights can be brought together, that interdisciplinary research can furthermore provide answers to increasingly complex issues, and that local perspectives must also be included to facilitate a better understanding of local conditions and their formation processes. Crumley's approach of historical ecology is not to be mistaken for the historical ecology approach outlined earlier in evolutionary ecology (Brooks, 1985) that had a clear evolutionary background and a disciplinary focus within the natural sciences. On the contrary, she views historical ecology as follows:

> Historical ecologists take a holistic, practical, and dialectical perspective on environmental change and on the practice of interdisciplinary research. Historical ecologists draw on a broad spectrum of evidence from the biological and physical sciences, ecology, and the social sciences and humanities. Together, this information forms a picture of human–environment relations over time in a particular geographic location. The goal of historical ecologists is to use scientific knowledge in conjunction with local knowledge to make effective and equitable management decisions. (Crumley, 2003, p. 1)

The historical ecology discipline attempts to understand human–environment relations over time, looking at the changes in the past and how these have informed current livelihoods and landscape formations. As William Balée describes it, 'historical ecology is a new interdisciplinary research program concerned with comprehending temporal and spatial dimensions in the relationships of human societies to local environments and the cumulative global effects of these relationships' (Balée, 2006, p. 75). The scientific representatives of this approach often distinguish it from other concepts, approaches and theories to create a better understanding of the scope of the historical ecology framework. It is therefore differentiated from environmental history, ecological anthropology, cultural geography, cultural ecology and cultural materialism (Balée, 1998), as well as from sociobiology and evolutionary biology (Balée

& Erickson, 2006). Compared to the popular approach of political ecology, historical ecology focuses more on the historical reconstruction of the socio-ecological transformations of a landscape before applying the insights of landscape development to current issues. Whereas political ecology often has a very strong focus on the examination of different actors and their inter-actions in the (political) field, historical ecology (at least the anthropological branch of it) is often concerned with gaining a better understanding of large-scale socio-ecological interactions. However, it must be emphasised that the boundaries between the approaches are very ambiguous, because both political and historical ecologies are concerned with changing environments, the actors involved and the effects of these changes.

I consider both political ecology – which is often referred to as having emerged from Blaikie's (1985) work on the political economy of soil erosion in developing countries and Blaikie and Brookfield's (1987) book on land degradation and society – and historical ecology, as described and further developed by Crumley (1994, 2003, 2018) and Balée (1998, 2006), as being interrelated and mutually influencing approaches (as can also be seen in the historical branch of political ecology that has been established by, e.g., Offen, 2004 and Mathevet et al., 2015). Whereas political ecology often focuses on analysing political decisions and the interaction and influences of different actors, historical ecology strives to look at today's conditions from a historical reconstruction perspective that refers to influences both natural and of human origin, at how these have influenced each other over time, and at how these continue to have an impact today. The focus on landscape changes and social transformations – in my understanding – is the strength of the historical ecology approach that focuses not only on humans and their views but also on environmental processes and explanations from different angles (pastoralists, scientists) that sometimes do, and sometimes do not, match.

I decided to address the history of pastoral landscapes from the perspective of historical ecology, because the integration of different scientific disciplines was necessary to understand the historical changes to Pokot pastoral landscapes. These could not be looked at in isolation, but had to be combined with local perspectives. In some cases, this went remarkably well – for example in the perception of land-cover change and the reduction of grass forage in the last decades. Herders can present a detailed picture of how their situation has changed, which grasses have disappeared, and which regions have been particularly affected; and, at the same time, they can describe the effects on pastoral livelihoods and the changes in the pastoral economy that followed. For instance, the geographic information system (GIS) analysis then clearly demonstrates the extent of these changes – and also makes them comprehen-sible to everyone who is not familiar with the situated knowledge in eastern African pastoral societies – and shows that this process has been and will continue to be rapid. Nonetheless, there are also results that do not match each other, such as the explanations for the reasons behind environmental change. Whereas scientific analyses refer mainly to environmental changes such as defaunation processes, changing fire regimes, or land-use changes as main drivers, Pokot elders usually state that the main cause of the environmental changes is internal social conflicts, and that such changes may also reverse themselves in the future. It is important to understand such discrepancies.

The focus of historical ecology on broader landscapes, their transformations and the diversity of human and non-human actors is probably one of the most important characteristics that differentiates it from other approaches. The landscape term is chosen as an analytic tool, because landscapes 'record both intentional and unintentional acts and reveal both humans' role in the modification of the global ecosystem and the importance of past natural events in shaping human choice and action' (Crumley, 2003, p. 2).

In 2017, an article was published by a group of researchers – among them Carole Crumley and Péter Szabó – who identify 50 questions that are key to the field of historical ecology. Although the framework of historical ecology is not yet institutionalised and has no definite methodology (Szabó, 2015), it unites several scientists from various disciplines with similar interests in human–environment changes in the past, present and future (Balée & Erickson, 2006; Swetnam et al., 1999; Szabó, 2015). Balée (1998, p. 14) describes historical ecology as a 'viewpoint, rather than as a field or a method per se' and Erickson focuses on a better understanding of human–environment relations to create a better future, as the following quotation shows:

> Humans do not adapt to a given natural environment, but rather are exploiting the past, complex human history of the landscape; partaking in the accumulated landscape capital created by their ancestors. Rather than passive responders or adaptors to a given environment as stressed in the traditional approaches, historical ecologists view humans as active agents in their interaction with nature who promote change and continuity through culture. The landscape, the central conceptual structure for historical ecology, is the physical manifestation of the long-term human history of the environment. The goal is to document and understand the long-term creation of the environment as we know it today. This understanding may provide models for strategies of conservation and management of the environment in the present and future. (Erickson, 2003, p. 456)

Historical ecologies and related approaches

The historical ecology framework is used in various ways to pursue different interests. Szabó (2015) identifies three main trends: the anthropological (referring to Girel, 2006), the ecological (referring to Bürgi & Gimmi, 2007) and the conservation/restoration trend (referring to Szabó & Hédl, 2011).

Whereas all three perspectives demand a detailed study of the landscape transformations to understand the dynamics that inform the current landscape shape,
the first two trends focus more on understanding specific historical–ecological
cases. The third trend, focusing on conservation and restoration, however,
goes one step further and claims to apply the results of historical–ecological
research in praxis to inform land-management processes. The representatives
of restoration ecology focus on the construction of future landscapes and the
extent to which humans can influence these transformation processes. This
'applied historical ecology' uses 'historical knowledge in the management of
ecosystems' (Swetnam et al., 1999, p. 1189). This branch of historical ecology
has expanded rapidly over the past two decades, indicating an increasing
interest in control over landscape construction and restoration. As mentioned
by Egan & Howell (2001, p. 1), 'a fundamental aspect of the work of ecosystem
restoration is to rediscover the past and bring it into the present – to determine
what needs to be restored, why it was lost, and how best to make it live again.'
The restoration of the landscape can happen in many ways such as wildlife
restoration (Morrison, 2002); prairie, savannah or woodland restoration
(Packard et al., 2005); or ex-situ plant conservation (Guerrant et al., 2004).

Interest in the restoration approach in historical ecology is increasing with
a growing trend towards systematic research and the practical application of
its results (Clewell & Aronson, 2007; Howell et al., 2005). Perhaps the most
famous project of recent times is the Pleistocene Park of Sergey and Nikita
Zimov in Siberia (Zimov, 2005). The two scientists are trying to restore a
steppe ecosystem that they identify as being the dominant ecosystem in that
area 14,700 years ago (Pleistocene Park, 2018). Their goal is to store carbon
dioxide in the permafrost soils of the tundra. They argue that the wild animals
of the tundra, such as mammoths and others, constantly demolished the snow
cover that itself created a cooling effect on the permafrost soils. Since the
wildlife populations have greatly decreased and the ecosystem has changed,
the two scientists have been trying to restore the former ecosystem by introducing new wildlife populations and imitating the mammoth inhabitation
with technological solutions. This project is linked to the claim that humans
must mitigate the consequences of global climate change and, in this case,
protect the carbon sinks of the permafrost soils through ecosystem control.
The results from the analysis of the past are therefore used to create and
design a better future.

However, the aim of my study is not to manage the East Pokot ecosystem
and construct a more suitable future. In line with the anthropological branch
of the historical ecology framework, I seek to better understand the complex
transformation processes of the landscape and all its inhabitants over the period
of the last two centuries since the formation of the Pokot pastoral people in
the Baringo plains. With the focus on landscape transformation and several
(human and non-human) agents of land-use and land-cover change, I argue

against the idea that pastoral land users are invariably and perpetually responsible for land-degradation processes (Hare et al., 1977). Rather, I would bring
forward the argument that historically grown trajectories continue to have
an effect on contemporary pastoral landscapes. The impacts of non-human
landscape agents such as wildlife or fire also have far-reaching effects on the
landscape and therefore influence the possible land-use opportunities that an
ecosystem provides. With regard to the history and use of fire, Kull (2004)
offers a particularly detailed account of the problem in Madagascar, outlining
the different facets and entanglements of a multitude of actors with conflicting
goals, and emphasising the acknowledgement that there is no simple 'for' or
'against' the use of fire. He describes the historical and present use of fire
in Madagascar for the harnessing of resources – for example, in the pastoral
context – but also the adoption of an anti-fire narrative that is used by national
and international actors to establish a link between fire and land degradation.

My research has been inspired by a variety of studies, both that have offered
in-depth accounts from the local context such as Anderson and Broch-Due
(1999), Anderson (2002), or Bollig (1992a), and those that were in the vanguard
of promoting local perspectives and situating these within scientific discourses
such as Fairhead and Leach (1996) or Leach and Mearns (1996). The last two
books demonstrate the importance of a scientific examination and contestation
of prevailing narratives over, for example, degradation processes and their
linkages to land management, as well as the assessment of local people's
positions in these processes and their responses to them.

The authors in the edited volume by Leach and Mearns (1996) describe
how much the degradation narrative was anchored in a variety of contexts and
taken up by so-called experts of different scientific, political or developmental
persuasions, thereby reinforcing the crisis perspective on the African continent.
This perspective of a 'natural' and 'pristine' vegetation and the disturbance
of a 'natural' balance is contested by the authors, as is the assumption that
any change in the landscape is a deviation from a state of equilibrium and,
consequently, a process of degradation. Fairhead and Leach (1996) likewise
use their book about misreading the African landscape to describe the history
of various experts' misinterpretation of the degradation of a larger forest based
on observing a patchy forest mosaic in the West African forest savannah. The
authors debunk these arguments, showing that no such degradation occurred,
but rather that the practices of local farmers helped to establish the forest
islands and not to destroy the forest area. Both books advocate the importance
of understanding the history of transformational processes in the local context
and integrating local perspectives on landscape change.

Anderson (2002) draws on the ideas of Fairhead, Leach, and Mearns and
describes how prominent the narrative of a 'land in decay' was in Baringo
County as documented by colonial officers, with its strong signs of degradation
due to drought events but also due to overstocking and ineffective pasture

management. Anderson delineates the extent to which colonial ideologies and development agendas have continued to shape the region's history, and how the colonial construction of the degradation narrative protected the interests of white settlers. Whereas pastoral groups were accused of overexploiting resources, the territories of the European settlements were kept exclusive, and pastoral groups were forbidden access to and use of these resources by prosecuting them for trespassing.

In the edited volume of Anderson and Broch-Due (1999), the authors furthermore emphasise the perspectives that pastoral groups take on their ways of life. In contrast to the external assumption that pastoralists in eastern Africa are subject to poverty often triggered by ecological crises, the pastoral views are emphasised that define poverty in a different way than outsiders assume. It is rather the stockless herder who is affected by poverty, and diverse strategies exist to protect the individual from it such as the redistribution of livestock along social networks. The strength of this work lies above all in the shift in perspective and the presentation of local positions on the topic of poverty, as well as in the explicit criticism and deconstruction of stereotypes and preconceptions about pastoral groups.

Bollig's (1992a) monograph explores the social organisation, the pastoral livelihoods, and the significance of intra- and inter-ethnic conflict among the pastoral Pokot in northern Baringo County. In this, the most detailed ethnographic work about Pokot pastoralists altogether, Bollig manages to cover both the history of the region and the formation of the pastoral Pokot in the eighteenth century. He takes a position that emphasises emic explanatory approaches and does not attempt to ascribe a priori a meaning informed by an academic orientation. The strength of his work lies especially in the description of local livelihoods, the organisation of the pastoral economy, and the role of intra- and inter-ethnic conflicts for the pastoral society.

I want to follow up on their examples and dedicate my attention to a region that was of less concern in Anderson's book: the area north of Lake Baringo. As I shall show, the narrative of degradation was also omnipresent there from a colonial perspective. However, I shall also explore how other factors influenced landscape change in the nineteenth and twentieth centuries, but were largely underestimated in the reports of the colonial administration. For instance, the processes of soil erosion and degradation cannot be understood from the perspective of overstocking and overgrazing alone, but must also take into account those influences that initially were not linked to them. These include not only big-game hunting by colonial Europeans and the associated local extinction of big game (defaunation) that altered the landscape composition, but also changes in the fire regimes that kept the savannah open. This shift in perspective will contribute to a better understanding of the complexity of the landscape history that has led to the current situation.

2

East Pokot: A Place and its People

The Tiaty Constituency,[1] formerly known as East Pokot District – is located in the north of Baringo County and extends over an area of approximately 4,500 km² in the East African Rift Valley with an official population number of about 153,344 (Republic of Kenya, 2019). Lake Baringo is located in the south of the constituency's boundaries, and the Rift Valley escarpment rises in the east and the west of East Pokot towards Elgeyo-Marakwet, Laikipia and Samburu Counties.

Fieldwork was conducted in Chepungus on the southern slopes of Mt Paka, an extinct volcano in central East Pokot right in the centre of the Rift Valley. Most of the research was done in the Paka community,[2] which consists of

---

[1]   The official naming of what I refer to East Pokot has continually changed over the past decades and especially in the course of the devolution process. Throughout this book I will refer to the region that is currently named Tiaty Constituency, and that today includes the sub-counties Tiaty East and Tiaty West (Republic of Kenya, 2020b), as East Pokot. In official accounts, it was also named Tiaty East and East Pokot (e.g. in the 2019 population census), which creates confusion in some cases, as the Tiaty Constituency has also been referred to as East Pokot District before (e.g. in the 2009 population census). The Tiaty Constituency currently consists of seven wards Churo/Amaya, Kolloa/Loiwat, Loyamoruk, Ribkwo, Tirioko, Tangulbei/Korossi and Silali, each represented by one member of the County Assembly (MCA).

Having the problem of continuously changing terminology in mind, I follow the tradition of earlier researchers such as Michael Bollig, Mathias Oesterle and Clemens Greiner, and use the name East Pokot to describe the region in the north of Baringo County that is inhabited by Pokot people. In contrast to the West Pokot County, where mainly agro-pastoral Pokot reside, the East Pokot territory with mainly pastoral Pokot constitutes the counterpart to its western neighbours. Furthermore, East Pokot resembles the term that is colloquially used on an everyday basis within the region..

[2]   The term 'community' is used to define the group of people involved in the research. The people on Mt Paka do not constitute a closed unit, but rather a group of people among the pastoral Pokot. The rigid concept of a community does not account for the high mobility of pastoral people. The mountain community on the southern slopes of Mt Paka is artificially defined and is by no means a coherent, self-contained community, but open to and in exchange with the surrounding pastoral Pokot people. Rather, the Paka community was specified to create a limited research unit that would be manageable during fieldwork and comparable to the agro-pastoral 'community'

approximately 600 people who speak the Pokot language and, to a limited extent, Kiswahili.[3] My interest focused on the pastoral ways of life, how environmental changes are having an effect on pastoral livelihoods and how both changes in the environment and social transformations influence each other. I decided to live in the pastoral parts of East Pokot extending from Lake Baringo in the south up to Silali and the Tiaty mountains in the north. Due to violent conflicts with Turkana pastoralists in the north and a rising conflict over pastures with Il Chamus and Tugen people in the south, I chose to live in central East Pokot.

The taste of fieldwork

Immersion into the field did not happen in a pre-determined, logical way, but, as in most anthropological fieldwork, largely intuitively. This intuition includes the senses, especially those over and above the visual dimension of fieldwork. Although visual experiences of the field often dominate in first impressions, tasting, smelling, and feeling the field are, in many ways, just as important. To live with the people in the field and share the same experiences and life-world, instead of imposing our own reasoning on them, makes an important difference for anthropological fieldwork. As Stoller describes for his research among the Songhay in the 1970s, people would lie to him if he did not 'learn to sit with people' (1989, p. 128). Most often, the preconditions of friendship and mere collaboration are shaped differently in the field. To be *with* people includes more than mere presence and frankness. It requires sharing feelings, understanding daily interactions and apprehending the context of everything that is said during fieldwork. Therefore, the researcher must learn both the verbal and the non-verbal communication as well as the implicit rules of daily interaction that are also learnt through participatory observation.

I consider participatory observation not as a technical method to gather data in the field but as an intuitively applied research method positioned between the extremes of participation and observation. With reference to the question 'How close is close enough?' (Coy, 1989, p. 107), we always have to ponder on our roles in the field. Nevertheless, participatory observation was the main approach with which to become acquainted with pastoral life in East Pokot. Spittler (2001) correctly claims participatory observation as an unsystematic approach that is able to explore the blind spots in systematic

---

in the East Pokot highlands located on the eastern escarpment towards the Laikipia Plateau.

[3]   At the time of fieldwork between 2013 and 2015. The rapid changes and social transformations described in this book are also occurring on Mt Paka; and especially the infrastructural projects of the GDC company are accompanied by a spatial reorganisation of households and the adaptation of language skills.

approaches. Furthermore, Ingold states that participatory observation itself is 'knowing from the inside' (2013, p. 5). Therefore, fieldwork can be considered to be a learning process and a transformational process in the researcher who aims to engage in research *with* a group of people instead of carrying out a study *about* this group (Ingold, 2013). In this sense, participatory observation was not used as a tool for data collection but as an approach with which to constantly learn with the people of Mt Paka; which in the case of a mobile pastoral group, also included walking long distances in the field. Walking as a method is described in the following as a distinct component of participatory observation, and its methodological implementation is demonstrated with a short excerpt of my walking diary compiled during a three-week walking trip through East Pokot.

The field walk

When the idea of an extensive walking trip first materialised, I intended to search for the greener pastures of the past that had been mentioned in many stories about former generations of Pokot pastoralists. Besides the descriptions of early colonial explorers in the nineteenth and twentieth centuries, Bollig (1988), who conducted research among pastoral Pokot in 1987/88, also describes the plains of East Pokot as open places with many grasses. At that time, some places, such as Mt Paka and the Moruase hill, still possessed special properties for the pastoral community. Mt Paka was a dry-season forage storage, and Moruase was a grassland reserved for calves during the dry season. However, since my arrival, I had never come across these beautiful pasture lands, and merely some parts of Mt Paka still give a glimpse of the pasture land that formerly existed in this region.

Against this background, together with Kudee and Kortin,[4] I went on an uncharted tour to search for the greener pastures, starting in central Pokot at Mt Paka. The everyday interaction with the land and its people and the exposure to life on foot made it possible to encounter a story along our way that gives an interesting account of what it means to dwell in East Pokot. This walking tour engaged in the subjective perception of, and immersion into, a landscape that was the object of my research in many ways though often difficult to approach methodologically.

---

[4] Kudee was my assistant during fieldwork in East Pokot and Kortin our friend from a neighbouring homestead who agreed to accompany us on our walk through East Pokot and explain to me the particular features we discovered on our way.

Walking through East Pokot

> We cannot simply walk into other people's worlds, and expect thereby
> to participate with them. To participate is not to walk into but to walk
> with – where 'with' implies not a face-to-face confrontation, but heading
> the same way, sharing the same vistas, and perhaps retreating from the
> same threats behind. (Vergunst & Ingold, 2006, p. 67)

Walking is an essential part of daily life in pastoral societies and was important
for my fieldwork at all times. Vergunst and Ingold (2006) explore the role
of walking for anthropologists during fieldwork and detect various ways in
which people interact with their environments.

With reference to their work, I similarly had to understand the mobility of
the people in East Pokot, and I wanted to understand the ways pastoralists
perceive and interact with their environment. The relatively slow speed of
walking enabled me to observe our environment in a more detailed way, and
the breadth of my observation was larger compared to that gained through
faster forms of movement (Vergunst & Ingold, 2006). During fieldwork, I had
to learn how to walk the rocky paths and hidden tracks in the way that others
did, and how to understand the landscape as my Pokot fellows instructed me
to do. Over time, I developed a routine and discovered a variety of stories
along different paths. Walking became a vital way of gathering and exchanging
information.

Therefore, walking was highly important during fieldwork and merits
methodological consideration. First, the pastoral Pokot move mainly on foot
every day; and hence, walking becomes an instrument for sharing experiences
and creating a shared space (Wikan, 1992; Tambiah, 1999). Second, walking
is not merely a form of movement. Walking with the people leads to encoun-
tering daily interactions, to gaining basic information about the community
and gossip about people and, finally, to becoming acquainted with the people
and the places of fieldwork. Third, extensive walking trips create unique, slow
and intense moments of discovery. Whereas anthropologists are often caught
between the acts of participation and observation, walking is an activity that
allows the researcher to assume a role that enables the surroundings to be
observed in detail.

The following describes a short section of the third option – the extensive
walking trip – and provides an insight into life on foot and the character of the
extended field. Some topics stood out at the time of the walk – for instance the
absence of the rains and its effects. Other matters address long-term developments, such as environmental changes and the introduction of crop cultivation.
The walk increased both my understanding of the current situation of Pokot
pastoralists and an awareness of the changes that have occurred in the past
that strongly influenced pastoral livelihoods.

Walking diary – epitome

Day 15 – 19 July 2015

Today we dedicate ourselves to Mt Paka right at the heart of East Pokot. Mt Paka is an important mountain, the home of the spirit of the rains (Ilat) and the highest mountain on our tour with an altitude of 1,700 metres above sea level. Since we started our research, we have dwelt on the southern slopes of Mt Paka in a place called Chepungus. This side of the mountain is densely populated, probably due to the permanent water source close by in Topogh. In Topogh, water gathers in a small crater along a riverbed and creates a small water body that also provides water in dug pits during the dry season. Oral histories refer to a comet that struck here long ago and formed the current water body. Other water sources are the dam in Lolemoi, the borehole in Adomeyon that opened at the foot of Mt Paka in 2014 as well as the water service of the Geothermal Development Company, which started its vast project in 2014. Nowadays, the natural shallow dams (takarai), which were often used in the past for water collection during the rainy season, are mostly silted up.

A high density of cultivation is found on the southern slopes of the mountain in the places called Lolemoi, Chepungus, Katapodin and Imampoet. This extensive area of cultivated gardens had dried up completely during the last few weeks. Moreover, the southern slopes of Mt Paka are overgrown by acacia species. Especially Vachellia nubica *is successfully infesting fallow cultivated gardens or abandoned homesteads. However, these impressions should not deceive us. Mt Paka has, like the other mountains in the region, a high diversity of plant species. The higher the altitude, the fewer acacias are observable, except for* Vachellia xanthophloea, *which grows at higher elevations. The inimitability of Mt Paka is also observable in respect to the last remaining pasture land in East Pokot, which begins at 1,300 metres above sea level towards the top of the mountain and extends over the complete northern slopes. All those grasses we missed during our journey over the past three weeks grow here.[5]*

In the crater, with all its gushing springs, another grass grows, called suswo kaa pa Ilat *(the grass in the house of Ilat). The crater is the home of Ilat, the spirit of rain, the messenger of the deity Tororot.[6] When the*

---

[5] These are identified as *chaya, koserinyan, churukechir, purteyon, cheluwowes, chesowoyö, awawatian, kipaupau, puresongolion, angoyelek, mukun, seret, moikut, amerkwoyon, pekonion, puyun, chepkaner* and *chemwania* (see Appendix).

[6] Peristiany (1951) describes the *sapana* initiation of men in the mid-twentieth century and locates the home of the Ilat as Mt Mtelo in West Pokot. This differs from my recent observations. Furthermore, Peristiany (1951) mentions that none of the

lightning appears in the crater during heavy thunderstorms, Ilat comes home and brings rain to Mt Paka. The lightning itself is part of Ilat.

*If fire breaks out on Mt Paka, a ritual must be performed for the mollification of Ilat. During the ritual, the men of Mt Paka gather in the crater and pray. They also bring four ostrich feathers (*songol*) and four lambs that are all left behind at the gate to the house of Ilat. Ilat takes everything and the next day the gifts are gone without a trace.*[7] *Some inhabitants of Mt Paka also believe that Ilat left the region long ago, as signified by the recent droughts and the misbehaviour of youths, alcohol production in the community and the GDC road construction. In the past, someone who caused a fire on Mt Paka had to sacrifice a big bull from his stock for the* kokwö *(assembly of initiated men). However, this is no longer practised nowadays.*

*To my surprise, I discovered the first cultivated garden in the crater. In recent times, this region was renamed Paren (Kipokot [the Kiswahili name for the language of the Pokot people]: 'garden'). Otherwise, the region around the northern slopes of Mt Paka is uninhabited except for the temporary houses of young herders (*kaa kapariök*) who live seasonally here with their cattle.*

Concluding, a respected elder, who was born in the region, tells the late history of Mt Paka.

In 1963, Mt Paka was open with plenty of grasses. No stone could be seen, only grasses. You walked until you hit a stone [hidden boulders]. Mt Paka was open, overgrown with grasses, and without trees. There were *chaya, churukechir*, even *cheluwowes*.[8] All grasses grew on Mt Paka, also the one called *puresongolion*, and *chemwania*, the bitter one, and another one called *nyuswo*.

Trees were scattered, such as *kram. Okop* was also available and *chuwuw*, but they were few. It was even hard to find branches to fence the calves. *Panyarit* was not around before, only *pelil*, at the foot of Mt Paka in a place called Apawoi. *Talamogh* was very scarce.

---

deities or spirits (Tororot, Ilat or Asis) were mentioned during the ceremonial killing of animals in the *kirket* (half-circle of men conducting the ceremony). Nowadays, this is also different in the case of pastoral Pokot in East Pokot who refer to all three of them.

7   Bianco (1996) gives a similar description of the interaction between people and Ilat when she recalls the constructive and destructive actions of Ilat.

8   The plant names in the text and in interview sequences are reduced to a minimum for better readability. On a few occasions, either the vernacular or the scientific names are used to illustrate specific processes – for instance biological invasions. The vernacular and scientific names are both listed in the appendix.

And today? Can you see the ground? You cannot see Mt Paka itself. When you go up the mountain, trees are all over, covering the place. You cannot even see down to the plains when you stand on a hill. All trees are growing in Mt Paka now and nobody knows who sent them. *Okop* is in full swing, even *renoi*. *Cheptuya* is another one that was present in Mt Paka in the past, which is gone now – just like *chuwuw*. Those that were here in the past are scarce now. In the past, *chuwuw* was used as a fence for calves. Cows were not fenced in; they were sleeping on the ground.

Fenced gardens just came recently, around the year 2000. Before, we had no cultivated gardens in the whole area.

Area history – 20 July 2015 with Nakan

Postscript

The walking tour led to interesting impressions that could be linked to many observations and narrations about East Pokot and the pastoral livelihoods there. I realised that pastoral livelihoods are presently going through a difficult time: water and grass forage are scarce. This scarcity leads to people and livestock migrating beyond the borders of East Pokot. Migration does not seem special in a pastoral society, but the out-migration often causes conflicts with neighbouring groups and is also affecting the people in East Pokot in other ways.[9]

Along with the perceived pasture reduction, the expansion of bushy vegetation is highly important to pastoral people. Especially, growth of acacia species seems to have expanded in most of the places in East Pokot. Although a general trend cannot be derived from mere observations, the stories about the past indicate a vast spread of bushy vegetation at the expense of grass.

The unique access to the field through this method makes it a valuable complement to standardised ethnographic methods. Following Spittler's (2001) claims that it is especially thick participation that shapes access to the field and to scientific knowledge in ethnographic studies, I would like to locate the method of 'walking' within the thick participation approach. Particularly in the context of research with pastoral groups, this method makes it possible to record unsystematic data – data that are particularly important due to their 'experience-near' character (Geertz, 1974) and their relevance in the local context. Of course, this method does not stand alone, but must be seen in the

---

[9] For instance, when conflict arose in Kapedo in 2014, the government sent the army to bring the situation under control. Furthermore, the only tarmacked road from Marigat into East Pokot is sometimes blocked when Tugen or Il Chamus are the target of Pokot raids. These road blocks then also affect every other person in the region when livestock markets remain empty.

context of a comprehensive ethnographic study based on not only non-standardised but also standardised systematic methods.

However, the methodological approach and the implementation of methods were not the only challenges I faced over the course of fieldwork. There were many situations and circumstances that not only influenced fieldwork but also challenged me in very different ways. These are described briefly in the following to make the context of fieldwork with pastoral Pokot accessible and the limits to such work easier to understand.

Reflections on fieldwork

When I started my research in Kenya, the idea of a conventional field experience exerted a strong force of attraction. I wanted to live with a small pastoral group in north-western Kenya for at least a year. In retrospect, I have the impression that my fieldwork was worthwhile, and I am confident that I opted for the appropriate fieldwork method. Nonetheless, the wonderful experiences I had were accompanied by intense situations for which I was not always prepared.

In the following, I focus on two very different types of challenge I faced during fieldwork: the ordinary, and the exceptional. Ordinary situations included everyday occurrences and ritual participation, and frequently involved dealing with what were, for me, unfamiliar Pokot conceptions of sickness and death. Adapting to different epistemologies resulted in me changing incrementally. While I gradually assimilated to my surroundings, my fieldwork also featured exceptional events that assailed me with surprise and feelings of helplessness. The sudden rupture of everyday life was epitomised by the 2014 execution of an army operation against some 'culprits' within the group of Pokot. Both everyday and exceptional experiences had profound effects on my understanding, on my writing and on me personally.

My intention here is to go beyond a mere description of experiences. Following Richardson & St. Pierre, I use 'writing as a method of inquiry' (2005, p. 959), as a cathartic process of reflection and a new access point to process my 'field data' and the stories I collected. I also intend to offer some insights into the unpredictability of fieldwork and my struggles to cope with physical, emotional and psychological dangers during this time. Through an exploration of my personal experiences, I intend to add to the already existing body of work on 'fieldwork under fire' (Nordstrom & Robben, 1995) and to Ansoms' (2010) approach to revealing 'the stories behind the findings' with its focus on emotional dangers and psychological trauma.

With reference to my own fieldwork experiences, I introduce the analogy of an *inner bell* that rings when there is resonance between people – for instance when a common understanding is achieved. In many situations, when there is little or no understanding, there is no such resonance, and this bell fails to ring.

In the following, I explore the extent to which my own bell resonated with those of various individuals and what that meant for my research. I begin with a description of the fieldwork and my immersion into the field and conclude with a discussion of the re-tuning of my inner bell when fieldwork ended.

Food, illicit brew and water

Immersion involves the discovery of, and dependence on, local food. Living with pastoralists, this food included many animal products: meat, milk (in many variations), intestines or blood – to name but a few. It was essential to share food with my host family, friends and strangers,[10] although it sometimes felt slightly unnerving to eat unidentifiable food, and sometimes I also had to be taught how to eat some specific food we were given.

Food also included the so-called 'illicit brew'. This refers to locally produced beer (*busaa*) and spirits (*changaa*). Stories about *changaa* are famous far beyond Kenya, and the negative effects of imbibing are notorious. Knowing this, I tried to avoid these drinks wherever I could. However, *busaa* and *changaa* had found their ways into everyday life in my field site. So, I adapted, and would have a drink or two, in this case a '*doli*' (250 ml of freshly brewed alcohol) with those with whom we lived. I decided that if I wanted to be here with my host family and friends, I could either adapt to my new environment or confine my research and myself in line with my own principles. I decided to eat and drink everything that came my way, including water from local sources. Most of the time we had sufficient drinking water, but it also occurred that people at Mt Paka would take any accessible water and share it with us. My assistant Kudee and I also dug pits if necessary, and the ability to drink any kind of water afforded us the freedom to follow pastoralists everywhere. It also legitimised us as equal counterparts and helped to close the gap between the people of Paka and 'us'.

Kudee

Kudee, who quickly became a good friend, assisted me during research for one year. The story of our collaboration is extraordinary, at least to me, and determined the whole fieldwork. I am convinced that this story would be completely different without him. During fieldwork, we became a well-cooperating team although, in the beginning, my plan had been to engage in an exclusive endeavour.

---

[10] By the term 'stranger' I refer to people we sometimes met along our ways. For instance, research on foot implies a lot of mobility of the researcher along different paths, and other people move as well. Hence, we often met all kinds of people in specific meeting places (*kokwö*), or in places where alcohol is brewed and sold.

After completing secondary school, Kudee assisted other anthropologists several times. Research assistance is a lucrative job in this part of Kenya, and he worked as an assistant three times before we started our collaboration. During all those projects, the researchers lived in some of the small centres of the region and started their fieldwork from there. This becomes more comprehensible when fieldwork conditions are considered. East Pokot is right in the Rift Valley and temperatures rise high not only during the dry season. Mosquitoes are ubiquitous to the lowlands and medical care is not available outside the centres. Electricity and drinking water (in the form of tankers and, later, community and livestock water points) did not reach the rural areas until 2015 and the roads are tough. Incentives for a research base close to a centre are therefore strong.[11] However, in our case we stayed in the remote region on Mt Paka so that we could do research and live with pastoral Pokot.

When I asked Kudee to assist me, he agreed; and after some time, it was no longer just my personal fieldwork, and Kudee became as motivated and keen on doing fieldwork as I was.[12] At the same time, we experienced some hardships, especially illnesses. Typhoid, pneumonia, malaria and gastro-intestinal diseases made our life in the village more difficult. One could imagine that this was hard to bear, but it also brought us closer together. We also agreed to have regular fieldwork times, from Monday to Friday, and the weekend was the time Kudee went to Nginyang to see his family. The responsibility I had for myself in the field now extended to Kudee and his family, while Kudee was responsible for me and introduced me to the implicit and explicit rules of everyday life. I might well have quickly despaired without his patient understanding, reflections and explanations of daily life, along with his empathy.

Kudee also embodies special characteristics that – in our case – fully fit our kind of fieldwork. He was not born in the Paka region, but he has a pastoral background. He is the first born from a pastoral family in Amaya, some 25 kilometres east of Mt Paka and he was sent to primary school and later to secondary school within East Pokot, after which he became a research assistant in several projects. When we met, he was already acquainted with research and the interpersonal relationships between researcher and assistant. The ways

---

[11] Conditions for research – like general living conditions – are changing rapidly in East Pokot due to the development plans of the Geothermal Development Company and the infrastructure development needed to implement this project. However, the descriptions of research conditions illustrated here always refer to the years 2014 and 2015 before GDC started constructing the geothermal wells in East Pokot.

[12] In the following, I often refer to 'our' fieldwork and the way 'we' explored the field and conducted fieldwork. This always refers to the constant debates Kudee and I had while engaging in the process of fieldwork and the situations we went through.

we discussed our work were not lopsided. Kudee intervened when my plans became unfeasible or touched sensitive issues. Several times, he proposed his ideas on how certain questions could be addressed, and we figured out alternative ways of investigating them. He quickly identified himself with the research. After a while, we both became acquainted with the people around us and adapted to local life.

Severe sickness

Health was another continual concern for us as much as for the people of our community. Kudee and I personally coped well with the difficult conditions. However, this was not the case when somebody close to us developed a critical illness and competing epistemologies of medicine came into play.

On one notable occasion, my neighbour told me about his sick baby boy at home.[13] I asked him how serious it was, and he said that he did not know exactly. I suggested taking advantage of the newly constructed road to take his son to the nearest hospital in Chemolingot, a distance of 27 kilometres, before the child's condition deteriorated.

Instead, my neighbour opted for *tapa* – a home-based healing ritual – and did not consider the hospital as an option. The next day we met again, and the boy was still sick; yet my neighbour still did not consider going to the hospital. Kudee and I continued with our work into the following day, when a heavy rain shower poured down. This rain shower brought us a lot of joy because we had long awaited the rainy season. The rains were so heavy that the whole area seemed to drown. That evening, another huge shower started.

It was at this point that my neighbour came to my hut. He told us that the condition of his son had deteriorated severely. He was worried whether his son would survive the night if he did not receive medical treatment. I was flung into a terrible situation. I had the only car available in the region, and while I would have taken anybody to the hospital at any time, it was pitch black outside and the sandy roads were completely flooded under the deluge of rain. To make this drive now would be very risky. I still recall sitting in the hut thinking about the boy, the impracticality of driving under these conditions and the perceived foolishness of my neighbour. In the end, I decided to make the journey, even though the risk of an accident was high. I was incensed, but concentrated on what I perceived to be the road.

We made it as far as a small homestead in Chemoril, halfway to Chemolingot, which we were familiar with, knowing there was a nurse based there providing health services for rural areas. Fortunately, she was around and agreed to treat

---

[13] Later, my neighbour told me the baby had caught malaria, but in the case of the Pokot the term 'malaria' could also refer to other diseases that result in fever and physical exhaustion.

the baby overnight. I was relieved but still felt anger towards my neighbour. Nobody talked during the drive, nor did my neighbour and I talk to each other for days. Although the journey and the treatment went well, the bad feelings persisted for some days until we settled the issue with a small assembly and some homemade beer.

My neighbour later became one of my closest friends in the field. This situation showed me how differently health care is perceived among the pastoral Pokot and how fragile human life is in an environment where access to conventional medicine is either restricted or not the first treatment of choice. Over time, I came to appreciate these competing worldviews, and fine-tuned my inner bell more towards local contexts and priorities. In general, I accept the importance of Pokot healing rituals in innocuous situations. But the evaluation of risk and danger is different, and it challenged my pre-existing ideas on health and sickness along with the danger and insecurity of being sometimes right and sometimes wrong. Situations in which my preconceptions were challenged were an important – if sometimes undesirable – precondition for a deeper understanding of Pokot life.

Raiding

Beyond the challenges of food and health that we coped with slowly, other more violent issues of Pokot pastoral life cropped up, such as raiding livestock from neighbouring communities. This is a strategy often contemplated by young Pokot men to accumulate livestock, and the pastoral Pokot are known for raiding members of neighbouring ethnic groups such as Turkana, Il Chamus, Tugen or Samburu. The character of these raids has undeniably changed over past decades, transforming from organised events with hundreds of warriors to small group enterprises. Now, fewer than ten men will band together to steal livestock independently of the wider community. Men now share only some of the captured livestock with friends and relatives, keeping the lions' share for themselves. The weapons used have also changed, from spears and bows and arrows to AK47 assault rifles.

Inevitably, raids happened during my stay in the field. On one occasion, someone who lived at the foot of the mountain and regularly visited the uphill *kokwö* next to our homestead participated. A few days before the raid, Kudee and I conducted an interview with five elders on the topic of prophecies. When the interview concluded, this person, who later came to be involved in a raid, joined Kudee, the elders and me as we listened to stories and shared tobacco in the *kokwö*. This was the last time we saw him.

Some days later, I learnt the details of his demise. Three men had gone to raid a neighbouring community on the southern border of Lake Baringo. They had captured some cattle and goats and had hurried back into East Pokot. But they were pursued by the offended party who engaged them in combat.

Our friend was shot in the leg and was unable to escape with the others. He shouted to his friend and said that he could not make it. He said he would shoot himself to escape torture and that the friend must take his gun home because it was worth a lot. So that is what was reported to us.

Only after some days did I really process his decision and begin to grasp the cruelty of life as a young warrior. A warrior's life is always prone to violence, and death can happen at any time through sickness or at the hands of an enemy. I questioned whether I would ever understand what it means to be a warrior, because I had never really been exposed to this life. My ability to resonate, so to speak, was limited, although I could comprehend the logic of the story. However, the full emotional extent of being in that situation was, and still is, inaccessible to me.

Encountering the slayer

As we spent more time at Mt Paka, we began to attend and learn rituals. One of these rituals is called *kolat* and aims to heal a household member from disease. *Kolat* involves slaughtering a goat and eating it with close friends and family members, and the person under treatment is painted all over with a mixture of clay, sand, water and ashes. Women must be separated from men while herbal medicine is given to the afflicted individual. The men sit within the cattle or goat kraal, and one elder distributes the pieces of meat and intestines to the group. The master of the ceremony must also embody a special characteristic: he must be a *slayer* (*kolïn*). A person becomes a slayer if he has killed an enemy during a fight. The slayer then undergoes ritual cleansing and can subsequently execute certain functions such as leading the *kolat* ceremony. When I learnt about this, I was astonished at how many of our friends hold the position of a slayer. The intensity of masculine ideals, and the rewards for striving to live up to these ideals among the pastoral Pokot, overwhelmed my imagination. Those few men I met on my ways who were freshly initiated *kolïn,* wearing a red coloured ostrich feather as hair decoration, always created an uncomfortable feeling in me and made me think about my own values and masculinity.

Of course, this insight challenged only *my* worldview. Nobody else found this particularly interesting, because it was normalised. For pastoral Pokot, it was a fact of life that people kill and die during conflicts. But for me, it was not easy to understand that killing an enemy is equated with ritual prestige.

Secret ceremonies

A few months after we arrived in the field, we had the chance to observe a special ritual. It was not like any of the ceremonies we had previously attended. This time it was a secret ceremony performed following the advice of a local prophet (*werkoyon*)[14] to ritually avert a dangerous situation. I was very excited because I had hoped to be included in a ritual such as this for some time. Our invitation seemed to be proof of our acceptance.

We went around with the men, from place to place, collecting more men as we made our way through the bush, all the while anticipating the ritual. Finally, we reached the location where the ceremony was to take place. The elders had already arrived, as had the goats that were to be slaughtered. As the ritual started, one of the younger elders, feared due to his connection to powerful forms of witchcraft, stood up. He was completely drunk. He complained about us – Kudee and me – being present: two boys, who had not been initiated and were not part of their community. According to him, our presence would cause the ritual to fail. We had to leave the scene.

Kudee was enraged. I was disheartened at our abrupt dismissal. We went home with a feeling of total failure, asking each other whether or not we could continue to stay with the group of people with whom we had been associating. We wondered whether we had actually shared any daily experiences with these people. This was a big setback, especially in light of our enthusiasm at being invited to the ritual. Kudee and I talked a lot about this situation and about the person who had dismissed us. We thought about his motives, his position in the community and his relations to the other people in Paka. It helped a lot to reflect on the situation and its aftermath. Nevertheless, we avoided working with this person for some time until the dust had settled.

In retrospect, the dismissal did not have negative consequences for our ongoing immersion in the field. In fact, other community members came to us afterwards to offer their consolations, advising that we should not listen to this one elder but rather to all the others who did want us to be involved. Later on, we were included almost as a matter of course in another secret ceremony of the same kind. However, the situation illustrates that connecting with people is not a linear process and may be accompanied by setbacks that can have a big, if passing, effect on the emotional state of the researcher and the assistant.

---

[14] The prophet is an important protagonist among the pastoral Pokot who connects the past, the present and the future. As in many East African pastoral groups, the prophet has a central position in the social organisation. In the case of the Pokot, this particularly involves interpreting current affairs, explaining the past experiences of other generations and providing concrete instructions for averting upcoming calamities. As Peristiany describes, 'the prophet knows the mind and the will of *Ilat*, the god nearest to humans. He also communicates with the minds of man, with the spirits of the deceased, and with animals and plants … He decides when a new age-set should be initiated, when war is to be waged, when people and cattle should be moved, the proper time for planting, settling on, or cultivating new lands' (Peristiany, 1975, p. 197).

A second case occurred at a later stage of fieldwork. This time we were no longer observers; we were part of the ceremony we wanted to conduct for the elders. Therefore, we asked a close friend to give us a goat for a ceremony. He agreed, and we fixed a date. Our host acted on our behalf because we were not eligible at the time – neither Kudee nor I were officially initiated into the community. On the day of the ritual, we gathered the elders, met close to the homestead of our friend and waited for him to come and join us. But he had left the homestead and abandoned us. Clearly, this is a major offence, and we quickly had to provide an adequate compensation to the elders. Although the ceremony went well, we were caught in a quarrel with our friend who deceived us, and deceived our host, for no obvious reason. A while later, he came to our homestead and asked for reconciliation, and we performed another ritual to appease the conflict. But the time between the first and the second ritual, when we did not know what kind of effect the denial could have on us, was full of uncertainties. The impact on our research was not foreseeable. In retrospect, the conflict arose because of our unspecific roles in the community. On the one hand, we were prominent members of the group, having a car and other means lying exclusively in our hands. On the other hand, we were uninitiated 'boys', unbound, like young warriors (*kapariök*) and not eligible to participate in official functions.

In the end, the dispute and the discourse around it helped us to find a more defined role in the community. But the search for acceptance has its limits, restricted both individually and by the group. It took us months to be accepted by most of the people, and every day we progressed a little bit while sometimes having to discover unexpected antipathy. Although we were slowly absorbed into the community, we were still aliens. We had no livestock, we did not live with our women, and although we went to many *kokwö* meetings, we never took sides for or against somebody.

Healing

At an advanced stage of the fieldwork, the people of the homestead that I belonged to decided to conduct a healing ritual for a sick baby from another homestead. Such approaches to healing are common. This one, however, raised some concern because it went by the name of *kisun* (blood). During the ritual, a baby goat is tied to a tree, and I was asked to cut its throat but not its neck.[15] To heal the baby, the goat needed to remain alive as blood gushed out of its

---

[15] In pastoral livelihoods, killing an animal is a fairly common routine, and I had taken part in the slaughtering of many animals before. The sacrifice of the baby goat, however, was an exceptional situation. On the one hand, I did not kill it immediately but left it alive and the baby goat struggled hard as it died. On the other hand, the severe sickness of the baby boy put me in dire straits.

throat so that the baby could be held in the stream of blood. To conclude the ritual, the goat was untied from the tree and, as it lay on the ground, my host made a deep cut across the peritoneum (abdomen) to remove its heart. The heart was then held to the front and back of the baby's chest. The ritual is performed to remove sickness from the baby. Another living being is required to take on the bad spirit responsible for causing harm to the baby boy. The heart was finally thrown far away from the homestead.

After the proceedings, the baby's condition continued to worsen. I urged my host and the parents of the baby to take the child to the hospital in Chemolingot about an hour's drive from our homestead. They agreed – but only after some time, because the ritual healing may take time to exert its influence on the baby; if the blood is washed off too early, it cannot develop its full effect. We drove off after a while and got to the hospital, mobilised the staff, and found a doctor. The doctor did some tests and diagnosed the child's illness, also mentioning that the baby might have to be transferred to the district hospital in Kabarnet. Sadly, the child never reached Kabarnet. The next morning, we met the parents on their way home, without their baby; they walked by without noticing us. It seemed we had failed. The ritual and the hospital treatment did not work. The despair and dejection of this situation seems obvious. I found it impossible to rely on participation, empathy or resonance as ways of making sense of what had just happened.

We did not meet the father of the baby in *kokwö* for some weeks, and Kudee and I tried to go on with our work. On our way to different locations, we often thought about what had happened and tried to make sense of it. It did not become more comprehensible over time; just less pressing.

Violence from outsiders

I was gradually beginning to deal with the everyday challenges and violence resulting from the masculinity of Pokot life when I came to realise that the scale of disruption was so much greater when outsiders intervened in this fragile system. The most intense fieldwork situation in East Pokot emerged during the first half of my fieldwork and showed me how rapidly and unpredictably situations can change.

In November 2014, the historically rooted Kapedo conflict between Pokot and Turkana people surfaced again, resulting in the killing of Kenyan Administration Police officers by some Pokot men. The Pokot conflict with the Turkana is nothing new, and clashes and raids have been frequent for decades.[16] At this time, Kapedo was still a central hub along a border zone. The conflict resulted in the displacement of many Pokot from the Kapedo area

---

[16] Bollig (1990b) describes the history of the violent conflict between Turkana and Pokot that began in the late 1960s.

in the 1970s. In the following years, Pokot communities pushed the Turkana north and continued to secure territory from them, although some Turkana stayed on in Kapedo under police protection. Tensions between these two groups have remained high in this region. In November 2014, the situation escalated once more when the Pokot around Kapedo denied anybody access to the town and ordered the remaining Turkana people to leave. The Kenyan government responded to the call for the removal of Turkana people from Kapedo with an elevated police presence on their side. The resulting clash between armed Pokot warriors and Administration Police left 22 officers dead.

Having been in the field for some time now, I had come to realise that the killing of people, especially during raids, had become a sad reality of life for pastoral Pokot, repeating itself on an almost cyclical basis every few weeks. However, the intervention of the Kenya Defence Forces (KDF) in response to the killing of the Administration Police officers created an entirely new environment of anxiety, different from that associated with cattle rustling. Whereas the raids take place mainly in the border zones between Pokot and neighbouring groups, the army intervention struck right in the heart of East Pokot. Furthermore, the appearance of military vehicles and helicopter gunships imposed a different magnitude of violence. From my field diary entries, I shall briefly try to reconstruct how the KDF operation influenced us during this highly tense period that forced Kudee and me to leave the region for a week.

27 October 2014

Two days ago, we sat together ... in the evening and a lot of bad news was exchanged. The Kapedo conflict flares up again and no vehicle is allowed to reach the town. Even the Chief [of Kapedo] was under fire when he tried to reach Kapedo with a lorry and a land cruiser. The situation is serious when Pokot start shooting at Pokot. Yesterday, Kudee texted me that rumours are going around that talk of three soldiers and two Turkana left dead, and it appears that the situation is growing more acute every day.

5 November 2014

The situation escalates! We had to leave Paka helter-skelter yesterday when the Deputy County Commissioner announced army interventions all over East Pokot on the radio if the ultimatum to return the weapons of the soldiers killed in Kapedo is not met. So far, six out of 23 G3-guns have been returned.

Therefore, I called the Deputy County Commissioner and asked him about the situation. He told me to drive to Chemolingot [which, in his view, was the only safe place in East Pokot in this moment] on the next day at the latest, because where the army interventions will take place has not yet been determined.

6 November 2014

The sudden departure from Paka yesterday still gives me collywobbles. We just left and evaded the coming danger. All the others, we left behind, merely telling them about the possible army intervention. The drive to Chemolingot was one of the longest of my life. My thoughts went in circles and I tried to imagine what could happen. Sadly, so much is possible. One tank is already in Kapedo and came into operation two days ago. During an interview, we heard four detonations, though Kapedo is relatively far off. Even the operation of helicopter gunships does not appear to be exaggerated ... With the appearance of the army and the threat of violence, the situation escalated completely and 22 soldiers have died so far. Hence, the president came to Kapedo to demand the culprits be disarmed, and he set a new ultimatum.

8 November 2014

It makes me sick! The situation is acute!

I was in Naivasha for two days to deal with some car issues and in the night from 6 to 7 November, the unimaginable happened. Apparently, soldiers or police set shops on fire in Chemolingot and Tangulbei, beat people up and imprisoned others. This is what people who we picked up yesterday report.

Chemolingot was a pitiable sight. Though we knew about the situation – and the army vehicles on the way into Pokot strengthened our impressions – the sight of burnt houses and streams of people fleeing the region left a feeling in me that is difficult to describe. These were merely the obvious sights of the terror of last night. I quickly picked up a (friend's) family, went on to the church to pick up the 'lost' missionary from Kapedo and his family, and moved on to find Kudee, who was hiding with his family in the bush.

The conflict between the government and suspected Pokot culprits went on for a few weeks until intermediaries returned most of the guns to government officials. During this time, the people in the small urban centres of East Pokot lived in fear of violence from government forces and spent their nights outside the town. The bad news spread all over Kenya.[17]

[17] In general, information coming from East Pokot often broaches the issue of violent conflicts. During the Kapedo conflict, the image of the situation changed over time. In the beginning of the disturbance, the newspapers focused on the massacre

The situation did eventually cool down in the following weeks. Surprisingly, the anxiety we felt seemed to disappear a few days after the incidents in Chemolingot. People quickly returned to their homes and stopped hiding in the bush. After this incident, I was glad for each day on which no news about Kapedo reached us. In retrospect, it surprises me how quickly we once again felt safe in the field, and how little violence ended up reaching us.

This situation differed from the other 'everyday challenges' described above, because Kudee and I were forced to immediately vacate the field and leave the people we dwelt with behind. I fell back completely into my more familiar worldview and did not undergo the same experience as everybody else who stayed. When I recall the story of Geertz's cockfight (Geertz, 1972), in which the renowned anthropologist hid from the police in the courtyard of some Indonesian villagers, I cannot help but think that perhaps I should have tried to handle the army intervention like everybody else did. But from my point of view, this would have been impossible and extremely dangerous. Getting in the car and driving away from the place and the people I was attached to was an extremely attritional situation, and being safely situated in the next town and disconnected from those who stayed behind was a disruptive feeling. These circumstances also led to the decision to return to Mt Paka as early as possible.

The adjustment of the inner bell

Kudee and I experienced some intense as well as many ordinary situations, all of which shaped our time in East Pokot. For every researcher, memories of fieldwork generate certain feelings – in my case, many good ones: warm welcomes; partaking of 'chai tea', milk and meat; and hours of walking together, aiming in the same direction, and reaching a destination as one. This way, we became part of the field and the people, as these became part of us. Moved by the urge to understand people and to create some resonance between some local perspectives and mine, I tuned my inner bell according to the vibrations of people in East Pokot.

---

of Administration Police officers by Pokot. After the incident in Chemolingot, they reported on the course of action taken by soldiers and the escape of people from the region. The national newspapers presented the incidents as follows:
'Soldiers hunt bandits over AP [Administration Police] massacre' (*Daily Nation*, 4 November, p. 1); 'Thirty injured as the military hunts for guns and warriors' (*Saturday Nation*, 8 November, p. 1); 'Residents flee as military hunts for guns and bandits' (*Saturday Nation*, 8 November, pp. 4–5); 'Pokot leaders declare "cold war" as military asked to halt arms mop-up. Legislators allege civilian harassment by security officers conducting the disarmament drive' (*Sunday Nation*, 9 November, p. 11); 'Court asked to stop arms mop-up. Law maker accuses soldiers of brutality against innocent civilians' (*Daily Nation*, 12 November, p. 10).

Although fieldwork is often perceived as a time of data collection, here I want to highlight the personal experiences. As anthropologists, immersing ourselves in other people's lives gives us the opportunity to create meaningful ethnographic accounts (as well as, in some cases, actively changing the course of events). Our sensual experiences, both bodily and mental, give way to a deeper understanding of the local context. Therefore, we use our bodies and minds as instruments of resonance that have to be fine-tuned over time. The more I tried to comprehend the lives of the Paka people, the more I had to leave my prior understanding of the world behind – and it took many months in the field until I understood things better.

3

Pokot Pastoral Livelihoods

Unlike many other pastoralists in East Africa, the origin of those in East Pokot has a rather short history. A pastoral section did not split off from the agro-pastoral Pokot in today's West Pokot County until the middle of the eighteenth century. Nonetheless, the Pokot pastoralists quickly became very successful herders, accumulating large flocks and effectively asserting themselves against other pastoral groups in the region.

In this chapter, I discuss the formation of pastoralism in East Pokot and describe the origin and history of the pastoralists in a contested region, their social organisation and land management over time and, finally, recent population developments and livestock herd transformations. To understand the transformation processes of pastoral livelihoods, it is first necessary to take a closer look at the term 'pastoralism' itself. Given a clear definition of the term, the pastoral livelihoods of the Pokot can, at a later stage, be compared with other livelihood approaches. Fratkin and Smith (1994) provide an elaborate definition that accounts for the complexity of pastoral livelihoods in East Africa. This also fits the pastoral Pokot who still depend on livestock husbandry, although farming, wage labour, trade and other activities have become more important in recent years.

> For the most part, this production is subsistence based, aimed at producing foods (primarily milk) for household members. Exchange is secondary. Pastoralists trade livestock, hides, or milk for other food products (or money to purchase them) including grains, tea, and sugar. Production is often organized within household units consisting of a male stock owner, his wife or wives, children, and other dependents. Seldom, if ever, do women have control of the herds … The household head is responsible for herd management and family subsistence and makes decisions to adjust to changing conditions in natural resources (i.e., land, including rainfall, vegetation, free water, salt, insects, and the presence of enemies or predators), livestock (individual feeding and watering regimens, reproductive behavior, and exposure to and treatments for diseases), and labor (access to which is influenced by changes in household composition, warfare, drought, education, urban migration, and wage availability). (Fratkin & Smith, 1994, pp. 93–4)

Fratkin and Smith's definition provides not only a better understanding of the characteristics and complexities of pastoral ways of living but also the insight that pastoralism is more than a lifestyle based on herding and subsistence. In the following, I shall describe the early, specialised pastoral livelihoods in East Pokot and use this account to show how these have transformed into diversified livelihoods that rely on various subsistence strategies.

Pastoral Pokot in Northern Baringo County

The Tiaty Constituency is located in northern Baringo County and is inhabited mostly by pastoral Pokot. The East Pokot territory, as it appears today,[1] covers about 4,500 km^2 and contains a huge lowland area in the Rift Valley, some volcanic mountain sites elevating from the lowlands, and the Rift Valley escarpment to the west and the east (Map 1). The four mountain sites are important places that traverse the region from south to north. Mt Korossi, the lowest mountain, is located north of Lake Baringo. Mt Paka and Mt Silali are the next highest mountains, with Mt Tiaty, the highest mountain, located in the north-east. The lowland area stretches along the Rift Valley bottom and includes the first three mountain sites with Mt Paka and Mt Korossi constituting the dry-season forage storage when lowlands forage is exhausted. The Rift Valley escarpment is still part of East Pokot.

The East Pokot semi-arid area is characterised by an average rainfall of 600 mm/m^2/year and strong inter-annual variations in precipitation.[2] The dominant vegetation is acacia bush savannah, mainly *Vachellia reficiens*, *Senegalia mellifera* and *Vachellia nubica*, together with *Senegalia senegal*, *Vachellia tortilis* and *Vachellia nilotica* in lower quantities. Grasses are scarce throughout the year, and, in general, the grass coverage is perceived as having greatly decreased (Vehrs, 2016).

The pastoral Pokot herd different types of animals but especially cattle, goats, camels and sheep. Many households also own donkeys that are used to transport goods or water during the dry season or when household members start their migration to other pastures. In the past, the most important animal was cattle. Goats were also part of the herd structures in times when pastoral Pokot were specialised herders, but their importance increased strongly in the second half of the twentieth century. Oesterle estimates the animal numbers

---

[1]   In the history of pastoral East Pokot, the de jure and the de facto territory nowadays occupied by the Pokot people was, and to some extent still is, contested. From time to time, Pokot, Turkana, Samburu, Tugen, Karimojong and Il Chamus people are involved in violent conflicts that also involve the loss or gain of territory.

[2]   Forty-two records from 1942–1991 gathered in Nginyang are considered here using data taken from Bollig (1992a). These range from 204 mm/m^2/year (in 1984) to 1,125 mm/y/m^2 (in 1961).

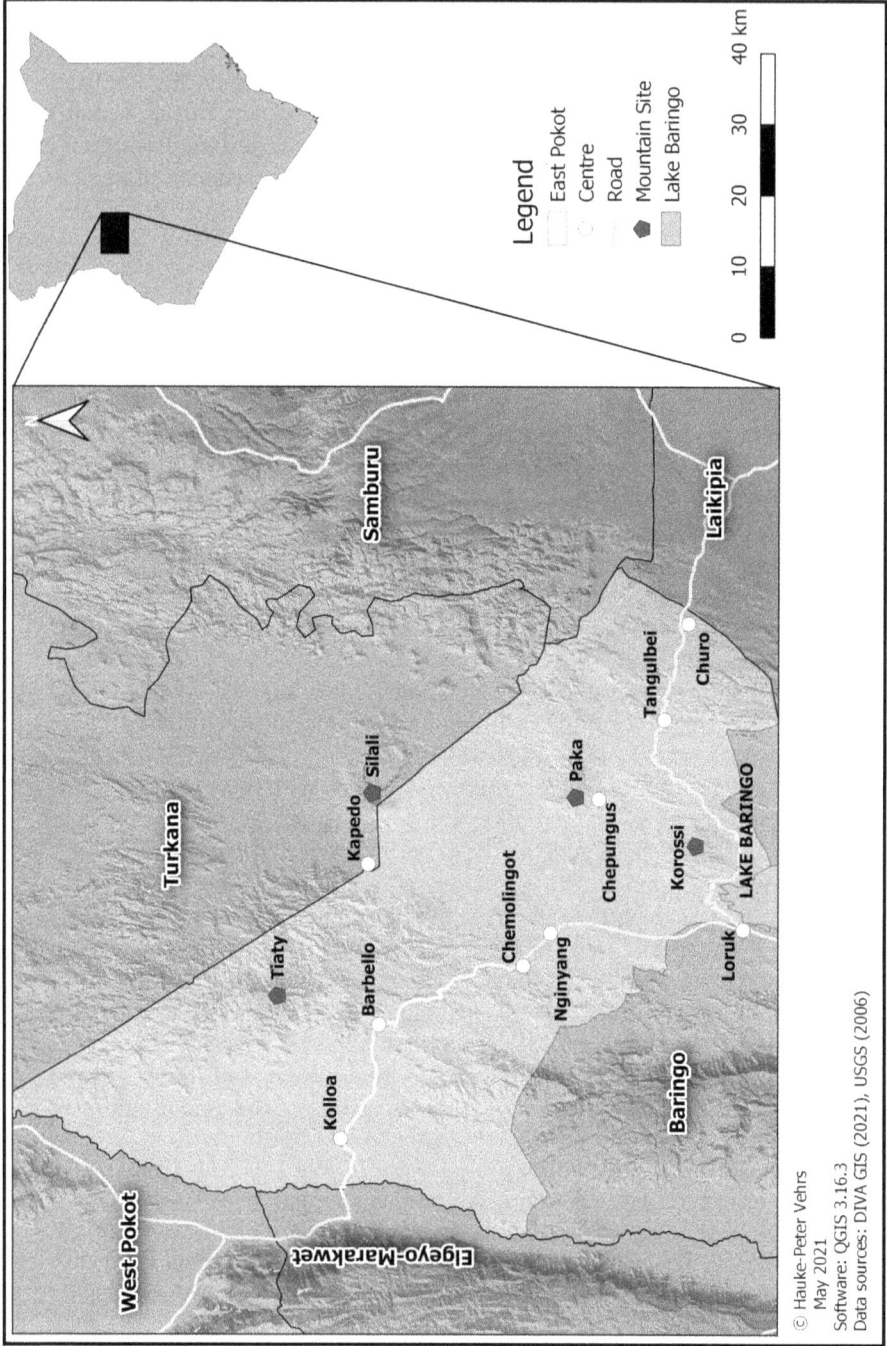

Map 1. Tiaty Constituency (East Pokot) in northern Baringo County (Hauke-Peter Vehrs).

© Hauke-Peter Vehrs
May 2021
Software: QGIS 3.16.3
Data sources: DIVA GIS (2021), USGS (2006)

in the early 2000s at about 117,000 cattle, 680,000 small stock and 8,000 camels, resulting in a total tropical livestock unit of about 211,000 for East Pokot (Oesterle, 2007). The exact number of goats and sheep is difficult to identify because estimations vary from 330,000 (Republic of Kenya, 2011) to 700,000 (Republic of Kenya, 2020a) head of small stock, amounting to 1.855 million goats and sheep in the estimation of the earlier livestock population census in 2009 (Republic of Kenya, 2009).[3]

Despite the wide range of estimations, the trend is towards an increase of browse-dependent small stock and camels. The shift in herd structure in East Pokot has been depicted by Oesterle, who also claims a twofold increase in camel populations over the last decades (Oesterle, 2008). These animals are associated with prestige, wealth and prosperity, because they also provide livestock services such as milk and meat during the dry season. Cattle, on the other hand, depend on the pastures, and these are under pressure due to a high degree of grazing on the one hand and bush encroachment on the other. Oesterle (2008) calculates the tropical livestock unit (TLU) for the 2000s in East Pokot to be 3.3 TLU/capita, and therefore still akin to other pastoral groups in Africa.[4] However, the TLU/km[2] is 35.4,[5] and therefore extraordinarily high in comparison to similar groups such as the Borana (17.4), Maasai (16.8) or Turkana (5.0) (Oesterle, 2008). Moreover, the person-to-cattle ratio has dropped from 1:14 at the beginning of the twentieth century to 1:2 at the beginning of this twenty-first century (Oesterle, 2008). These results are clearly related to the restriction of territorial expansion, the enormous population increase of the last decades and the comparably moderate increase in livestock numbers. Hence, livestock numbers per square kilometre are astonishingly high, whereas the livestock numbers per person are average. The recent population estimations of about 153,000 people in East Pokot (Republic of Kenya, 2019) leaves a per capita TLU of 1.39, which is extremely

---

[3]   The debate about livestock data and tropical livestock units (TLU) will be taken up again towards the end of this chapter when discussing livestock population developments over the past decades.

[4]   22TLU is not always used consistently. Whereas Oesterle follows Galvin and Little (1999) and calculates the TLU as follows: Camel = 1.25 TLU, Cattle = 1.0 TLU and Goat/Sheep = 0.125 TLU (with reference to the FAO Production Yearbook of 1967), many other authors use the following conversion factors: 1 head of cattle = 0.7 camels = 10 sheep = 11 goats (see, e.g., McPeak & Little, 2006, who refer to the Range Management Handbook of Kenya). For reasons of comparability, I use the conversion factors chosen by Oesterle.

[5]   Based on the official Pokot territory of about 4,500 km[2] (not the 6,000 km[2] assumed by Oesterle), the TLU/km[2] would be 47. Oesterle calculates a TLU/km[2] of 35.4, which might be more reasonable, taking the recent expansion of grazing territory into account.

low compared to the Turkana (3.0 TLU/capita) or Maasai (3.3 TLU/capita) (Oesterle, 2008).

Because the accuracy of the official population figures is subject to considerable criticism, as will be discussed in detail in later chapters, the precision of the TLU/capita calculation must also be viewed with caution. Besides doubts about the official population and livestock numbers, the changing livelihoods and the disparate distribution of livestock ownership among the pastoral and agro-pastoral Pokot in the region must also be considered in order to assess current conditions for pastoralists.

The origin of the pastoral Pokot

The history of the pastoral Pokot is difficult to reconstruct from oral accounts, and only a few elderly people can still remember stories about the formation of Pokot pastoralism. Bollig and Oesterle (2013) assume that they formed about 150 to 210 years ago. During that time, the cattle people (*pi'-pa tich*) emerged from different small groups with a pastoral background in the Baringo region along with agricultural Pokot from the western escarpment (Bollig & Oesterle, 2013). Beech, one of the early colonial administrators, narrates the formation of the pastoral Pokot, wrongly referred to as 'Suk' by the coloniaists, as follows:

> While the Suk nation was being evolved in the mountains of the Elgeyo escarpment the Kerio Valley was occupied by the Sambur [*sic*]. If ever the Suk descended from their fastnesses they were raided and harried by this tribe, until there arose a wizard among the Suk who prepared a charm in the form of a stick, which he placed in the Sambur cattle kraals, with the result their cattle all died. They thereupon left the Kerio Valley, and formed a large settlement at En-ginyang [*sic*]. Perceiving that Kerio had become evacuated, the Suk descended from their hills in some numbers, and occupied Tiati [*sic*] and the hills as far south as Karuwon. From here they successfully raided the Sambur [*sic*] and captured a great many cattle. ... From this event dates the origin of the pastoral Suk. Hitherto they had been a purely agricultural people... However, when once the pastoral Suk had originated, it became, and still is, the aim and ambition of the hill Suk to amass sufficient livestock to enable them to descend into the plains and join the pastoral Suk. Hence the latter section is continually increasing at the expense of the former. It must be therefore borne in mind that, although written of here as two distinct sections, the hill and the pastoral Suk are essentially the same. (Beech, 1911, pp. 3–4)

Beech describes the origin of the pastoral Pokot as coming from West Pokot agriculturalists who established their pastoral livelihoods successfully in a competitive landscape. During their formation, they must have been successful in capturing and defending the contested region north of Lake Baringo. Early accounts of Pokot people emphasise descriptions of their

livestock and livelihoods as von Hoehnel adds in his personal view on the
agro-pastoral and the pastoral Pokot.

> Half the Suk are nomad cattle-breeders, the other half sedentary agricul-
> turists, cultivating chiefly dhurra, gourds, and tobacco. Probably they
> were all originally cattle-breeders, but were driven to agriculture through
> loss of cattle from disease. The sedentary Suk are restricted to the eastern
> slopes of the mountain, and dwell in pretty little round huts made of hewn
> tree trunks with a conical thatch of dhurra stalks. Most of their settle-
> ments are rather hamlets than villages. The nomad [*sic*] live on either
> side of the valley watered by the Kerio, between the parallel chains of
> mountains on the east. They own cattle, goats, sheep, many of the latter
> with black heads, donkeys, and a few camels, the last-named probably
> stolen from the Turkana. ... They dwell in kraals containing numerous
> huts made of brushwood and plaited osiers, and enclosed within a thorn
> hedge. (von Hoehnel, 1894, pp. 270–71)

In contrast to von Hoehnel's assumption that West Pokot agriculturalists
derived from the pastoral Pokot in a kind of cultural evolution, the real case is
the reverse. Davies & Moore (2016) date the separation of the pastoral Pokot
from the agricultural Pokot to around 1750 at a time when agriculturalists
specialised their agricultural production and a section of Pokot moved to
Baringo and specialised in livestock husbandry.

In Map 2, Beech illustrates the territory occupied by Pokot groups in the
early twentieth century. The description of the boundaries around Lake Baringo
is interesting. Beech draws the Pokot territory towards the southern regions
around Lake Baringo on both the east and the west sides of the lake – neither
of which are officially occupied by Pokot to this extent nowadays. Remarkably,
the sites of Mt Silali, Naudo and Amaya (all in the upper right corner of the
map) are excluded from Pokot territory. Nowadays, they are all occupied by
Pokot pastoralists.

In summary, the pastoral Pokot formed in the mid-eighteenth to early
nineteenth century and successfully contested for the land north of Lake
Baringo. They were also successful herders and warriors. But, how can we
imagine the early pastoral Pokot? Photo 1 shows some Pokot men in the
early twentieth century.[6] Their appearance often impressed the observer, in
this case, a big-game hunter, who emphasised their weaponry, animal skin
clothes and hair dress. In the case of the pastoral Pokot, their style of head
dress also signifies belonging to different generation sets and having the
right to wear different hair styles or certain feathers that is transferred from
the older generation to the younger during distinct ceremonies to this day

---

[6] Pictures of Pokot women and children do not seem to be available from that
time.

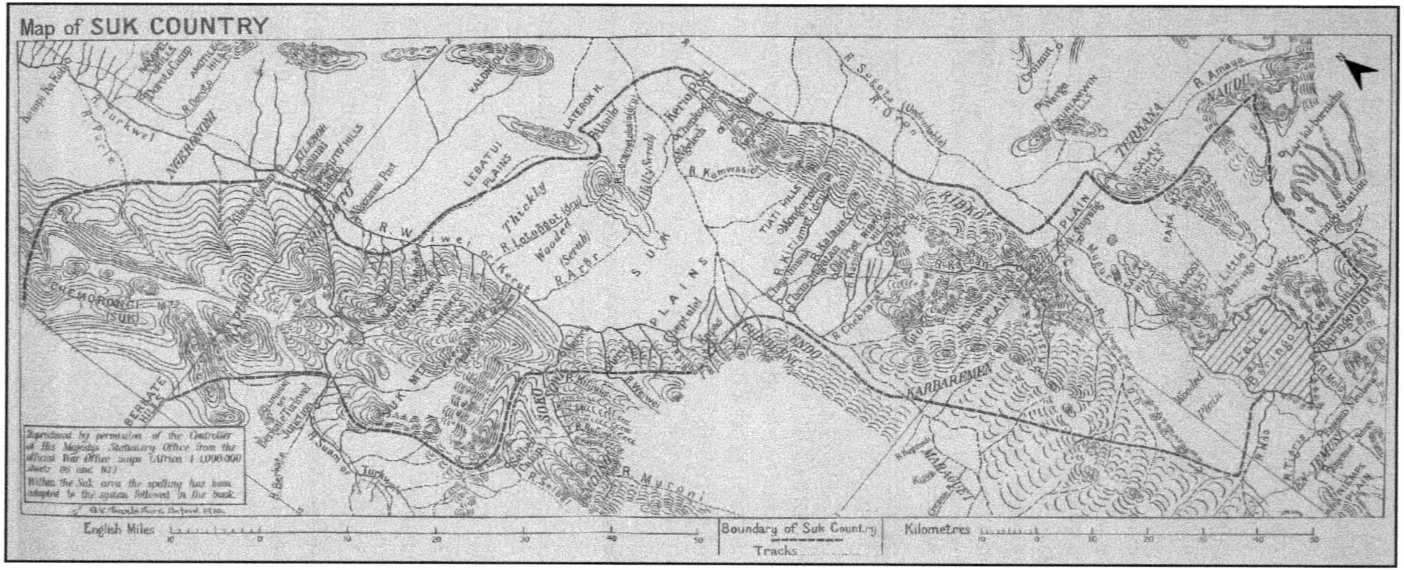

Map 2. Pokot territory in the early twentieth century (Beech, 1911: appendix). Geographical north is as indicated. Lake Baringo and the East Pokot plains are located on the right-hand side; West Pokot on the left-hand side and extending to the Ugandan border. The most important feature is Mt Seker, nowadays called Mt Mtelo, in West Pokot County. Beech's description of the Pokot territory ends at the Ugandan border, though Pokot people also dwell on the Ugandan side.

(Bollig, 1990a). Photo 1 was taken around Lake Baringo. Besides portraying the warriors, the open landscape catches one's eye, an environment that seems suitable for pastoral purposes.

Early accounts of the pastoral Pokot also highlight their preference for cattle husbandry: "The pastoral Suk keep and breed cattle, sheep and goats, ... As with the Nandi, cattle-herding is the favourite – indeed the only – occupation of the pastoral Suk" (Beech, 1911, p. 8).

In the late nineteenth and early twentieth centuries, the Pokot pastoral livelihoods were focused strongly on cattle husbandry. Bollig and Oesterle describe this period of successful cattle herding as 'specialisation' and the following period, when cattle became less important and browsing species more important, as 'diversification' (Bollig & Oesterle, 2013). In the nineteenth century, the strategy of specialising in cattle husbandry paid off, Pokot pastoralists became rich and prestigious and, as Beech described earlier, even agricultural Pokot aspired to transform their livelihoods. This change is also mirrored in the cattle-to-human ratio of 14:1 at the beginning of the twentieth century. The origin and success of the pastoral Pokot is also remembered and narrated by some Pokot elders, who still rhapsodise about their ancestors' large cattle herds, such that one could not see each end of a herd at the same time.

Photo 1. Suk warriors (Powell-Cotton, 1904d, p. 115).

The history of the emergence of the pastoral Pokot

Oral accounts still report incidences in the past that had a strong impact on Pokot livelihoods. One example is the occupation of the region north of Lake Baringo, at a time when the lake completely dried up. This statement about the desiccation of the lake delivers important information about the time of the formation of the pastoral Pokot. As mentioned before, Bollig and Oesterle (2013) recall the past generations in the generation-set system of the pastoral Pokot and date the emergence of Pokot pastoralists back to about 150 to 210 years ago. Furthermore, climatic accounts indicate an extreme dry period in the late eighteenth century and again in the early nineteenth century when Lake Baringo desiccated (Bessems et al., 2008; Kiage & Liu, 2009). One elderly person in East Pokot narrates the oral history of the emergence of the pastoral Pokot. He dates the situation back to a time when Lake Baringo was dry. At that time, three groups of Pokot could be differentiated – who might today be referred to as the West Pokot agriculturalists, the agricultural Pokot in the highlands of north-east Uganda, and the pastoral Pokot who occupied the plains along Lake Baringo north of the lake and the plains in the Kerio Valley. In the following, the narration of the early times of the pastoral Pokot and that during the last desiccation of Lake Baringo, the pastoral Pokot already occupied the region and were surprised by the replenishment of the lake. It also gives some insights into how the pastoral Pokot imagine the richness of their ancestors, as well as their arrogance and the punishment of their misbehaviour.

> Pokot originated from the land of Seker [Mt Mtelo]. This is where the division of people started. Some people moved west side to Kitale and Kapenguria. Others moved east, and another group moved north. So, some Pokot moved east to Loruk and Kampi ya Samaki, and Chemarigat. By then there was no formation of Lake Baringo. Pokot were very rich by then, they were lending milk to others like water. They had so many cattle that you cannot see the end of the herd. So, life continued and people were proud because of their richness. They insulted the poor and many bad things happened. One night in the kokwö hill [the Ol Kokwe Island in the middle of Lake Baringo] an unknown sound was heard in the night.

> Siyeyi Lomut, siyeyi Lomut,   Women of Lomut,
> Owuweno kayu, owuweno kayu,   move from the surrounding,
> Tunturo Kositei, Tunturo Kositei.   Kositei will burst.

> Someone asked: 'Did you hear the song?' But other men responded: 'How can you pay attention to birds singing?'
> 'Is that really a bird? Go and check it', the other responded, but nobody went.

After two days, the singing repeated. But now, a deep bass sound was singing.

Oruko Lomut, oruko Lomut,	Men of Lomut,
Owuweno kayu, owuweno kayu,	move from the surrounding,
Tunturo Kositei, Tunturo Kositei.	Kositei will burst.

Now, some men paid attention and moved towards the rocky part of the region, which is called Kampi ya Samaki today, and some moved south to Marigat and some moved east. The stubborn people stayed in the plain grazing area. After the second song was sung, it took two days and heavy rains started, which came from the east. It rained two days without stopping and on the third day at midnight there was a strong lightening and the people say the rain fell in red colour from the sky. In the morning after the rains had stopped, people woke up and suddenly Lake Baringo was full of water and the stubborn people drowned with their animals. (Interview with Riteluk – 4 September 2014)

Riteluk, an elderly Pokot, describes the origin of the pastoral Pokot in a prosperous time. The Pokot pastoralists were able to generate wealth and adopted an arrogant behaviour towards less wealthy herders. This hubris led to their death. From the perception of the current elderly generation of the pastoral Pokot, unmannered behaviour, such as adultery or disrespect, must have a negative impact on either individuals or the whole group. In the story narrated above, only the arrogant people were cursed and drowned in the lake. But the misbehaviour of some people can also be interpreted as a curse on all Pokot and their land.[7]

Another source on the formation of the pastoral Pokot comes from Dundas in 1910 and refers to a time long before the first explorer Joseph Thomson reached the region. Dundas recalls a narration of the migration of Il Chamus people to the southern shores of Lake Baringo that took place in the early nineteenth century. He illustrates the story of a pastoral group of people from Samburu County in search of pasture during a severe dry spell and their move towards Lake Baringo, an area which was uninhabited at that time. The following quote underlines the unique character of the Lake Baringo pastoral landscape in the nineteenth century and shows the occupation of the land north of Lake Baringo at the time of the Il Doigo migration.

The greater portion of the present Njemps [Il Chamus] population are survivors of a Samburu tribe called Il Doigio. About seventy to a hundred years ago the Doigio were settled on Loroghi [Plateau – southern

---

[7]   This framework of interpretation will be discussed further in Chapter 7 on the Pokot explanations of environmental changes.

Samburu County]. Loroghi is a high lying plateau above the Rift Valley … the descent into the valley below is most precipitous; the traveller crossing this plateau from the north will not catch his first glimpse of Lake Baringo until he reaches the very edge of the escarpment. The grazing is magnificent, but the country is subject to long spells of drought, and, at the time of which I am speaking, the Doigio cattle were dying for want of grass. Now it happened, that one day, when the drought was at its worst, an old man lying under a tree, as is the custom of old men, saw a bird come to the tree holding in its beak a blade of green grass. In the evening, therefore, he summoned the tribe to assemble by blowing the village horn, and when all were gathered together, addressed them thus: 'Today, the heat of the sun being very great, I went and lay under a tree, and presently I saw a bird come to the tree in which it was building a nest, and in its beak it held a blade of green grass. Select therefore forty young warriors and let them follow this bird and see whence it obtains the green grass.' The following day a party of young men set out accordingly, and proceeding due west came to the edge of an escarpment, from whence they beheld a wonderful view of a great lake and in the far distance at the south end a plain of fresh green grass. Far below they saw Naudo and the Ngingyang [sic] River, its banks lined with great trees, and nearer at hand Mt Paka. Descending into the valley and passing by this mountain they came to the north end of Lake Baringo. Skirting its rocky shores they proceeded onwards and at length reached the plains of green grass; seeing here, however, the smoke of fires they decided to return and report to the old men of the tribe their discoveries; but the old men said, 'Return again and find out who the people are whose fires you saw, and what rivers flow into the lake where you saw the green grass.' So the young men went again, and passing this time along the east shore of the lake came first to the River Tim and a little farther on to the Rivers Molo and Tigrish,[8] where they found a colony of hunters and fishers. Returning again to their villages they related all that they had seen, and it was immediately decided by the elders of the tribe to move to this El Dorado of rivers, lakes and green grass. The old men, however, went first and made friendship with the Geroi, explaining to them that their only desire was to graze their stock and live in peace. Thus the Doigio came to Baringo, and though I think we may relegate the greater part of this story to the region of other similar myths and fables, it bears witness perhaps to two significant facts; namely, that the Doigio on their first arrival were but a very small tribe, and that they found the shores of Lake Baringo uninhabited. (Dundas, 1910, pp. 50–51)

Dundas describes the migration of today's Il Chamus people and dates its origin 70–100 years further back, between 1810 and 1840. At that time, the shores of Lake Baringo were repopulated, and because the Il Chamus people

---

[8]   The rivers are located south of Lake Baringo.

found the northern region of Lake Baringo already inhabited, they migrated to the southern end of the lake.

In both the mid-eighteenth and early nineteenth century, scientific accounts record extreme dry periods at Lake Baringo (e.g. Bessems et al., 2008; Kiage & Liu, 2009). These dry periods were accompanied by the absence of humans and herbivores (wildlife as well as livestock) in the region before 1650 and again between 1750 and 1830 due to droughts, famine and migration. In paleo-ecological records of Lake Baringo sediments, Kiage and Liu (2009) detect an increase in pollen and spores again after the 1830s, and refer to it as a sign of increasing human activity around Lake Baringo by both pastoralists and agriculturalists. Anderson (2016) calls the dry event in the Baringo-Bogoria basin in the early nineteenth century the 'Great Catastrophe', which was then followed by a rapid recovery of local livelihoods. During the recovery phase, the southern shores of Lake Baringo were then inhabited by the Il Chamus and the northern slopes by pastoral Pokot (Bollig & Oesterle, 2013). This was the beginning of a successful era for Pokot pastoralists.

In the twentieth century, the Pokot sustained their pastoral livelihoods despite coming under pressure. In reaction to a changing environment, they diversified their herd structures and were able to adapt to the incremental changes occurring. The external social changes, however, had very little impact on their livelihoods. British colonial rule, which ended in 1963, had only few effects on pastoral Pokot in East Pokot, apart from one famous revolt that was quelled. Bollig and Oesterle describe this period as follows:

> In 1902 the British established a station in the region, first in the Kerio Valley and then at Mukotani near Lake Baringo. In 1911 headquarters were relocated to the Tugen Highlands, and colonial impact on the Pokot pastoral community remained rather ephemeral until the early 1950s. (Bollig & Oesterle, 2013, p. 297)

In the second half of the twentieth century, the town centres in the region slowly grew and school education and church activities increased over time. Both processes exerted little influence on the rural pastoral areas. More important were the wars with Turkana pastoralists from 1969 to 1984 and the consequent loss of Pokot territory and their arming with automatic guns in reaction to the armament of Turkana pastoralists (Bollig, 1990b).

> On the 18th June, 1975 at about 06.00, a group of about three hundred (300) Pokots from Baringo armed with two (rifles) and one pistol, raided Turkana Manyatta at Lomelo in South Turkana and stole unkown [*sic*] number of cattle, goods, sheep, donkeys and camels. During the raid thirteen (13) Turkanas and eight (8) Pokots were killed. The stolen stock were taken in two groups, one group to Kolloa area and the other to Nginyang area.

The G.S.U. [the Kenya Police Service paramilitary General Service Unit]
pursued the raiders and on the 19th June, 1975 recovered 200 herds [*sic*]
of cattle, 20 camels, 35 donkeys and 150 sheep/goats. ... This raid was
rather serious because it is the first time Pokots have used firearms in a
raid. (Nasieku, 1975, p. 1)

During the long-lasting conflict, the pastoral Pokot regained their territory
and expanded further north. The war is still remembered vividly by Pokot
elders, and many of the changes that can be seen today are ascribed to the
consequences of the war. When it ended, a new generation set was initiated.
However, the conflict with the Turkana people still flares up from time to time
in the border zones between Pokot and Turkana territories.

Moreover, the pastoral Pokot contest access to land and resources with
other pastoral and agro-pastoral groups (Il Chamus, Tugen, Samburu and
Karimojong people). In the north, pastoral Pokot often clash with Turkana;
during the dry-season migrations in the early 2010s, they occupied the southern
border zones at Lake Baringo that are inhabited by the Il Chamus and Tugen.
In the west, the expansion of pastoralism is confined by West Pokot agro-
pastoralists; and in the east, by Samburu and the ranches of the Laikipia
Plateau. As Letai and Lind (2013) describe for the Maasai on the Laikipia
Plateau, pastoralists are 'squeezed from all sides' in this part of Kenya.

The arrival of religious and political actors in East Pokot

External interventions in East Pokot have a comparatively short history.
Whereas the pre-colonial and colonial period was ostensibly characterised
mainly by encounters with Europeans and ivory traders, there were very few
intensive interactions with the colonial powers. What has been termed the
'Kolloa Massacre' in the early 1950s was one of them: a very short episode
of resistance against the British that was suppressed violently (Bollig, 2006;
Oesterle, 2007). The massacre was preceded by the symbolic burial of a pen
on the way from Nginyang to Kolloa as a sign of resistance to external interventions and education efforts (Oesterle, 2007). Bollig (1992a) outlines the
few interventions by the colonial power in the affairs of the pastoral Pokot
up until the declaration of independence. These included the collection of
taxes by colonial officials, which, however, did not provoke further resistance,
along with the colonial exploration of the region. In some respects, this
colonial penetration of East Pokot is even described as being beneficial to the
Pokot pastoralists, because the British drove Turkana pastoralists back from
previously conquered Pokot territory, and the Pokot received compensation
for the violent occupation of their lands.

The first profound external influences came mainly from church institutions.
First of all, in the late 1940s, the Africa Inland Mission (AIM) was established

in Nginyang where it started to educate Pokot children in the first primary school in the region (Bollig, 1992a). However, the first more intensive efforts began in the post-colonial period. These continued to be initiated by church leaders who were active in various regions located along the established roads, thereby concentrating their work in the few built-up centres in the region. In the 1970s, this was especially along two roads: the Loruk–Nginyang–Kolloa–Tot highway and the Loruk–Tangulbei–Maralal highway with 'rural access [being] poor' (Catholic Diocese of Nakuru, 1980, p. 4). But even the already established roads were far from being in an ideal condition, and the northern Baringo County in general was poorly connected to the rest of Kenya. In the 1970s, a proposal was made to re-route the B4 road through the Rift Valley from Nginyang to Kapedo and Lokori (Republic of Kenya, 1975). However, the route actually chosen was to connect Nginyang via Kolloa up the escarpment to Lomut. Access routes to rural areas, such as the Marigat–Amaya road were, on the other hand, designated only as 'carriage ways' that were 'to be improved' (Republic of Kenya, 1975, p. 164).

In the 1970s, the education efforts of the missionaries in Nginyang became more successful; and in the late 1970s, the Catholic mission was founded in Kositei. Further religious institutions followed such as the AIC (African Inland Church), which was closely connected to the AIM, the FGCK (Full Gospel Church of Kenya), the Holy Ghost Fathers, the Anglican Church, then known as the Church of the Province of Kenya (CPK), the Pentecostal Assemblies of God (PAG) and the Seventh-Day Adventists (SDA) (Oesterle, 2007). These initiatives had many plans to improve the lives of the people in the region by, for example, educating youth, improving access to water for people and animals and educating and empowering women. One of the most successful examples is certainly the establishment of schools in the region. Whereas school infrastructure was almost non-existent in the early 1970s (Republic of Kenya, 1975), this changed quickly. By 1991, the Full Gospel Church – with funding from the Finnish Free Foreign Mission (FFFM) and the International Relief and Development Agency of the FFFM – had established the first secondary school in East Pokot along with eight primary schools and 18 pre-primary schools (Full Gospel Churches of Kenya, 1991).[9] In 1996, there were officially 36 pre-primary, 26 primary and one secondary school in East Pokot (Republic of Kenya, 1998).[10] Hence, the churches had a large share in developing a formal educational infrastructure in East Pokot, also by building a hospital and dispensaries (Full Gospel Churches of Kenya, 1991).

But the churches also had a strong impact in other fields. For instance, the Catholic Diocese of Nakuru built dams in Seretion, Tangulbei and

9   The schools were taken over by the government in the 1980s.
10 Today, eight secondary schools and 114 primary schools can be found in the entire region (Republic of Kenya, 2018).

Kolloa,[11] and it also set up centres for agriculture in Chepkalacha, Mkutani, Seretion, Chesemerion and Nginyang in the late 1970s (Catholic Diocese of Nakuru, 1980). The programme objectives of these centres covered all facets of crop production, women's development (especially health issues), range management development and soil management, as well as grass reseeding and bee-keeping (Catholic Diocese of Nakuru, 1980). They also addressed water supply, adult education, foodand income production, skills training for youth and tree nursery and planting (Catholic Diocese of Nakuru, 1994).

The government projects, however, remained rather limited to plans for one health centre in Nginyang and the construction of dispensaries in Kolloa and Tangulbei in the mid-1970s (Republic of Kenya, 1975). In the field of water supply, there were also very few utilities. For instance, in the early 1980s, there were only three boreholes in Nginyang, Tangulbei and Chemolingot (Republic of Kenya, 1982) sponsored by the Ministry of Water Development (Republic of Kenya, 1975). As stated in a government report, it was the church institutions that were largely responsible for the development of infrastructure in East Pokot.

> Church of the Province of Kenya C.P.K. [now the Anglican Church of Kenya (ACK)] also provided help in the supply of water to East Pokot. Based in Nginyang, the Mission proposed to construct about 18 water structures including dams, steam jets, trenches, weirs and stream walls, all to cost about 86,000/=. Should this materialise, a breakthrough will have been made in East Pokot for water supply. (Republic of Kenya, 1977, p. 55)

Plans to construct offices and staff houses in Chemolingot and to post government personnel came only in the late 1990s (Republic of Kenya, 1998). This shows the marginal character of East Pokot from a political perspective.

Some of the most important developments were the agricultural projects that were initiated from different sides. In the late 1970s and the 1980s, the Baringo Pilot Semi-Arid Areas Project started work in the Churo highlands and vicinity as well as in Chepkalacha in the lowlands (both along the Maralal highway) and Chemolingot (on the B4 to West Pokot). This project particularly targeted water harvesting and agricultural extension (World Bank, 1990). The Kenya Freedom from Hunger Council also successfully aimed to rehabilitate dams and shallow wells, crop development and livestock development in the 1980s and 1990s, and it set up livestock markets during the 1980s. As

---

[11] Later, other churches were also involved in the provision of water. An example is the AIC in Loruk that built a total of 26 water tanks and six shallow wells with the assistance of UNICEF (Republic of Kenya, 1998). The Church Province of Kenya (CPK) also built 70 water tanks to provide water (Republic of Kenya 1998).

Bollig (2006) points out, there was even a weekly livestock market set up in Nginyang in 1988 with the help of the German Agro Action aid organisation that invested in the livestock sector, but withdrew its involvement in the late 1990s. However, the livestock markets were established all over East Pokot, and livestock selling became an important livelihood strategy to generate cash income and to provide goods and food for pastoral households.

The actual impact of the projects on the ground is difficult to assess precisely. However, what is visible from today's perspective, and is also reported by many Pokot, is that three major aspects have had an impact on livelihoods in East Pokot: these are the effects on land use in the highlands where agriculture has taken on a pioneering role in the transformation process; the access to water in the form of area-wide pan dams and boreholes, which arrived to some extent in rural areas as well as at the trading centres; and the consolidation of formal education and church institutions in the region's settlement centres. But it must also be noted that the influence of these on most pastoralists has been very limited.

Management of the land and conflicts over pasture land

The history of land tenure in Kenya has a deeply entrenched relationship with colonial history and the colonisation of large areas by white settlers. Furthermore, it can be described as a tangled history since the declaration of independence with political elites failing to reform and redistribute land rights (Manji, 2012, 2020), but, instead, grabbing large areas of land for themselves, as revealed by the so-called Ndung'u Commission (2004). The political elites have been subject to heavy criticism for their misconduct and land grabbing. This collective history of injustices led to the emergence of demands for decentralisation of the political administration and for a new land law to be incorporated into the constitution. This was enacted in 2010.

Following the adoption of a new constitution, a political devolution process was implemented in Kenya that not only affected the political organisation in the country and strengthened the position of the 47 counties that were established along the former district boundaries, but also had far-reaching effects on the land tenure system and administration. Under the devolution of governmental power and the reorganisation of land tenure, a National Land Commission (NLC) was established including land-management boards on the county level that organise legal issues over public land such as its administration and redistribution, security of land rights, changes in ownership, land subdivisions, and conservation-related issues, while also addressing historical injustices and community land issues (Bassett, 2017; Klopp & Lumumba, 2017). In 2012, The Land Act (Republic of Kenya, 2012a) and the Land Registration Act (Republic of Kenya, 2012b) came into effect and created a system to register public land, private land (including freehold and lease), and community land. Four years later, in 2016 the Community Land Act was adopted, emphasising the communal use of land that 'means holding or using land in undivided shares by a community' (Republic of Kenya, 2016, p. 529). It intends to provide those communities that manage land on the communal level with more security of land tenure and its allocation.

In East Pokot, the land is currently under trustee ownership and the process of official recognition as a community land is currently (in 2021) under way. Already in December 2020, six community committees were established in the sub-counties Tirioko, Kolloa, Ribkwo, Tangulbei/Korossi, Loyamoruk, and Churo/Amaya with each board consisting of 15 community members. These boards are responsible for defining communal pasture areas, community recreation points, or places for government institutions. They further discuss the administration of land issues such as the private allocation of land titles; or they engage in the demands for compensation in cases of compulsory acquisition of land – for instance by the Geothermal Development Company (Klagge et al., 2020). These payments, which are still under negotiation, are expected to result in private payments for those persons directly affected by construction activities such as roads, pipelines or drilling sites. With the Community Land Act, it becomes possible to register land privately, and especially in those regions of East Pokot in which agricultural farmland was established in the last decades that has been used in a de facto private way, it is expected that private title deeds will be issued soon after the establishment of the community committees. This also includes payments into the community trust land account that will then be available for community measures in the respective sub-counties.

In the county context, the devolution process is also prone to criticism (see, e.g., Lind 2018 for the case of Turkana County), because many questions about contested territories remain unanswered, and the effects of the devolution are not entirely understood. Indeed, it might even seem that it fosters local conflicts. Although devolution helps to acknowledge the perspectives of regional political representatives and their interests, it also generates new struggles, especially in regions in which the discovery of oil reserves has created new questions of accession and distribution (Orr, 2019).

The new land legislation is also subject to critical assessment (Boone et al., 2019; Manji, 2014, 2015, 2020), and the Community Land Act inaugurated in 2016 seems to have further loopholes that allow many difficulties to arise (Alden Wily, 2018). But from the perspective of many pastoral Pokot, participation in political decisions and the opportunity to participate in the decisions about land and also about regional development measures are also viewed positively, because they at least hold the promise of involvement and ownership.

For the early 2000s, Oesterle (2007) still describes the land tenure system in East Pokot as an openly accessible territory that ensures access to resources to all Pokot. Although pastoral Pokot refer to the land as communal property, land access is de facto limited in certain areas by social demarcation and exclusion (Greiner et al., 2013). When referring to pastoralists in Cameroon, Moritz (2016) discusses the difficult term of open access in the literature about the commons and suggests using the terminology 'open property regimes' instead of 'open access' to indicate that these systems also have – often informal – structures and regulations that determine land use. Moreover, Galaty (2016) describes the difficulties in the de jure designation of land tenure for East Africa that does not always describe the de facto land use by pastoralists. He emphasises the dynamics of the transitions between different property regimes such as common, private and state-owned, claiming that 'each form of property-as-use is susceptible to boundary erosions that at the limit create conditions of open access' (p. 715). This also holds true in the case of East Pokot, where access to land and resources is generally open, but, under certain conditions, also restricted and managed. This includes the enclosure of land used for individual or group purposes (such as on the household level), or the establishment of homesteads, which are changed at irregular intervals, as well as the demarcation of fields used for agriculture and for feeding calves that are not sent on seasonal migration to other grazing areas.

For agriculture, gardens are demarcated by fencing a piece of land with acacia branches. These plots are often extensive parcels cultivated only partially with maize. In the remaining area of the fenced plots, grasses grow abundantly – in contrast to commonly used land – and owners of gardens create small grass storages for their own exclusive use.[12] Whereas, once implemented, enclosures create a de facto ownership of land, which is accepted by all Pokot (see Photo 2), establishing new gardens is often accompanied by contentions about recent land use and former land occupation. For instance, garden boundaries are perceived not only in terms of the physical fences around them but also by the catchment area that provides additional water for cultivation. Therefore, the allotment of land sometimes also results in conflicts among pastoralists over the enclosure and demarcation of land for private purposes.

In general, land access in East Pokot is open, land-use rights are performed *inter pares*, and the only official restriction to pasture is the closure of mountain sites for dry-season pasture – something that is decided by the council of elders. When livestock forage, especially grasses, are exhausted in the plains, herders move to the mountain sites of Paka and Korossi and use water from Lake Baringo or dams to water their animals. Highland pastures on Mt Korossi

---

[12] Women have their own gardens. Mainly these are established in the homestead to grow some vegetables during the rainy season. Nevertheless, women can also fence bigger plots outside the homestead and establish their own gardens for maize and other crops.

Photo 2. Pastoral farming in an enclosure in Lolemoi, Mt Paka (Hauke-Peter Vehrs).

and Mt Paka are protected after rainy seasons (in years of high precipitation) to ensure the recovery of the vegetation. When these pastures are exhausted, the herders must move further afield. Surrounded by other pastoral communities, Pokot herders then often enter 'enemy' land to the north, east and south in search of pastures. Little et al. (2009) estimate that Il Chamus lost 30 per cent of their seasonal grazing area in the eastern region of Lake Baringo in the period 2004–09 due to Pokot raids and encroachment.

Over time, Pokot migration routes change depending on the availability of forage and water and the magnitude of violent conflicts with neighbouring Turkana, Samburu, Il Chamus and Tugen, because the territory inhabited by pastoral Pokot is limited and surrounded by other ethnic groups. Hence, dry-season movements often evoke violent conflicts in the border zones with the Turkana (Kariuki, 2015), Tugen (Koech, 2017b) and Il Chamus (Little, 2016). The decision to move to a certain grazing area is accompanied by inquiring about the prophets' opinion and any existing inter-ethnic conflicts. In the 2010s, Pokot violently raided beyond their southern border areas towards Mukotan and Arabal, east of Lake Baringo. These areas are characterised by good pastures, water accessibility and the least resistance to Pokot warriors. However, warriors cannot arbitrarily occupy 'enemy' land, and frequently clash with members of other groups, the local police and the Kenya Defence Forces (KDF) that are sent to secure the area. The severity of fighting increased over the years and the Kenyan government employed a union of different units, consisting of Government Administrative Officers, the Rapid Deployment Unit, the General Service Unit, the Anti-Stock Theft Unit, the Directorate of Criminal Investigations and the National Intelligence Service to deal with the security situation and lead a mission to disarm the 'Pokot bandits' (Macharia, 2021). From such a 'bandits' perspective, the ongoing conflict with governmental and military units, the situation appears as follows, referring to a 2015 military intervention.

> It is peaceful.[13] We are the ones who moved to Losadan with all the cattle. That is the place where we fought with Tugen and the government. Last time we fought with the helicopter, until we defeated the soldiers last week. … We stayed until last Wednesday. Some men were on patrol in the conflict zone in the night. Next morning, we took the animals to the water place. Four Njempsi [Il Chamus] men stole animals and we followed them. The fire started and it was good we got support from men behind us. The fire continues, fire continues, until we returned our animals.
>
> We slept until 2 am in the morning, ready to move. Gunshots were all over – paw, paw – the gunshots were all over. We got worried and people said it is time to move: 'Let's move completely, we cannot live in this area anymore.'
>
> Then, we were on the road [cattle track leading back to East Pokot]. The road was really squeezed until morning time – you can imagine all the Pokot cows. (Interview 11 March 2015, anonymous)

The focus on the territory of Il Chamus people is not completely new, but the intensity of fighting has increased in the recent past. Limited water and pasture during the dry season lead to regular contestations about land during the migration of pastoral Pokot. The conflicts in the past differ somewhat from the recent conflicts at Lake Baringo. From the 1960s to the 1980s, Pokot fought against the Turkana in the north. Bollig describes this conflict in detail and draws the links between weaponry, conflict and the importance of masculinity and braveness in battle. He describes the deep-rooted conflict between Turkana and Pokot as a 'bush war' (1996, p. 148). He also depicts the practice of raids with large groups of several hundred men who prepared for the raid, asked for permission, were blessed by the elders and strictly adhered to rules of purity.

In recent times, these structures of organised raids in larger groups have changed, and now small units of young men secretly enter enemy land and steal small quantities of livestock. Furthermore, the young warriors often delay the rituals attached to combat. Apart from ritual blessing, these involve

---

[13] Opening phrase in the beginning of a conversation.

the purification of those who have killed an enemy during a fight. Bollig emphasises the masculinity and warrior ideals among the pastoral Pokot that are part and parcel of the ongoing conflicts with neighbouring groups. The vilification of a man by another Pokot – man or woman – often resulted in a situation where the vilified person had to prove his masculinity. This also includes killing an enemy during combat, which is acknowledged with special *kola* scars and a red ostrich feather, acceptance among the Pokot community and the prestige of being a slayer (Bollig, 1996). The warriors with *kola* scars, so-called *nyakan*, had to prove themselves further through courage, discipline, determination, courtesy, rhetoric talent, skilful use of weapons and intelligence (Bollig, 1996).

This example shows that the prestige of the individual also determines his or her position in society. In general, both men and women have rites of passage that follow strict rules and must be passed to access different stages in life. The following section describes the social organisation of the pastoral Pokot acephalous society.

Pokot social organisation

The community life of the pastoral Pokot is structured along patrilineal descent and inheritance (Edgerton, 1964). Totemistic clans (*lilö*), patrilineal lineages (*ortïn*) and age sets and generation sets provide the basis of the social structure in East Pokot (Bollig, 1990a). With reference to Schneider (1953) and Huntingford (1953), Bianco (1991) mentions the existence of 36 different clans of pastoral and agro-pastoral Pokot, each equipped with a totem sign often in the shape of an animal or another feature of life such as the wind (*yomöt*) or the sun (*asis*). Each clan consists of several lineages, and exogamous marriage rules apply for every clan. In the early twentieth century, Barton identified and listed 15 clans, their lineages and totems, as well as their specific characteristics (Barton, 1921). Oesterle identifies 22 East Pokot clans (Oesterle, 2007). Bollig (2006) also explains rules of affinal relationships that are mainly but not exclusively oriented towards lineage and clan exogamy, and he comes to the conclusion that, through marriage, new ties are forged between two sets of people who had no relations before. These affinal relations are also used to establish new networks among each other.

The egalitarian society of pastoral Pokot is furthermore constituted around the age sets (*asapantin*) and generation sets (*pïn*). Every man belongs to both – one generation set and one age set. The men gain membership of an age set during an initiation ceremony that normally takes place in the late teens of a young warrior, the so-called *sapana*. Often, subsequent initiation cohorts are consolidated into one age set, which is named after a specific event of that time (Bollig, 1990a). Second, men are initiated into a generation set during circumcision, which takes place only every 25–35 years for each generation-set group. The generation- and age-set groups are organised in a gerontocratic political system. Figure 1 displays some age and generation sets of pastoral Pokot since the early nineteenth century.

It is important to point out an inconsistent use of the term 'age set' for the pastoral Pokot. In many East African pastoral societies, the respective age sets and their implementations follow strict rules of either circumcision or other rites of passage (such as killing an ox, camel or goat in Pokot or Turkana pastoral groups). Previously, both types have been described as age

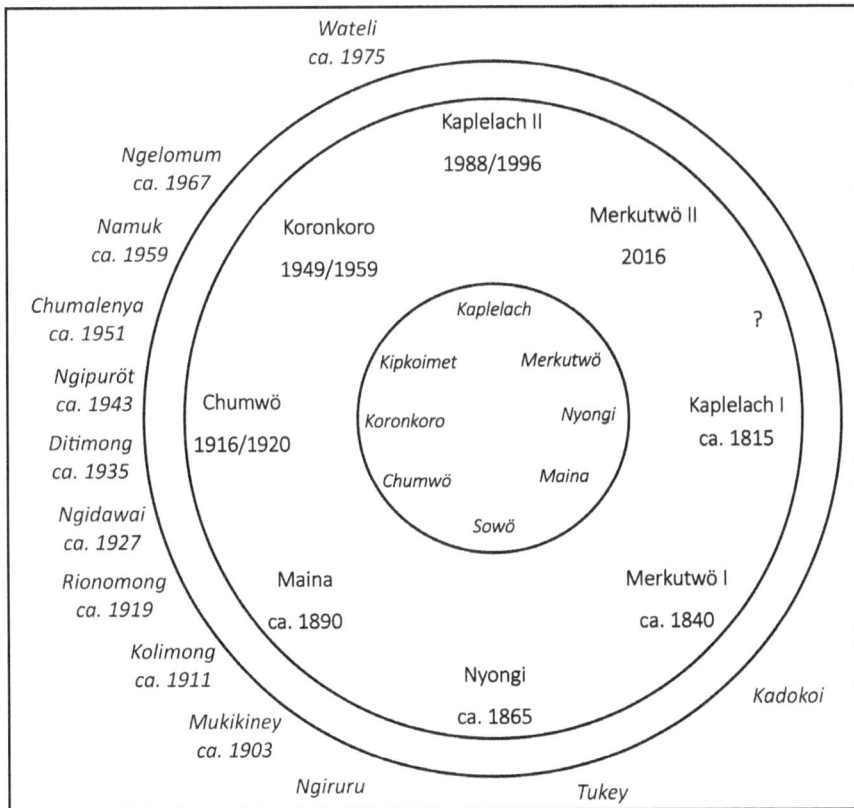

Fig. 1. Pokot generation- and age-set names, early 1800s (adapted from and courtesy of Bollig, 1992a, p. 85); the inner circle describes the regular sequence of generations sets, the middle circle the actual sequence including initiation periods, and the outer circle age sets as specified by Bollig.

set, as can be seen in the case of the Turkana (Gulliver, 1958)[14] or the Il Chamus, Maasai and Samburu (Spencer, 1997).[15] However, in the case of the pastoral Pokot in East Pokot, both types of male initiation are performed and therefore must be differentiated from each other. In line with Bollig (1992a), I use the term generation set for initiated men who undergo circumcision and hence are put together as one generation. This practice is very similar to the initiation of age-set groups of Il Chamus people. In total, seven generation sets exist and appear in a cyclical way that Bollig (1992a) identifies as Nyongi, Maina, Chumwö, Sowö, Koronkoro, Kaplelach and Merkutwö. The current generation sets are Koronkoro (circumcised 1949–59), Kaplelach (1988–96) and Merkutwö (2016). In contrast to Bollig, Schneider (1953) uses the term age set when referring to the circumcision of men. Peristiany again turns it the other way around, and refers directly to the Pokot age-set system when describing the initiation of men during the *sapana* ceremony and remarking on the complication of there being two initiation ceremonies for pastoral Pokot men (Peristiany, 1951). In general, age-set terminology could be used to describe both ceremonies, because both are 'rites de passage' – or 'puberty rites' as van Gennep (2010) calls them. To make a clear distinction between the two different initiation ceremonies, the circumcision of men and the more individual *sapana* ceremony, the first is referred to through the term generation set because it determines the different generations within Pokot social organisation; the second is referred to through the term age set because initiands from different initiand sets (undergoing the *sapana*) are clustered within one age set.

However, generally, the term 'age set' is used to describe the ways in which boys pass through a rite of passage to become fully acknowledged members of their societies. Spencer (2018) defines age sets as follows:

> Analytically, it is necessary to distinguish between age sets (or age groups), which incorporate all men within a broad age range regardless of personal wealth, and age grades (or age classes), which refer to a fixed scale of seniority inhabited by specific age sets at defined points in their careers. The overarching characteristics are, first, the notion of strict equality and sharing within an age set and, second, rigid inequalities in status between age sets. It is useful to envisage age sets climbing an 'age ladder' in which successive rungs are the age grades to which age-set members aspire. Entry into an age set normally occurs through initiation onto the bottom rung in youth. The relevance of affiliation to an age set often dwindles with age, but in the most developed systems

[14] Gulliver (1958) describes how young Turkana, similar to the *sapana* initiation of young Pokot, are initiated into an age set to become fully acknowledged members of society.

[15] Maasai, Samburu or Il Chamus, on the other hand, initiate their men periodically into an age set by circumcision of all boys in a certain wet season after a sequence of years (Spencer, 1997).

it is lifelong, and an age set only dies when its last surviving members die. (Spencer, 2018, p. 1)

Spencer distinguishes here between the general description of different age sets characterised by a strong internal identification among their members and an internal differentiation of age grades that determines the internal hierarchy of age-set members. He further reports that the generational sequence might also be important, and suggests that it is reasonable in some cases to classify the newly initiated set of men as 'age and generation systems' (Spencer, 2018).

In the case of the pastoral Pokot, we face a terminological dilemma, because both systems – the circumcision of boys and men every 25–35 years and the *sapana* initiation – are highly important for Pokot social organisation and are undertaken at different stages of a boy's or man's life. However, they cannot both be referred to as age set. Former scientists already caused some confusion by doing so (see, e.g., both Schneider and Peristiany). Therefore, as noted above, I follow Bollig's use of the terminology for the description of pastoral Pokot social organisation.

> Through separate initiation rituals each man becomes a member of an age-set (*asapantin*) and of a generation-set (*pïn*). Membership of one set involves egalitarian, almost brotherly relationships with one's peers on the one hand and submission under an age-based hierarchy on the other hand. Initiation into generation-sets only takes place every twenty-five to thirty-five years when numerous young men and boys are circumcised together and from then on constitute one generation-set. (Bollig, 2006, p. 33)

Women are excluded from membership of both generation and age sets. They undergo female circumcision before the usual marriage in their teens. Edgerton describes the importance of both male and female circumcision for Pokot communities (Edgerton, 1964). Although officially illegal, female circumcision is still practised among pastoral Pokot, and girls are often circumcised to attain full membership status in the community. When girls and boys become full members, they can take on the full rights and obligations attached to their new position. Women can marry and enter a new phase of life. Men can also marry after completing their *sapana* and are then allowed to raise their voice during official communal meetings (*kokwö*) meetings and sit among the men in the *kirket*, the half-circle of men that is formed during ceremonies.

The pastoral Pokot separate men's and women's worlds strongly from each other and both sexes have their specific obligations in the household. Women mostly take care of domestic work as well as a small share of livestock keeping and farming, whereas men organise the husbandry of livestock and the activities attached to it such as tick spraying or watering the animals and attending *kokwö* meetings.

Population development in East Pokot since the mid-twentieth century

One of the most difficult issues to understand is the historical reconstruction of population dynamics in East Pokot. Because in the past, it was nearly impossible to collect exact population figures for the pastoral areas in Kenya, one has to compare existing data and try to identify trends. It is not possible to provide exact figures at this point either, but at least a trend can be identified that can be used to define the orders of magnitude for further calculations.

The official data published on the national level in Kenya (especially the 2009 and 2019 census data) stand out through their high estimates of population figures that need to be treated with caution. The census data from the Republic of Kenya from 1979 to 2019 suggest that a population of 26,917 people increased by 570 per cent to 153,347 people within merely four decades. Against the background of both the inter-ethnic conflicts in East Pokot that ended at the beginning of the 1980s and the region's continuing marginal status in terms of economic development, I do not consider it plausible for immigration into East Pokot to have accounted for a large share of the population increase. In 1953, Huntingford (1953) estimated the population of Pokot people in Baringo at between 6,500 and 7,350 people in an estimated area of 1,000,000 acres (about 4,000 km²). Table 1 shows the population development for East Pokot between 1953 and 2019 according to Huntingford and the Kenyan census data for the period 1979–2019.

Table 1. Population development in East Pokot, 1953–2019.

Source	Huntingford (1953)[16]	Census data 1979	Census data 1989	Census data 1999	Census data 2009	Census data 2019
Population number	6,500–7,350	26,917	40,670	63,659	133,189	153,347
Area (km²)[17]	4,047	4,441	n.a.	4,431	4,517	4,663
Population density (people/km²)	1.6–1.8	6.1	n.a.	14.4	29.5	32.8

Sources: Huntingford (1953); Republic of Kenya (1981); Republic of Kenya (1994b), data taken from Oesterle (2007); Republic of Kenya (2001) – data taken from Oesterle (2007); Republic of Kenya (2010); Republic of Kenya (2019).

---

[16] Schneider (1953) gives a similar population of 7,000 for East Pokot, referring to estimations by Hennings (1951).

[17] The administrative units in East Pokot varied over time, and density calculations were made according to the respective area under study.

What is particularly notable about these official numbers is that the population appears to have increased tremendously over the past two decades. Weitzberg (2015) discusses the questionable census data from 2009 with regard to estimates of strongly increasing numbers of people with Somali ethnic affiliation in Kenya – an increase of more than 140 per cent in the census within merely one decade (for the Pokot case, the increase is 'only' an additional 109 per cent). The indication of the inaccuracies of the census data led to the nullification of the results in eight districts (Weitzberg, 2015).

Moreover, the challenges when trying to gather valid census data in pastoral communities are also wellknown. In the 2009 census, the enumeration of pastoralist populations was highlighted as problematic in a number of districts that appeared to have experienced unrealistic population growth since the 1999 census (Randall, 2015). There could be several reasons behind this (lower counting in the former census due to drought conditions, high mobility of pastoral groups, or higher incentives that attracted people for the 2009 census etc.), but a comprehensive picture cannot be drawn from all the discontinuities. What can be assumed, at least for the case in East Pokot, is that estimated population numbers do not match extrapolations based on reasonable growth rates. One can, furthermore, assume that the number of households (however defined in the census), and the population figures given, are lower than those stated in the official 2009 and 2019 census data.

Figure 2 compares the population data of the Kenyan census (1979, 1989, 1999, 2009 and 2019) to extrapolations made on the basis of the 1979 figures. Assuming that the 1979 population data are more robust than the estimations in the following censuses, I have calculated two trends based on the following assumptions: for both cases, I assume that immigration does not play a significant role and that natural growth rates are the main contributor to population development in East Pokot. One extrapolation is based on data from the SALTLICK (1991) survey that states that an annual growth rate of 3.47 per cent per annum was taken for extrapolations in their survey. The second extrapolation is based on empirical data published by Bollig and Lang (1999) who state that the growth rate among the pastoral Pokot was 2.4 per cent per annum in the 1990s.

As can be seen in Figure 2, the official data and the extrapolated data show similar trends in terms of a strongly growing population, but the official estimations are far higher than the two extrapolated trends based on reasonable growth rates for the region of East Pokot. A population number between 69,506 (estimation based on an annual growth rate of 2.4 per cent)[18] and 105,343

[18] Less widely acknowledged official projections for the years 2008, 2010 and 2012 were made on the basis of the 1999 census data of 63,659 people in East Pokot (Republic of Kenya, 2008). Figures are projected as follows: 2008: 78,495 people, 2010: 82,236 people, and 2012: 86,155 people (Republic of Kenya, 2008). With an

(based on an annual growth rate of 3.47 per cent)[19] seems more plausible if one wants to estimate the current population numbers for East Pokot, with estimated household numbers between 10,000 and 15,000.[20]

Therefore, I would question not only the overall population figures displayed in the official census data but also the number of households in East Pokot. This is given as 26,651 households for 2019 (Republic of Kenya, 2019). Because SALTLICK (1991) calculates less than 3,000 households for East Pokot,[21] the sharp increase to more than 12,000 in 1999, more than 21,000 in 2009, and finally more than 26,000 in 2019 is inconceivable.

According to the extrapolations in Figure 2, an educated conjecture can be made on the basis of more reasonable population and household figures. These are also used to estimate livestock numbers in the next section.

The contradiction presented here cannot be resolved finally at this point. However, I want to argue that the number of households in the region is most likely to be far below the officially stated figures. I would attribute this to a higher average household size than that stated in the official census data and to incomprehensible population estimates in the recent Kenyan census publications. Furthermore, the Kenyan national trend of decreasing fertility rates since the 1970s (the World Bank 2021 reports a decrease from an average of 8.1 children per woman in 1970 to 3.5 in 2018) can also be taken into account when assessing population trends in East Pokot, even though specific data on the district level are lacking. Whereas county-level data were released for 2014 (KNBS & ICF International, 2016), these did not account for disparities between regions in the counties. Therefore, a clear and predictable statement about the impact on population growth in East Pokot is not possible. However, the general trend in the fertility rate speaks equally to the argument elaborated here about a numerically lower population in East Pokot than that stated in official reports. I hope to have shown that the high official figures are not reliable and need to be examined closely.

---

underlying annual population growth rate of 2.355 per cent, the projection for 2019 is a total of 103,789 people in East Pokot.

[19] An annual growth rate of 3.47 per cent is a fairly high assumption, but in the national Kenyan context, the average growth rate was 3.17 between 1960 and 2019 (World Bank, 2020).

[20] Average household numbers in the pastoral and agro-pastoral context have been measured in a large survey in 2019. This revealed an average number of people per household of 7.0. This household size is still low compared to data collected in 2015, when the average household size was 10.4 ($n = 151$).

[21] The 1991 survey also referred to higher estimations of up to 4,211 households for the entire region, but is not as high as the 12,712 households published in the 1999 census.

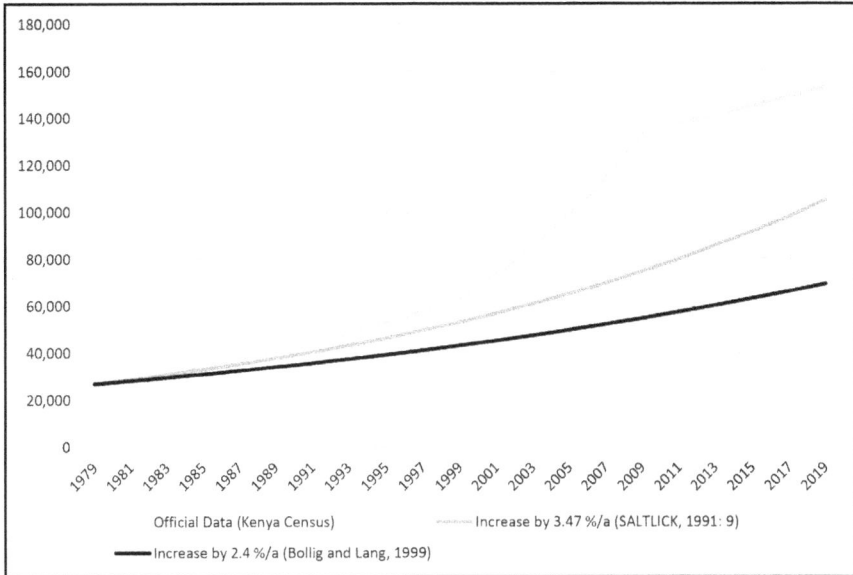

Fig. 2. Extrapolations of population development in East Pokot, 1979–2019, in comparison to official census data compiled from the population data of the Kenyan census, suggest lower population growth (Hauke-Peter Vehrs).

However, the general trend towards growing population numbers in East Pokot and increasing population densities is clearly evident and is also emphasised by elders who see a clear trend of a constantly growing population.

Livestock populations

The same problem of unrealistic population statistics also applies to the official livestock population estimations. Whereas moderate livestock figures from previous research and surveys suggest numbers of around 100,000 cattle, 600,000 to 700,000 small stock, and under 10,000 camels, official figures from the Kenyan government over the past two decades are substantially higher (especially the 2009 census). I address this issue in the following, and begin by assessing and deconstructing recent figures from the livestock censuses of 2009 and 2019 (see Table 2) before subsequently extrapolating more realistic estimates on the basis of more reliable livestock data and the revised population figures from the previous chapter.

In the 2009 Kenyan livestock census, the numbers of livestock are given as follows: 787,209 cattle, 1,854,742 shoats (sheep and goats are counted together) and 67,036 camels. This equates to a total tropical livestock unit

(TLU) of 1,102,847. Even if we consider the high official population estimations of 133,189 people (Republic of Kenya, 2009), this would lead to a TLU
of 8.3 per capita or in terms of area to a TLU/km² of 244.2.[22] These figures
do not suggest a realistic picture of livestock populations in the region.

The last Kenyan livestock census of 2019 (Republic of Kenya, 2020a)
relativises the high figures from 2009: 185,840 cattle, 699,835 shoats and
38,175 camels, resulting in a total TLU of 321,038; out of a total population
of 153,344, this results in a TLU/capita of 2.1 and a TLU/km² of 69.7 (total
area in 2019: 4,663 km²). There is no explanation for these extreme fluctuations in livestock numbers – 1/4 of cattle, almost 2/5 of shoats and 2/5 of
camels compared to 2009. Nevertheless, it can be assumed that these data
are much closer to a realistic estimate of the livestock data in East Pokot
than the figures published previously, although the value of 69.7 TLU/km²
(for 2019) is still extremely high compared to other pastoral groups in East
Africa. Nonetheless, when considering this value, one must still bear in mind
that the pastoral Pokot are very mobile during the dry season, allowing their
cattle to graze far outside their own territory (which would also result in
lower TLU/km² figures).

Table 2. Livestock population data in East Pokot 1991, 2009 and 2019.

	Cattle	Shoats	Camels	TLU (total)	TLU/ capita	TLU/ house-hold	TLU/ km²
SALTLICK 1991	69,980	175,783	4,443	97,507	2.4	35.1	22.2[23]
Census 2009	787,209	1,854,742	67,036	1,102,847	8.3	51.8	244.2
Census 2019	185,840	699,835	38,175	321,038	2.1	12.0	69.7

Sources: SALTLICK (1991), Republic of Kenya (2009, 2020a).

To obtain a realistic assessment of earlier livestock numbers, Table 2 also
contains data from the 1991 SALTLICK survey. These data are based on a
survey conducted in October 1991 and give a more realistic snapshot of the
situation in East Pokot in the early 1990s. The number of cattle might be
slightly underestimated, because the authors estimate the cattle population
using average livestock numbers per household and household number estimations. The estimations are discussed against the background of the 1988
rinderpest vaccinations in Nginyang and Tangulbei in which 73,323 cattle were
vaccinated. Especially, the TLU/km² value reflects a reasonable estimation

---

[22]   The area is indicated as 4.517 km².

[23]   In the SALTLICK survey the size of the area under study is estimated as being
4,400 km² (SALTLICK, 1991).

when compared to the Kenyan livestock census data reported in Table 2. The SALTLICK survey from 1991 gives a detailed account of how data were estimated and provides a robust data assessment for livestock populations.

To evaluate recent livestock data and reasonable estimations of the current stock situation in East Pokot, I shall discuss a series of survey data sets in the following (based on data gathered between 2015 and 2019) that give a very detailed picture of livelihoods in East Pokot. Table 3 compares these data to the official census data of 2009 and 2019.

The two surveys in 2015 were conducted in different regions of East Pokot: one characterised by predominantly pastoral land use (Paka); the other, by agro-pastoral land use (Churo). All livestock numbers for the Paka region (pastoral) are much higher on average compared to the other data displayed. Only the 2009 livestock census data record comparable values. However, because the Paka community does not represent the average per capita or per household distribution for the entire region, these data cannot be used for general extrapolations. The same bias holds the for the Churo survey data (in an agro-pastoral context) that also do not reflect a cross section of the society in East Pokot. The most recent and comprehensive data were gathered in a broad survey conducted by a group of researchers in 2019. This had a larger sample and did not focus on pastoral or agro-pastoral land uses. These data are taken for the calculation of current livestock population estimations.

Table 3. Population and livestock population growth in East Pokot, 1991–2019.

	SALTLICK 1991	Mt Paka 2015	Churo 2015	Tiaty East 2019	Census 2009	Census 2019
Households	2,777	54	97	361	21,291	26,651
People	40,000	600	966	2,541	133,189	153,347
People per household	14.4	11.1	10.0	7.0	6.3	5,8
TLU total	97,507	3,011	3,073	7,924	1,102,847	321,038
TLU/ household	35.1	55.8	31.7	21.9	51.8	12.0
TLU/head	2.4	5.0	3.2	3.1	8.3	2.1
Cattle per household	25.2	37	23.7	13.2	37.0	7.0
	SALTLICK 1991	Mt Paka 2015	Churo 2015	Tiaty East 2019	Census 2009	Census 2019
Cattle per head	1.7	3.3	2.4	1.9	5.9	1.2
Shoats per household	63.3	134.1	57.8	63.8	87.1	26.3

Table 3 continued.

	SALTLICK 1991	Mt Paka 2015	Churo 2015	Tiaty East 2019	Census 2009	Census 2019
Shoats per head	4.4	12.1	5.8	9.1	13.9	4.6
Camels per household	1.6	1.6	0.6	0.65	3.1	1.4
Camels per head	0.1	0.15	0.06	0.09	0.5	0.2

Sources: SALTLICK (1991), Survey Data 2015 (Paka Survey [n = 54], Paka Network Analysis [n = 56] and Churo Survey [n = 97]), Survey Data 2019 (Nshakira-Rukundo et al., 2021 and Census Data Republic of Kenya 2009 and 2019).

Even considering that cattle numbers in East Pokot are very high and that, due to degradation of existing pasture land, herders resort repeatedly to grazing areas outside their territory during the dry season (see also the ongoing conflicts with the Il Chamus east of Lake Baringo), a value above 50 TLU/km² is inconceivable. [24] This is also true in view of the fact that Oesterle and Bollig have published much lower values for East Pokot of 35.4 TLU/km² (Oesterle, 2008) and 15.4 TLU/km² (Bollig, 2006). Moreover, supplementary data for other pastoral groups in eastern and southern Africa indicate that TLU/km² values in the range of single-digit or low double-digit values would seem more appropriate.

Whereas the SALTLICK data provide a robust account of stock numbers for the early 1990s, the most reliable data with which to extrapolate current livestock numbers come from the 2019 CRC228 survey (Nshakira-Rukundo et al., 2021). Because the 2015 surveys both had a certain focus on pastoral and agro-pastoral land uses, the CRC228 survey has the advantage of a high *n* value with participants from a broad social background who therefore do not merely have a pastoral or agro-pastoral focus. I extrapolated livestock numbers using the population figures from the previous section. For Scenario 1, I assumed a total population of 69,506 (as discussed and extrapolated in the section before with data taken from Bollig) with a total household number of 9,874; and in Scenario 2, 105,343 people and 14,966 households (with data taken from SALTLICK). Results are displayed in Table 4.

---

[24] Rosati et al. (2009) compared livestock densities in different regions of the African continent for the year 2000 and made projections of livestock population developments for the year 2030. Highest numbers are reached in the Horn of Africa and in East Africa, with 46.4 and 38.9 TLU/km² respectively (for the year 2000).

Table 4. Extrapolation of livestock populations in East Pokot, 2019.

Survey Data 2019	Population	Households	Cattle	Shoats	Camels	TLU total	TLU km²
Scenario 1 (Bollig data)	69,506	9,875	132,061	630,007	6,419	218,836	48.6
Scenario 2 (SALTLICK data)	105,343	14,966	200,152	954,836	9,728	331,666	73.7

Sources: Hauke-Peter Vehrs, based on data from Bollig and Lang (1999); SALTLICK report (1991).

Livestock figures vary between 130,000 and 200,000 cattle, 630,000 and 950,000 shoats and 6,000 and 10,000 camel for the entire region of East Pokot.[25] These numbers are still high compared to Oesterle's livestock estimations published in 2007. He estimates livestock numbers as high as 117,332 cattle, 671,474 shoats and 8,008 camels (Oesterle, 2007). The data from Table 4 also show that small stock and camel numbers have risen compared to 1991 (SALTLICK). This trend also mirrors the opinion of Pokot elders, who indicate a strong rise in browsing livestock species (goats and camel) over the past decades. However, they also stated that cattle numbers have not risen significantly compared to the past,[26] even though the extrapolations in Table 4 suggest a moderate increase since the 1990s. Interesting are also the TLU/km² figures in Table 4 that are much lower than the 2009 Kenyan livestock census data suggest, but still depict a fairly high figure for pastoral regions in East Africa. Oesterle argues that the official territorial extent of East Pokot does not mirror the actual situation. Pastoral Pokot make use of territories north and south of East Pokot. In the north, they occupy regions north of Mt Silali that officially fall into Turkana County. In the south, land is occupied temporally for grazing purposes east of Lake Baringo during the dry season. Therefore, Oesterle assumes an extent of 6,000 km² rather than 4,400 km² (Oesterle, 2007). Taking this into consideration, TLU ratios would fall to 36.5 (Scenario 1) or 55.3 TLU/km² (Scenario 2), but still present high values.

---

[25] The 2019 population census might cause some confusion here. The area under study in this case (that was also referred to by other authors before, such as Bollig, Oesterle or Greiner) is named East Pokot and reflects the territory of the former Tiaty Constituency. In the 2019 census, the region in the north of Baringo County is now split into two areas – Tiaty East and East Pokot. However, the 'East Pokot' area from the 2019 census accounts for merely 2,500 km² and constitutes together with Tiaty East the region under study here that is also named East Pokot.

[26] In this case, 10 elders gave their opinion on rising or decreasing livestock numbers in East Pokot in 2015 compared to the year 1975.

So far, I have described the formation and establishment of Pokot pastoral people as well as their social organisation, population trends in the twentieth century and livestock developments. In the following, I want to address a specific case in more detail and delineate the pastoral livelihoods that currently exist in East Pokot using the example of the Mt Paka community to gain a better understanding of today's pastoral modes of living and compare them to other livelihood approaches.

4

The Paka Community

Mt Paka is an extinct volcano in the centre of East Pokot, a region characterised by its pastoral livelihoods. As mentioned before, in the nineteenth
century the pastoral Pokot were specialised cattle herders who established
their territory north of Lake Baringo and in the Kerio Valley. This chapter
describes the pastoral livelihoods at Mt Paka in detail in order to provide a
better understanding of today's pastoralists. Contrary to stereotyped assumptions, these are not geared exclusively to life with and from livestock, but are
characterised by a high diversity of livelihoods. Nevertheless, the focus on a
life with cattle, goats, camels and sheep is very clearly visible – on the one
hand, for own consumption; on the other hand, for market-oriented production.
The following description of Paka pastoral livelihoods also provides a basis
for a later comparison with agro-pastoral livelihoods. In this chapter, I focus
on describing the household and community structures and relationships and
explaining those elements that are particularly important in the daily life of
this pastoral community.

The population of the Paka community consists of approximately 500
to 600 people. Fluctuations in population numbers can be explained with
seasonal mobility and in- and out-migration of households from the study
area. During the main fieldwork from 2013 to 2015, I counted 92 married
women, 50 married men, four independent women and 412 children, resulting
in a population of 558 people. The official population density in the former
Paka/Korossi sub-location is 27.8 people per km^2 for the year 2019 (Republic
of Kenya, 2019), whereas the average population density in East Pokot has
been calculated as 32.8 people per km^2 for the same year (Republic of Kenya,
2019). Population numbers in East Pokot have increased strongly over the
past 60 years but, as mentioned in Chapter 3, official population figures must
also be viewed with caution.

The pastoral people at Mt Paka organise their living in households
consisting of the husband and at least one wife living together with children
and sometimes other members of the family such as the husband's mother or
siblings.[1] Each wife has her own self-built hut and several small shelter huts

---

[1] In terms of the definition of the 'household' unit, each family is counted
separately as including the husband, the wives and children. Sometimes, young families

for the goatlings, and she owns specific usufruct rights for milking certain livestock given at marriage (Sassoon, 1994). In general, the ownership of stock, as Schneider (1953, pp. 320–21) depicts, '[is] held by adult males, followed by young men who have passed through circumcision. Women have rights over stock although most of the stock in a family herd belong to the husband.' This is true in most cases, although a few exceptions are observable at Mt Paka. One widow living independently in the community exemplifies the exact opposite by owning her own stock and also exchanging it with men for ritual purposes. This example is illustrated further in the next section on social networks.

Every homestead has an open meeting place (*aperit*) in a central part of the homestead. Here, the day starts for the household head, visitors come and wait here, and tea is offered. In some cases, there is even an *aperit* hut in which guests can stay overnight. Photo 3 shows a typical pastoral homestead in the early afternoon.

The small stock and cattle are herded at some distance from the homestead during the rainy season, but they return there overnight and stay in specially constructed cattle and goat kraals. If somebody owns camels, a separate kraal is also constructed for them. The goatlings and calves also often get a separate small shelter. These kraals are sometimes moved within the homestead when the household head perceives a malaise or illness among the stock. If the stock continues to be ill, or sorcery against the household members or the herd is suspected, even the complete homestead can be moved to another place.

Often, the homestead is located next to a temporary water source that provides small quantities of water during the rainy season. In this case, it is an ephemeral channel next to the homestead, whereas the next reliable water source is a small spring (only during the rainy season) 500 metres away or the borehole at Adomeyon 3 kilometres away at the foot of Mt Paka. The women of the homestead collect water and almost all other goods (food from the markets,[2] firewood, etc.), whereas men deal mostly with livestock issues and community cases in the assembly of men, the *kokwö*. These meetings are

still live in the same homestead as the father of the husband. In these cases, both the father's family and the son's family are considered separately. Furthermore, four households of independent women were part of the research community. These women have separated from their husbands' homesteads and live with their oldest sons.

[2]   The women must walk to the nearest market – either in the closest centre or in 'bush markets' – once a week: a distance of 10–15 kilometres (one way). This applied for the time of research in 2015, but has changed profoundly in recent years since the Geothermal Development Company built up road infrastructures in East Pokot. Since then, small centres have been established along the roads and more goods have become accessible in the closer vicinity around Mt Paka.

Photo. 3. A Pokot homestead in Chepungus, October 2014 (Hauke-Peter Vehrs).

held regularly to discuss issues of importance, and decisions are made among the initiated men in the community.[3]

However, these *kokwö* meetings are slowly eroding and the consumption of alcohol by all adult members of the community is omnipresent in daily life. Oesterle describes the rising importance of alcohol production and consumption in East Pokot (Oesterle, 2007), a trend that is also observable beyond this region (Mieth, 2007; Smith & Little, 2002). Although both pastoral Pokot and researchers evaluate the general impact of alcohol consumption negatively (Becker, 2014), the production and selling of locally produced beer and spirits represent an opportunity for women to earn their own money, which is otherwise under the men's control. Everyday alcohol production through brewing beer and distilling spirits is a women's domain (Oesterle, 2007). In contrast, the production of *kipketin*, the local honey beer, which is used mostly during several ceremonies, is still in the hands of the men, but this is brewed only for non-commercial purposes. The rising consumption of alcohol, which, some decades ago, was restricted to the production of honey beer and its consumption by elders, is also perceived as a cause of

---

[3]   The right to speak in the *kokwö* is gained after carrying out the *sapana* ceremony and being initiated into an age set.

rude behaviour and adultery. From the perspective of the elderly Koronkoro generation, the consumption of alcohol and the behaviour of men and women in the community is interpreted as a decline of respect towards elders and a general erosion of the current gerontocratic political system.

In general, two or more households can cohabit. Often, the youngest of the married sons of the household lives together with his father and wives. Friends also establish households in close vicinity and form a kind of common household providing mutual support. In the dry season, these ties continue; the cattle herds are merged and sent to the protected grazing areas in East Pokot – such as Mt Paka and Mt Korossi – or to the better grazing ground outside East Pokot.

Bigger households with two wives or more often split into two parts during the dry season. One wife accompanies the household head on the transhumance migration for two to four months together with most of the cattle, a good share of the goats and sheep and some donkeys for transport. The remaining wife or wives stay in the main homestead with the rest of the livestock as long as minimum needs such as water, food and animal forage are met. Only during heavy droughts would all household members move out of their homestead to migrate for the period of the dry spell. Although mobility is still an important characteristic of pastoral livelihoods, the community structure at Mt Paka is relatively stable. It would be misleading to apply the notion of highly mobile herders who are constantly on the move in their search for pasture and water to Pokot pastoralists.

Table 5 shows the composition of households in the Paka community based on membership of generation sets. The older a man is, the more wives he might have married and the more children belong to his household.[4] With reference to the difficulties associated with the use of the household term, I would like to briefly discuss the term household and explain what this unit means in the case of the pastoral Pokot.

---

[4]   Clearly, this applies only to those men who successfully embark on a conventional pastoral way of life. However, it is not to be assumed that this applies to all men, but rather that some of them are involved in wage labour within the group – for example seasonal herding for well-established households – or work in the small centres on a variety of non-pastoral activities. They may also try to obtain the necessary capital for a pastoral life in the form of livestock through illegal activities such as raids, or they might even perish in the attempt.

Table 5. Households sorted along generation-set memberships at Mt Paka, 2015.

Generation set (n = 50)	Wives (range)	Children affiliated to the household head (range)
Sowö[5] [n = 1 (older than 90 years)]	4	26
Koronkoro [n = 4 (69 –84 years)]	4 (3–5)	20.5 (13–33)
Kaplelach [n = 26 (30 –76 years)][6]	2.3 (1–5)	11.4 (1–30)
Merkutwö [n = 19 (22–39 years)]	1.3 (1–2)	2.5 (0–9)

Source: Hauke-Peter Vehrs.

Beech (1911) refers to *kô* (pl.: *kor*) as a house or a hut that is normally built by the woman in of the household. If the man marries more than one woman over time, each wife builds her own hut in which she lives with her children. The man himself normally does not build a hut but sleeps in the huts of his wives. Furthermore, the mother of the man can also build a hut in the household if she has decided to live with him. The household itself is referred to with the term *kau* in Kipokot. Beech notes it as 'village' (*kau* in the singular and *kiston* in the plural; Beech, 1911, p. 146).[7] However, the notion of a village does not accurately describe the household that I am using here as an analytical unit. Rather, *kau* describes the homestead where the members of a family live. This family is organised around the household head (usually male). He lives in the village with his wives and children and sometimes with his mother. As noted above, it is often the case that the most recently married son also lives in this homestead with his wife and his (still few) children, so that the newly formed, small family can establish itself. The aim of the married son, however, is to build his own homestead and move out of the father's homestead with his wife and children as soon as possible. For this, he needs a place that is suitable for establishing his own homestead, as well as a certain number of animals with which he can sustain his family. For analytical purposes, I have considered

[5] The Sowö generation set is associated with the Chumwö generation set illustrated in Figure 1. It is named differently but refers to the same generation of people.

[6] Age-wise, overlaps between generation sets can be explained with the rule that a son cannot be of the same generation set as his father. From the perspective of a son, for instance, if the own father was not initiated in the Koronkoro generation set in 1949 or 1959, the father would have to have waited until the next initiation took place 29 years later. This was an exceptionally long interval due to the violent conflicts with Turkana between 1969 and 1984 (Bollig, 1990b). The father would then be initiated into the Kaplelach generation set, which was circumcised in 1988 and 1996. The only option for the son would be to wait for the circumcision of Merkutwö, which took place in 2016, 20 years after the second initiation of Kaplelach. Hence, the oldest initiand of the Paka community was 39 years old, when the Merkutwö were circumcised.

[7] A common phrase is *Kepe kau*, which literally means 'Let us go home'.

these two families as two households, because the separation from the paternal household is only a matter of time and the two families (that of the father and that of the son) already have clearly defined separate ownership over animals. Moreover, if the next younger son were to marry and also want to live in the paternal household with his wife before becoming independent, the older of the two would also be forced to separate from the father's homestead.

In general, it must be emphasised that the household unit is not a rigid, invariable construct. Rather, it is a constantly changing element, as Randall and Coast describe it with reference to Guyer (1981) and Guyer and Peters (1987):

(1) ... households are not discretely bounded groups and different household members can draw on different personal networks to access resources; (2) households are not fixed forms but constantly evolving; and (3) households are differentiated along lines of gender and generation. (Randall & Coast, 2015, p. 163)

The definition of the household concept has been criticised considerably, especially with regard to the use of this category in national censuses (e.g. Coast et al., 2016; Randall et al., 2015). In the case of census data, there is justified criticism of the application of rigid categories. In Chapter 3, I have already discussed the obstacles associated with the collection of quantitative population and livestock data and the inadequate representation that this entails. However, I shall use the household unit for two reasons: on the one hand, it is used in a wide range of scientific literature dealing with pastoral groups and therefore offers the best possibility to make comparisons with other groups. On the other hand, I hope that the detailed description of the household unit for the pastoral Pokot also contributes to an understanding of the livelihoods I want to describe.

The number of family members in Table 5 might be misleading at first glance, because it displays the de jure household affiliation. In general, households grow smaller the older the household head, because adult sons and older wives leave the household and adult daughters marry and live with their husbands' families. In my experience, households of Merkutwö men are comparably small, with mainly one wife and a few children. The biggest households are the ones of the Kaplelach generation with many wives and their children still present in the household. The Koronkoro households are becoming smaller again, because some wives and many children have already left the household. The only Sowö household consisted of merely five people in 2015.

Livestock and bridewealth

Livestock husbandry is central to all households at Mt Paka, and they keep different species of animals. Cattle are still the most valued livestock in pastoral households, followed by goats, sheep and camels. In general, the different livestock species are valued for their very specific characteristics. This is based partly on the idea that they complement each other. Whereas cattle and sheep rely mainly on grazing forage, camels and goats rely mainly on browsing forage. Only donkeys have a less important status, are not exchanged for ceremonial reasons and are also not consumed. Their main purpose is to carry the loads that need to be moved during mobile phases at the end of the dry season or to transport large quantities of water from the water points back to the homestead. Camels are prestigious animals that are valued for their meat and milk. Their milk is available in the dry season, when the amount of milk from cows and goats is low. Furthermore, camels are perceived as resilient animals, especially in dry periods. Goats and sheep are often kept together in one herd and the number of goats far exceeds the number of sheep. The small stock also provide milk (from goats) and meat, which is available more frequently because slaughtering a goat is more practicable than slaughtering an ox. The small stock also reproduces faster than cattle or camels and can easily be sold for a reasonable amount of money (for instance a two- to three-year-old male goat for 2,000–3,000 KSh).[8] Cattle or camels are sold only for major investments, or in cases of sickness – and then preferably the male ones because they do not reduce the herd's reproductive potential. Furthermore, most households own donkeys, but these are not kept in the household. Because donkeys are not prone to predators, they form larger independent herds and are retrieved before the dry-season migration starts.

Table 6 shows the distribution of livestock wealth in the Paka community and the ownership of livestock. The TLU/household is by far highest for the Kaplelach generation rather than the Koronkoro who represent the current elderly generation. This difference can be explained by the fact that wives and their children often leave older household heads, because older wives often go to live with an adult son. In this case, the last wife stays with the husband and a small herd of animals. The other wives and their sons have taken some part of the stock and established another homestead independently of their husband and/or their father. The Merkutwö generation consists of many young men who have married recently and started to increase the family herd. In these young marriages with relatively few household members and smaller stock, daily labour must be shared among the few members of a homestead.

---

[8] In 2014 exchange rates averaged as follows: Euro €1: 110 KSH; USD $1: 85 KSH; GBP £1: 140 KSH.

Table 6. Distribution of livestock numbers among households based on generation sets, 2015.

Generation set	Cattle numbers (range)	Small stock numbers (range)	Camel numbers (range)	TLU per household
Sowö	3 (3)	39 (39)	3 (3)	11.6
Koronkoro	33 (11–66)	103 (25–300)	0 (0)	45.9
Kaplelach	54.7 (0–370)	186 (40–850)	1.8 (0–13)	80.2
Merkutwö	17.5 (1–42)	90.4 (0–350)	1.5 (0–15)	30.7

Source: Hauke-Peter Vehrs.

In households with more people and livestock, this labour is easier to share and they can keep larger livestock herds. With average TLU/capita numbers of 5.5 (Kaplelach generation) and 6.4 (Merkutwö generation), the pastoral livelihoods at Mt Paka are above the average East Pokot livestock numbers of 3.1 TLU/capita (Nshakira-Rukundo et al., 2021).

People's livestock wealth is also reflected in the bridewealth payments (*kanyoy*) made before and after marriage when a group of men visits the homestead of the bride's father to make arrangements for the marriage. In the mid-twentieth century, bridewealth payments in East Pokot varied between 30 and 60 head of cattle – more than in any other region with Pokot inhabitants such as West Pokot (Schneider, 1953). However, current bridewealth negotiations vary at around 12 to 15 cattle, 30 to 36 head of small stock and sometimes one or two camels depending on the status and wealth of the man's household.[9] These numbers have not changed much in the past decades, as Bollig (2006) mentions an average bridewealth of 12 head of cattle, two to three camels, 30 goats and some additional sheep in the late twentieth century.

---

[9]   These bridewealth figures do not include any still outstanding payments that have not yet been made. In this case these are 3.3 head of cattle, 3.7 small stock and 0.3 camels (still to pay). The overall average bridewealth at Mt Paka consists of 17.3 head of cattle, 43.9 head of small stock and 1.0 camel.

   I calculated the average on the basis of two average data: the bridewealth paid for a wife and the bridewealth received for a daughter. For some reasons, the number of livestock received was slightly lower in average than the information obtained for bridewealth payments. There can be different reasons for this: on the one hand the negotiations about bridewealth payments are highly competitive and differences might occur between the first agreement on the livestock to be paid and the de facto amount of livestock paid in the end. On the other hand, differences possibly occur because the Paka community is relatively wealthy and therefore expected to meet the high bridewealth expectations of outsiders and the lower (perceived) need to pay extraordinary bridewealth to people who are well off.

Exchanging livestock is of major importance, and not just during bride-wealth agreements. Indeed, cattle, camels and small stock are exchanged for several reasons. The following section looks at the networks established along livestock exchange and along kinship ties. The underlying question is whether the dense social networks, which Bollig (1992a) describes for the end of the 1990s, are slowly eroding.

Social networks

Social network analysis was a method used during the initial phase of the research; and, in this case, my aim was to investigate whole networks in contrast to ego-centred networks (McCarty & Molina, 2014). I included 50 households in the Paka community in my social network analysis. Livestock exchange (*tilya*) constitutes the basis for friendship relationships. These complement the strong kinship relations arranged along clan (*lilö*) and lineage (*ortïn*) affilia-tions (Schneider, 1957). Schneider refers to the exchange of livestock, *tilya*, as 'joint cow ownership' (Schneider, 1953, pp. 264–65). He describes how a man who needs an ox for ceremonial purpose requests it from a friend's or a relative's herd and must compensate the owner with a cow in return.

I investigated the exchange of livestock in terms of its particular purpose, such as healing (*tapa* and *kolat*), official functions (*pution, ilat* or other kinds of *kirket*), initiation ceremonies (*sapana*), presents (*kipich*), bridewealth payments (*kanyan*) and return reciprocal gifts (*ghosyö*). If a man decides to give a male goat or an ox to a friend, he must be compensated with a female goat or a heifer. Only the bridewealth contribution between father and son are unidirectional in terms of livestock exchange.

For the East Pokot *tilya*, an animal is exchanged for a certain purpose and, in many cases, a return gift is obligatory. For instance, if a young male goat is provided for a healing ritual, the beneficiary is expected to return a young female goat after a time. The obligatory return gift is called *ghosyö*. This practice of giving male animals and receiving females in return aligns with Schneider's observations (1953) that distinguish between the 'instrumental capital' – oxen and male goats and sheep – used to purchase money and the 'capital goods' – cows, ewes and female goats and the few bulls – necessary for reproduction.

However, the specific rituals I observed in East Pokot differ widely from those Schneider (1953) lists for West Pokot in the mid-twentieth century. In his listing, it is mostly oxen that are slaughtered, something that does not currently apply to many ceremonies in East Pokot because small stock numbers are high, and using a goat or a sheep during ceremonies is common and accepted. Table 7 summarises the occasions and functions of livestock exchange for ceremonial reasons.

Table 7. Ceremonial functions of livestock exchange.

Name	Exchange	Note
Kanyan	Small stock or cattle	*Kanyan* is the exchange of bridewealth payments among family members. For instance, if a household head has received a bridewealth payment, brothers or sons can request their share.
Tapa	Goat	*Tapa* is a home-based ritual. In most cases, goats from the household herd are used. Moreover, the household head can request a goat from a good friend.
Kolat	Goat	*Kolat* is also a home-based ritual and exchange is arranged similar to the *tapa* exchange.
Kirket	Small stock or cattle	Livestock, which is killed in the *kirket*, can be used for several reasons. In all cases, initiated men identify a ceremonial place outside the homesteads (often in hidden, bushy locations) and kill an animal to conduct different functions. Whoever donated the animal must be compensated (*ghosyö*).
Sapana	Oxen, male camel, castrated goat	The *sapana* is the initiation ceremony for young men. Often the livestock is offered by the father of the boy. In other cases, the livestock is requested from a friend. If the latter donated the animal, it must be compensated (*ghosyö*).
Kipich	Small stock	*Kipich* can be requested only by sisters from their (independently living) brothers. For instance, a married woman visits her brother's homestead and requests a goat or a sheep. Cattle are seldom given. No compensation is expected.
Pution	Small stock	When the community is seeking the prophet's advice during times of hardship, the advice given is sometimes to ritually kill specific animals. These are identified among all the community's animals and taken for the ceremony. The person killing the animal is obliged to compensate for it accordingly (*ghosyö*).
Ghosyö	Depending on the kind of compensation	Compensation in terms of small stock, cattle or camel for certain exchange functions: *kirket*, *sapana* or *pution*.

Source: Hauke-Peter Vehrs.

Figure 3 shows the livestock exchange network at Mt Paka containing all male-headed households and one female-headed household in 2015. The household heads are marked according to their generation-set memberships. Most exchanges are executed by the Kaplelach generation that constitutes the central points in this network.

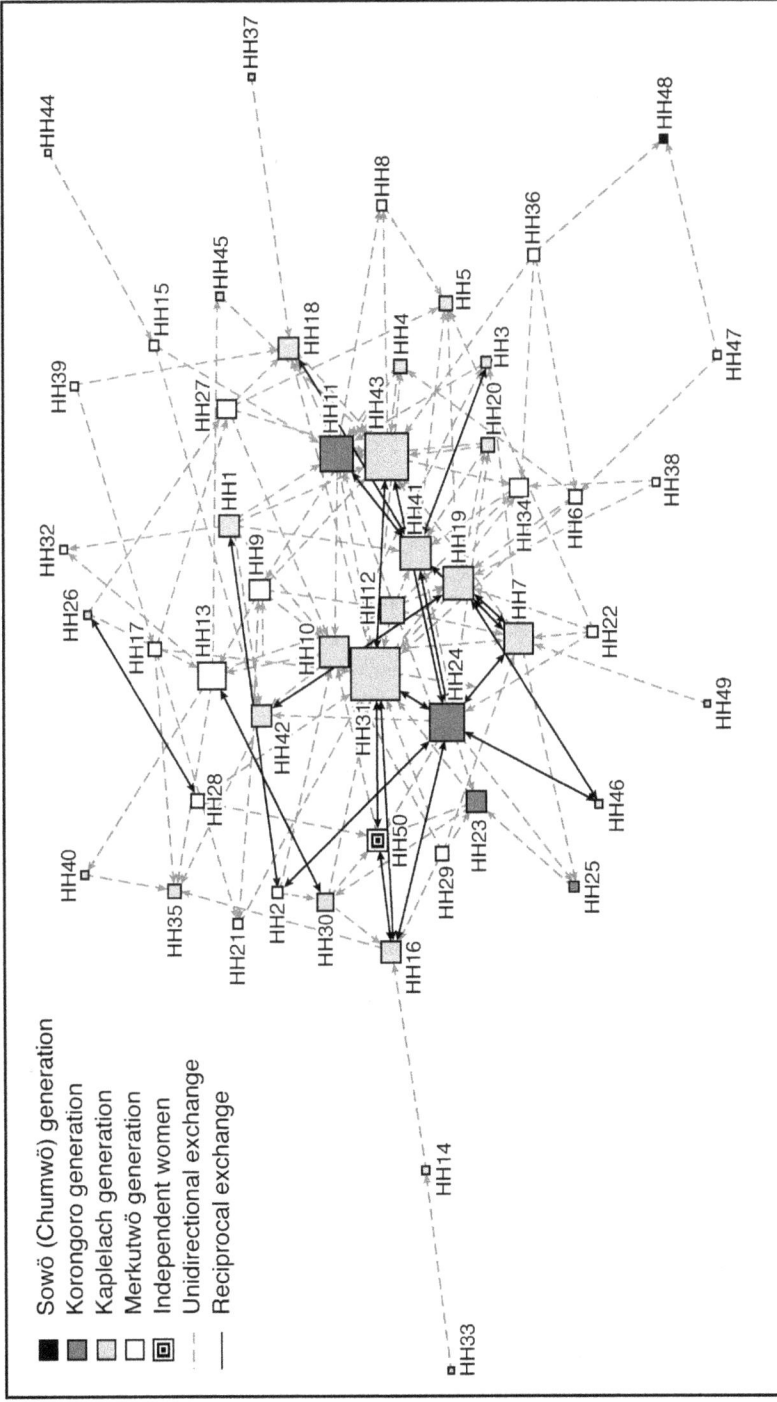

Fig. 3. Livestock exchange relations between household heads in the Paka community, 2015 (Hauke-Peter Vehrs).

Sowö (Chumwö) generation
Korongoro generation
Kaplelach generation
Merkutwö generation
Independent women
Unidirectional exchange
Reciprocal exchange

The older generation set (Sowö – in the bottom right corner) and Koronkoro are slowly retreating from the centre. Taking the livestock population results from Table 6 into account, results are not surprising. The generation with the most livestock is the one that is exchanging most animals within the Paka community.[10] On the one hand, this exchange is based on friendship ties between household heads. For instance, men from the same age set might have close friendship relations and exchange livestock between each other. Furthermore, exchange happens between generation sets – for instance in the case of a *sapana* request for an ox. A friend might not be able to provide such a highly valued animal, but an elderly person can. Therefore, the exchange of animals works between generations and strengthens the social network within the community.[11]

Fieldwork revealed a further change in today's social network: an independent woman is now included in the social network at Mt Paka. In a previous study on social networks on pastoral Pokot, Bollig (1992a) describes the dense networks in East Pokot and includes 35 households all led by men. The appearance of a woman acting independently of a male household head, owning her own large stock and exchanging livestock with men of the community, has not been described before. The case of this independent woman is unique in the Paka community, and exceptional compared to other independent women living at Mt Paka. She was once married to a successful herder. When her husband died, she decided to live with her oldest son – a common step taken by independent women when widowed or separated from their husbands. Together they took a share of the husband's stock, which was split among the widows and sons of the deceased husband. In the course of a dispute, she split from the son's homestead and took the animals that belonged to her. Although she is not allowed to participate in ceremonies during which

---

[10] The 'community' displayed here is not a closed system as it might appear in Figure 3. For reasons of illustration, I have considered only those ties that are established between the research 'community' of Mt Paka. Although relations among people in the same place seem to be more intense than those to people in other places, relations to other pastoral Pokot are well established. In general, I assume that the pastoral society of Pokot in northern Baringo constitutes a large network of social relations including both kinship ties and livestock friendships. The following figures exemplarily show the composition and density of these networks that constitute the basis for a successful pastoral livelihood.

[11] The structure and organisation of pastoral groups along the principles of kinship (clan and lineage), age groups (generation and age sets) and friendship ties is not unusual. Bollig (1992a) describes it for the case of the pastoral Pokot, but in many pastoral groups, the organisation of the community and the collaboration between its members is based on close connections within the group. As Vries et al. (2006) describe, pastoral Turkana rely on social network and livestock exchange in order to survive in the non-equilibratory environmental system.

an animal is killed by men in the *kirket*, she can exchange animals for healing rituals and receive the official compensation (*ghosyö*). Compared to most other households at Mt Paka, she possesses a relatively central position in the network.

In general, the social networks among the pastoral Pokot not only constitute the background for friendships with each other but also make it possible to distribute animals among people, which again contributes to livelihood resilience and the mitigation of risks (Faas & Jones, 2016). The general assumption that the social networks have decreased over time at the expense of individualisation and the establishment of a market-oriented livestock economy does not hold true for the case of pastoral Pokot at Mt Paka in the year 2015. Network relations are manifold between all households, including kinship affiliation (men's and women's relations are considered) as well as livestock friendship ties (mostly between men). Compared to Bollig's 'multiplex relations of the local network' (1992a, p. 326), which also deals with kinship and livestock exchange in a Pokot pastoral community in 1988–89, the social network still appears to be similarly dense.

In general, social network ties among the pastoral Pokot are strongly established and provide the basis for successful pastoral livelihoods. Kinship relations along lineage and clan membership, as well as the friendship bonds described above, often constitute the legitimate background for land occupation. Although pastoral Pokot land management is characterised by open-property regimes, the people at Mt Paka have a dense web of social and kinship relations. This web includes those people who are perceived to be insiders and it excludes outsiders from social activities such as certain ceremonies or access to land for establishing homesteads or small gardens. Although almost every household at Mt Paka in 2015 performed agricultural practices, further examined in Chapter 6, these were comparably small scale with very low outputs. Herding of cattle, camels, goats and sheep still constitutes the most important asset for local livelihoods that depend on livestock for both the subsistence products and revenues from trading.

In this chapter, I have described the pastoral livelihoods at Mt Paka ranging from the details of the single homestead to the interaction between households in the Paka community. My description has focused on livestock herding and exchange. However, there are also some points at which the changes that are occurring in East Pokot have already shone through. In the following, I turn my attention towards the environmental changes in East Pokot over the past 200 years and illustrate the social transformations of pastoral livelihoods in the past and the present and relate these to different kinds of environmental changes.

5

Environmental Changes in East Pokot

The changing environment and social transformations in East Pokot are not a recent phenomenon. Indeed, changes on different levels have always been part of pastoral landscapes. These are not only the long- or short-term climatic and environmental changes that have had strong influences on pastoral groups in East Africa at different times, but also other challenges such as inter- and intra-ethnic conflicts, confrontations with the colonial government or the struggle for access to land and resources. In this chapter, I want to highlight one of the various processes of socio-ecological transformation – namely, the transformation of the landscape in East Pokot. The brief description of the ecological conditions at Mt Paka in Chapter 2 already indicates that the pastoral Pokot perceive a change in their environment. However, this description is confined to personal experiences in East Pokot in 2015 and does not necessarily deliver a general picture. Therefore, in this chapter, I want to draw a broader picture of the environmental changes by using different methods to triangulate results that will lead to a better understanding of not only the environmental changes of the past but also recent dynamics.

Regarding the environmental changes described here, I need to distinguish between two different types of environmental change. On the one hand, the extensive grass vegetation in the region has been declining over centuries, while the bush vegetation strongly increased, and this process has accelerated considerably in recent decades. This change particularly affects the pastoralists' cattle husbandry with its strong dependence on the availability of feed. On the other hand, a second process can be observed: the rapid expansion of different invasive species in certain regions of East Pokot. I will discuss this process in more detail in Chapter 8 when reporting on the links between current land-use changes and human-induced land-cover changes.

In the following, I concentrate on the first process of incremental bush encroachment and explain it in detail by integrating and discussing results from three different research approaches and methods. I start by reviewing the results of archival research to gain an overview of landscape changes as well as the composition of landscape actors. This will show that the disappearance of wild animals plays a particularly important role in landscape design at the beginning of the twentieth century.

After describing these historical conditions, I turn to the present situation and how the herders in the region evaluate it themselves. This evaluation will be based on the results of the herders' forage rankings for different grazing and browsing animal species. By including these subjective perceptions and aggregating many perspectives in a multidimensional scaling, I identify general trends in the environmental changes over the last 30–40 years.

The results of the first two steps can also be compared with results from analysing remote sensing data going back to 1985. Findings from a time-series analysis of land-cover changes in East Pokot can be juxtaposed with the perceptions of pastoralists and used to quantify the latter. The magnitude of this change is surprising and illustrates the critical situation currently facing the pastoralists.

Baringo pastoral landscapes

The area of the Baringo basin was not only the destination of several early explorers of East Africa such as Joseph Thomson (Thomson, 1887), Count Teleki (von Hoehnel, 1894), Emin Pasha and Carl Peters (Peters, 1891; Tiedemann, 1907) but also home to colonial officers such as Mervyn Beech (Beech, 1911). Lake Baringo became a famous destination for big-game hunters at the end of the nineteenth century who reported their hunting experiences in *The Wide World Magazine* (Bright, 1899; Chapman, 1908; Dickinson, 1908; Eastwood, 1903; Powell-Cotton, 1904a, 1904b, 1904c). They all portrayed the landscape in different forms, from vast pastures and bushy forests to eroded sites and gullies.

But before turning to the descriptions of the landscape, I should like to comment on the relevance and tenability of these descriptions, especially in light of the countless atrocities either committed by many of these explorers or carried out on their behalf. A great number of the written sources from the nineteenth and early twentieth centuries that are examined in this book were composed largely by those people who are often referred to as the 'early explorers'. This collective term also includes names such as Carl Peters who committed all sorts of atrocities in East Africa in the cruellest of ways and whose racism is clearly evident in their writings. The discovery of new territories was driven by different interests: whereas many expeditions were motivated by the interest in gaining more knowledge about the regions and the geography, economic interests – including the ivory trade – were also of great importance. As Seidler (2016, p. 627) puts it, 'the material output of elephant hunting was one of the most important financial resources of colonial rule'. Moreover, personal interest in the heroic exploration of the 'wild continent', the perceived adventures, and the almost unlimited chances to hunt big game were of paramount importance. Big-game hunting served to reinforce the colonial structures, and, as Gissibl describes, 'hunting was an indispensable part of land occupation and use; served for the provision of food, scientific research, entertainment and the ritual orchestration of domination over nature and territory' (Gissibl, 2011, p. 15; own translation).

From most of the early travellers, only limited useful information can be gleaned when it comes to aspects of, for example, human habitation, histories, or economies. The implicit and explicit assumptions about the people being 'savages', their 'natural' or 'primitive' ways of life, and the ideology of racial supremacy are inherent to the descriptions of that time. Only a few people, such as Mervin Beech (1911) who lived in the region for a longer period, attempted to learn the local language and acquired knowledge about the history and the different ways of living. Although not free of undertones, these descriptions, unlike the overt racism of other early travellers, are inspired by a sincere interest in the pastoral Pokot. Consequently, while reviewing the materials, it was necessary to differentiate between those materials that present a comprehensible and adequate description of the people and those that clearly lack this quality.

Racist declarations and derogations along with exoticising descriptions of the people and places can be found throughout the documents, and these generally reveal more about the racist mindset of the authors than actually describe what is portrayed. The porters who accompanied the expeditions were constantly humiliated, exploited, and regarded as mere instruments either unworthy of attention or forced into obedience through chastisement. This assumption of racial supremacy is omnipresent in many accounts of the late nineteenth and early twentieth centuries.

Despite the intricacies and ideological baggage inherent to the racist descriptions of European travellers, I have chosen to include certain elements in this work, especially those concerning the environmental features and wildlife populations of that time. This is important, inasmuch as these descriptions are less influenced by the ideological framework of their time – if one disregards the idealisation of 'wild Africa' – and they may give us credentials for a time when the region around Lake Baringo was structured fundamentally differently from that today. This concerns, on the one hand, the surface vegetation and the accounts of seemingly infinite grazing areas containing an abundance of forage for grazing animals – both wildlife and cattle. It also allows conclusions about the abundance and diversity of wildlife in the late nineteenth century that no longer inhabit the region today, and most of which perished as a consequence of the activities of the big-game hunters and early travellers. The stories that the travellers present with such pride speak of this senseless slaughter of wildlife in unbelievable dimensions.

I decided to reflect briefly on the character of these descriptions and address the ethical dilemma of relying on these sources. In terms of descriptions of the people in the region, I cannot use these sources with the exception of the unproblematic accounts of, for instance, Beech and Dundas. With regard to the descriptions of the other early travellers, I have decided to make use of their accounts only to depict the landscape and wildlife populations without reproducing their racist stereotypes.

In the following, I reconstruct the pastoral landscapes of the late nineteenth and early twentieth centuries based on the views of the early explorers and European big-game hunters. I illustrate some impressions of the Baringo flora to show the character of the former pastoral landscape and its suitability for cattle-centred pastoralism. These include descriptions of the fauna, especially elephants, rhinoceroses, lions and ungulates – animals that hardly exist in today's East Pokot, with the exception of smaller antelopes. This description therefore includes the intensive wildlife hunting in Baringo that enjoyed 'the reputation of being one of the most favoured regions in the British Protectorate in respect of its big game' (Chapman, 1908, p. 74) in the early twentieth century – a reputation that led to the immense reduction of large mammals in the Baringo region.

The grasslands in northern Baringo

The initial idea of this research was to understand the environmental changes of the past and their effect on pastoral livelihoods today. Nonetheless, the extent of change that was discovered for the past two centuries during research was overwhelming. The Pokot elders do not tire to recall the pastureland of the past that consisted of grasses that even grew head-high.[1] However, it is sometimes difficult to imagine the landscape from stories about the past. Therefore, I provide a visual impression of the changes. Photo 4 shows Lake Baringo with the central island nowadays known as Ol Kokwe Island and the surrounding landscape at the beginning of the twentieth century. The picture shows how the littoral zones and slopes around the lake were abundantly covered with grasses, interrupted by small islands of bush vegetation.

In the early twenty-first century, one hundred years after Chapman's record of Lake Baringo and in stark contrast to that grass-dominated landscape, Photo 5 displays a similar view of Lake Baringo in which the surroundings are completely different. In 2014, the lake level was extraordinarily high and some of its shores were inundated.[2] However, Ol Kokwe Island is still visible

---

[1]   The memories of the elders must be interpreted as a reference to the abundance of grass forage vegetation. The head-high grasses are not suitable as cattle forage, but they are even more useful for burning the sites to stimulate the growth of a new grass vegetation.

[2]   The ecology of the lake has still not been understood fully, especially the reasons for the varying lake levels across even short time periods. Lake Baringo is a freshwater lake fed mainly by rainwater that possibly 'dilute[s] waters by subsurface seepage through permeable sediments and faulted lavas' (Tarits et al. 2006, p. 2027). Although there has been some debate about whether the lake level is decreasing, the ongoing danger in 2020 was that the freshwater lake Baringo and the saline, alkaline lake Borogia in the south may merge again. This would probably have far-reaching effects on the ecology of both lakes.

Photo 4. Lake Baringo from the north-east, early 20th century (Abel Chapman, 1908, p. 77).

Photo 5. Lake Baringo from the north in 2014 (Hauke-Peter Vehrs).

in the distance, while new islands have been created by the rising level of the lake and the flooding of lower areas. What is most conspicuous is the land-cover change around Lake Baringo. Grasses have disappeared and bushes have become the dominant vegetation with scarce ground cover. Some herbs constitute the meagre ground vegetation and black volcanic stones cover the ground.

In the accounts of the early explorers the lake is also described and resembles their views on the landscape. Thomson reached Lake Baringo in the late 1880s and was amazed by the magnificent sight and its wildlife inhabitants.

> Best of all, there was the mysterious Lake Baringo, gleaming apparently at our feet, though several thousands of feet below. ... When we had thoroughly engraved on our minds the main outlines of the scene, we began to cast about in our thoughts how to descend to the lake. It seemed as if a couple of hours should bring us to its shores. But, alas! we reckoned without our host. ... The country was most horrible, with sharp angular boulders hid by grass and thorns of the most fearful description. The afternoon was now far spent, and after tramping along in that dangerous waste for about an hour and seeing no sign of a place where my men could descend, I began to get a little uneasy in my mind. Not a soul could be seen, and buffalo and rhinoceros were in great numbers, starting up indeed in more than one instance quite close to me. (Thomson, 1887, pp. 228–31)

A few years later, Peters published the experiences of the Emin Pasha expedition by referring to Thomson's accounts and describing the extensive pastures around the lake.

> Thomson had drawn seductive pictures of Lake Baringo. We hoped to find food there in abundance, and to regain the feeling of security for life and limb. Patiently, therefore, we accepted the fact that we had to march for hours through the parched prairie, and then to ascend towards the last circumference around Lake Baringo. Towards eleven o'clock this was reached; and there, in truth, lay the lake before us! A green grassy steppe extended far and wide, shading off, here and there, into brownish and reddish tints. (Peters, 1891, p. 267)

Hobley also draws attention to the quality of pasture and the scarcity of water in the region. Lake Baringo is the only reliable freshwater source in northern Baringo, and hence many herders rely on the lake water during the dry season. Hobley also notes that the high mobility of pastoral nomads in this region is attributed to the distribution and temporal scarcity of fresh water.

> In spite of the aridity of the area, the grazing is declared by the natives to be marvellously good, especially for sheep; but, owing to the precarious

water-supply, they are forced to adopt a nomad existence and move on from one water-pool to another. In some places they depend on brackish springs, and often dig wells in the dry watercourses to a depth of over 20 feet. (Hobley, 1906, p. 472)

Similarly, Little describes how, in the eighteenth century, the southern region of Lake Baringo was advantageous for the Il Chamus people, but 'over time, the concentration of good grazing and water proved to be a curse in one critical respect – it attracted to the region larger, more powerful herding groups who frequently raided the community' (1996, p. 41). These included the Pokot herders who successfully asserted themselves on the northern shores of Lake Baringo and established their livelihoods specialising in cattle husbandry.

Wildlife in Baringo and its extinction

The Baringo pastoral landscape described above was characterised by not only extensive grass plains and few people inhabiting the region but also its abundance of wildlife such as lions, leopards, rhinoceroses, elephants, ostriches, buffaloes, giraffes and a variety of different antelopes. This abundance of wildlife also attracted several big-game hunters to Baringo, who reported on their extensive hunts and the killing of a vast quantity of animals (Bright, 1899; Chapman, 1908; Dickinson, 1908; Eastwood, 1903; Powell-Cotton, 1904a, 1904b, 1904c). Photo 6 shows the hunt of the 'five-horned giraffe' and gives an impression of the land cover around Lake Baringo in the early twentieth century.

The early explorers also give several accounts of the abundance of wildlife in the region. Thomson, for example, states:

> We were ordering our steps for Lake Baringo ... Next day we began the descent of the western aspect of the Lykipia [*sic*] plateau, and our hopes were greatly raised on striking a small stream and valley which evidently ran towards Baringo. ... Buffaloes, zebras, elephants, and rhinoceroses were in astonishing numbers. (Thomson, 1887, pp. 226–27)

Some two decades later, Dundas wrote about the extensive herds of elephants roaming in the Kerio Valley:

> The greatest glory, however, of this region was the magnificent herds of elephant that throughout the year were to be found roaming over it. I should be afraid to say how many elephants once lived in this bush, but I should think that a thousand head would not be a very exaggerated estimate. I myself have on two occasions met with a great herd that covered three or four square miles of country. ... It would be no exaggeration, I think, to say that we saw fully three hundred elephants that day. (Dundas, 1911, p. 64)

Photo 6. Baringo giraffe and Suk elder, early 20th century (Powell-Cotton, 1904d, p. 137).

With the exception of small antelopes, such as the dik-dik, ostriches and a few predators, wildlife became extinct in the first half of the twentieth century. The clan totems of several Pokot clans still reflect the diversity of wildlife in East Pokot such as eland antelope (*ptuko*), buffalo (*soo*), rhino (*kipau*), elephant (*pelion*) and lion (*ngotiny*). Furthermore, some places are still named after the former gathering of wildlife, for instance Chemoril (*moril* – leopard), Chepelion (*pelion* – elephant) or Kokwö Kales (the meeting point of *kales* – ostrich). Beech (1911) also describes the use of elephant, giraffe or rhinoceros skin for footwear. However, all these big mammals are no longer to be found in East Pokot, with the exception of a few giraffes that are protected on the Lake Baringo Island and had to be surrendered to a nearby conservancy due to the rising lake water levels. In the following, I shall explore the reasons for the extinction of these mammals.

The Pokot people were known as hunters who had land tenure rules around the killing of elephants.[3]

---

[3] In contrast to the clan-based management of territory exemplified here, the pastoral Pokot in East Pokot changed towards a group-based management of their territory with common access rights.

Elephants are the chief prey of the hill tribes. Indeed, each section has its own particular hunting-ground for this animal. The man who first wounds the elephant may claim the tusks for himself, but the meat belongs to the section in whose ground the animal actually dies. Thus if a Suk of the Cheptulel section wounded an elephant which ran away and subsequently died, say, at Merich, the Cheptulel Suk would have the tusks, but the meat would belong to the men of Merich, even if the slaying had been entirely carried out by pursuers from Cheptulel and not a single Merich man was present. (Beech, 1911, pp. 24–25)

The local hunting of elephants did not just provide food; ivory traders also visited the region to buy elephant tusks, as von Hoehnel describes in the 1890s:

An equally trying march along the picturesque mountain slopes brought us, the next day, to the settlement of Maricha [south of Nasalot National Reserve]. Close to our right rose an unbroken series of rugged mountains some 3,000 feet high, belonging to the Suk [Pokot] range, whilst on the east of the Trrawell [Turkwel] plain the chain, running from north to south, narrowed to a breadth of some thirteen miles. The Trrawell [sic], which here receives many brooks and rivulets, flows through a dark greyish-green, impenetrable, and uninhabited primaeval forest, which, however, evidently harbours a great many elephants, as the natives have quantities of ivory for sale every year. (von Hoehnel, 1894, p. 267)

However, Pokot people were far from being the only ones hunting the elephants. Even in 1887, Thomson was already mentioning the organised troops of hunters who had only one goal: ivory.

Our first march took us across the mountains, and our second to Baringo, where I had the satisfaction of finding everything right, with the exception that one man had died.

The elephant-hunters left by Jumba had met with two accidents, one of them having ended fatally. In the one case a wounded elephant had turned and caught its tormenter and shaken him … and then thrown him aside breathless and nearly dead. In the other the same thing had occurred, but the man was killed outright. Strangest thing of all, the unfortunate man's gun was never found, though several days were spent in search of the valuable article, and the only conclusion that could be arrived at was that the elephant had carried it off to the mountains. The other men had been more fortunate, and had shot some elephants with fine tusks, several being considerably over 100 lbs. each. (Thomson, 1887, p. 311)

Somerville (2016) examines the origin and development of elephant hunting and ivory trade from African countries to Europe, Asia, Russia and the Americas in pre-colonial and colonial times up to today's treatment of elephants, for example in conservation projects or big-game hunting businesses. He describes how there was already an early demand for and trade in ivory in Asia, especially in the region of today's China and India, going back a few millennia BCE. After the elephant population decreased drastically, although the demand for ivory was still high in the first millennium BCE and the first centuries CE, hunting shifted to North African regions. Later, the sub-Saharan areas were also made accessible and ivory was delivered increasingly to Europe and the American west as well (Beachey, 1967; Somerville, 2016). The Portuguese did a lot of trade on the west coast of the continent, but had limited reach to the East African coast that was controlled mainly by Arabic and Kiswahili-speaking traders who obtained ivory through local groups and their middlemen (Somerville, 2016). Along the east coast, various groups played a prominent role in the ivory trade such as the Wakamba in Kenya, the Nyamwezi in Tanzania or the Yao of Malawi and Mozambique (Somerville, 2016). Somerville emphasises that although local groups hunted elephants for subsistence purposes, commercial trade and the stimuli from outside Africa pushed elephant hunting towards a previously unknown dimension that also prompted local groups to increase their elephant hunting and ivory trade. In common with the Waliangulu, Wakamba hunters used poison obtained from plants to coat arrows for elephant hunting. During the 1820s, they extended their hunting areas to Mt Kenya, towards Lake Baringo and as far north as Samburu country near Lake Turkana. Wakamba caravans of 200–500 men would bring ivory and slaves from the Nyika and other areas to the coast. In mid-century, they were supplying about 45 tons of ivory a year to Swahili and Arab dealers at Mombasa (Somerville, 2016).

However, the impact of local hunters was limited, and it was only through the 'large-scale introduction of firearms and the development of more organised and lucrative globalised ivory trading' that the killing of elephants reached a new level in the early nineteenth century (Somerville, 2016). The exploitation of elephant populations was thus exacerbated enormously, and many of the early European explorers on the African continent shot hundreds if not thousands of elephants and other wildlife as they traversed the regions. In the late nineteenth century, the effects of the huge demand for ivory and the extensive elephant hunts became obvious: 'the area between the coast and Lake Tanganyika had largely been cleared of elephants' and 'the experience of hunters and travellers indicated that Kenya and Uganda still had huge herds of elephants that were to become the new sources of ivory as demand soared in Europe and America' (Somerville, 2016, p. 38).

The depletion of the elephant population subsequently also took place in Kenya including the Baringo region, as described earlier. Gissibl (2016, p. 41) emphasises the importance of elephant tusks 'that were by far the most important commodity derived from the grand-scale slaughtering of East Africa's wildlife', while also mentioning the importance of hippopotamus teeth, rhinoceros horn and gazelle hides for European markets. In the late nineteenth century, when European explorers reached Lake Baringo, the economic and strategic importance of the region was recognised by Peters, who also remarks on the status of the Baringo region for the ivory trade.

> I expressed myself on this point in a report which I prepared at Baringo, on January 10th, for the German Emin Pasha committee, and which was not published for a long time: A Baringo nation would be of the very greatest importance for the general opening up of Central Africa, and for the great plateaus, over which our way led. Here, in what resembles a peaceful oasis, the expeditions which, approaching from the east, are making their way to the north and west, can rest and gain strength for the further difficulties that lie before them. It is also known that Njemps and the Baringo form one of the great centres of the ivory trade of Eastern and Central Africa. ... In a word, I consider the establishment of a strong European station by the Baringo to be called for in the interest of the whole further development of civilisation in Eastern and Central Africa. Five white men and twenty-five well-armed Askari, with a piece of ordnance, would, according to my estimate, be quite sufficient to secure this charming valley in a military point of view; and I also believe that such an establishment would very soon pay for itself as a commercial factory. (Peters, 1891, pp. 272–73)

A few years later, a permanent station was indeed established at Lake Baringo, not by the Germans, but the British, who opened a government station under the direction of Hyde Baker. Both the early explorers and the big-game hunters at the end of the nineteenth century and the beginning of the twentieth century had decimated the wildlife populations. However, the extent to which the Pokot were involved in elephant hunting is uncertain. Bollig (2006) describes their general political and economic position as marginal, and argues that, although the pastoral Pokot also exchanged ivory for cattle (between two to five cattle per tusk) in times of crisis, this was by no means comparable to the trade relations of other groups in the region, such as the Il Chamus in the 1870s (Anderson, 2004). Under colonial rule at the beginning of the twentieth century, it was realised that the huge elephant populations and other wildlife – despite the earlier depictions of their incredible abundance – were endangered, and first conservation efforts were made – such as the first international conference for the protection of game, in London in 1900 (see Beachey, 1967); or the 1903 proclaimed 'Society for the Preservation of the Wild Fauna of the Empire' (see Somerville, 2016).

Somerville shows how early the trade in ivory began and how the demand from all parts of the world led to the slow decimation of the large African herds of savannah and forest elephants. Contrary to the image that local hunters were particularly responsible for the drastic reduction in elephant populations, he illustrates how massively the European hunters and early explorers inflicted damage on wildlife populations (Somerville, 2016). In the early nineteenth century, it was already reported that the Rift Valley had no more elephants of its own, but only elephants who came to visit from neighbouring areas such as Laikipia, although even there, only a few hundred animals were counted (Somerville, 2016). Whereas it was still possible for European settlers to acquire a few hunting concessions, hunting by local groups was prohibited and declared illegal. However, the low wildlife numbers also led to a decrease in the hitherto legal big-game hunts, and a growing conviction that the protection of animals must stand was more important than the opportunity to hunt. But for the Baringo region, this did not result in the recovery of elephant numbers, and the herds finally disappeared. Although the pastoral Pokot also took part in elephant hunting, their impact can be considered small compared to that of European hunters and explorers. Hunting by other local groups was larger, but was also driven by the international demand for ivory and contributed to the decline of elephant populations that first descriptions had represented as being nearly endless, but were now reduced to only sparse populations.

However, the demand for ivory does not account for the extinction of all wildlife species. The large European expeditions and 'sport hunters' who visited the region also killed countless other animals apart from elephants. During the late nineteenth and early twentieth centuries, hunting was initially not much restricted, and the hunting experiences reported in *The Wide World Magazine* illustrate the malpractices of big-game hunters who even shot several animals in a day and took advantage of the established government station at Lake Baringo. Over time, these trips became more popular, and an expedition to the Baringo region promised the desired trophies and exceptional specimens such as the 'five-horned giraffe' (Powell-Cotton, 1904c), as well as extraordinary adventures, such as 'a battle with a rhino' (Eastwood, 1903).

Over time, the big mammals became locally extinct in northern Baringo County, a process that will be referred to as defaunation in the following. Today, they can be found only in the conservation areas of the Laikipia Plateau, but no longer in East Pokot. Little dates the end of the wildlife extinction back to the 1940s when district officials reported only small stocks of wildlife in Baringo due to 'uncontrolled hunting by European parties' (Little, 1996, p. 43). Reports from the Baringo District Range Officer Edmondson in East Pokot in the 1960s and 1970s show impressively that, with the exception of a few smaller species, wildlife populations were almost non-existent in the region east of Nginyang. Compared to the descriptions of early explorers mentioning hundreds of elephants and other large mammals, Edmondson's account of wildlife seems negligible.

Saw 6 or 7 score Impala & aprox [*sic*] same number Grant's Gazelle.
Some dikdik, some guinea fowl (2 of which I shot & ate. I have a license),
some jackals, some greater bustard. (Edmondson, 1965b, p. 2)

It must be noted that the East Pokot pastoral landscapes underwent several
changes in the nineteenth and early twentieth centuries, and the defaunation
of wildlife and the bush encroachment of the grass-dominated savannah went
hand in hand. The linkages between herbivory and grass–savannah establishment and maintenance are further discussed in Chapter 7.

The rinderpest panzootic in the late nineteenth century and its effects on pastoral livelihoods

It is not only human interventions into the ecosystem that have left their
marks over time; the effects of diseases on humans and animals also left
their signs. Particularly towards the end of the nineteenth century, pastoral
groups throughout the African continent came under pressure when the
rinderpest, originating in Ethiopia, spread in sub-Saharan Africa with devas-
tating consequences.

For the region in East Pokot, there is little evidence of the exact effects of
the panzootic, but the detailed reports on the extremely high losses of cattle
and sheep (and other wildlife species such as buffalo and eland antelopes and
bushbucks; Rowe, 1994) in other regions can give a picture of how strong the
negative effects on the pastoral Pokot must have been, because these, like many
other pastoral groups, had few alternatives to livestock-based subsistence.

In East Africa, rinderpest spread mainly towards the end of the nineteenth
century and probably came through East Pokot in 1890. Matwetwe (2017)
dates the time of a huge catastrophe told of in Pokot oral history to the period
1878–82, referring to huge livestock losses (more than 90 per cent of cattle;
see for instance Lugard, 1893) and a smallpox outbreak. The existence of an
extremely difficult period for pastoral groups in the form of drought, rinderpest
and smallpox is beyond question, but the period must be considered to be
the late 1880s and early 1890s and not earlier (Rowe, 1994; Spinage, 2003,
2012). The elders of Mt Paka, for example, still remember the disaster of
that time and recall the period when many people died of a disease called
Molmoloy. This does not refer to rinderpest (Kipokot: *Kiplok*), but probably
to the smallpox epidemic, the outbreak of which can be found in historical
records shortly after the great rinderpest of the early 1890s. The impact of the
rinderpest on livestock and wildlife during that large outbreak was enormous,
as Lugard describes:

The hills [of the Kamasia range – in western direction from Lake
Baringo] consist of rocky shale, at a high angle of dip, together with
black volcanic rocks and boulders. Here, for the first time, we began

to find carcasses of buffalo, recently dead of the plague,[4] and, as we passed onwards, they daily became more numerous, and we found that this dreadful epidemic had swept off all the cattle and the wild buffalo, and much of the other game beside. The vultures and hyenas were too surfeited to devour the putrid carcasses, which lay under almost every tree near water. (Lugard, 1893, p. 356)

Whereas cattle and sheep populations recovered quickly, the combined pressure of intense hunting and diseases on the region's wildlife was probably another reason for their steady population decline in the nineteenth century and a contributory factor to the region's defaunation in the twentieth century.

Not for thirty years has a plague like this been known in the country, and even then it was not to be compared in virulence to the present one. Never before in the memory of man, or by the voice of tradition, have the cattle died in such vast numbers; never before has the wild game suffered. Nearly all the buffalo and eland are gone. (Lugard, 1893, p. 527)

This is not to underestimate the human responsibility for the disappearance of the wildlife, especially the colonial administration, as well as hunters from overseas and the local population, but the effects of the rinderpest panzootic must likewise be acknowledged at this point. This does not, of course, apply to certain animal species such as gazelles, hippopotami and elephants (Spinage, 2003) that were not affected by the rinderpest, but certainly by hunting and the intense trade in ivory.

After the cattle plague and the smallpox epidemic at the beginning of the twentieth century, the numbers of cattle recovered in a surprisingly short time; and for the year 1909, Beech already describes the growing herd sizes of cattle of the pastoral Pokot in the area of today's East Pokot as follows:

'But it doesn't matter', they say, 'If their cattle become too numerous, Tororut [sic] (God) will send a disease and take some away so that it will be all right!' Since writing the above note the disease has come and carried off in some cases as much as 50 per cent. of their cattle. The calamity is borne with Stoicism. But the fact that the disease was introduced by a Somali trader is not. (Beech, 1911, p. 8, footnote)

Spinage (2003) describes the spread of cattle plague on the African continent since the end of the nineteenth century in great detail, including the case of Kenya. Recurrent outbreaks until the 1990s furthermore led to the decimation of livestock, but never again to the same extent as in the 1890s. Despite the fact that the cattle plague had such an enormous impact on livestock and wildlife

---

[4] Rinderpest is often referred to as 'cattle plague'.

as well as on people, people and livestock are exposed to many more threats. The greatest impact on cattle populations has certainly been from diseases such as rinderpest, East Coast Fever or anthrax from among the at least 37 different animal diseases that Bollig (1995) reports as being important in East Pokot.

Bollig (2016) furthermore states that the rinderpest was followed by a contagious goats' disease (called *Simpiriyon*) that, in turn, increased the pressure on pastoralists and resulted in many people losing their lives during this period. The decreasing stock numbers and rising pressure on local livelihoods also led to increasing attacks on neighbouring groups to replenish the surrounding herds (Bollig, 2016). Because all pastoral groups in the region were affected by the negative consequences of the cattle plague, the epidemic also led to the territorial allocations being questioned.

For example, the Maasai were very much affected by the rinderpest, as described in numerous sources (Klingspor, 1909; Lugard, 1893; Schillings, 1907; for a comprehensive overview see Waller, 1988). As Homewood et al. (2009) report, this massive disruption to the pastoral life of many Maasai groups also led them to lose their military dominance in some regions after the great cattle plague of the 1890s. This might have also been the case in East Pokot where in some locations towards the Laikipia Plateau, the names of places are reminders of Maasai occupancy (for instance Kokwö Maasai – the meeting place of Maasai).

It should be noted that not only the cattle herds and the pastoral groups of East Africa but also the wild animals of the region suffered severely from the effects of the rinderpest panzootic. However, this radical impact on the lives of the local people and animals was only just one extreme event in the history of the region. Living with different livestock species also involves a constant confrontation with diseases that can affect not only cattle but also goats, sheep and camels. The pastoral Pokot, however, were very successful in replenishing their herds after severe losses and successfully continuing their pastoral life. In the following, I further examine the development of the pastoral landscape and its effects on local livelihoods during the second half of the twentieth century.

Limits of specialised cattle husbandry in the twentieth century

When cattle numbers recovered and reached high levels again in the early twentieth century, pastoralism was a lucrative business. By that time, it was not forage that was the limiting factor, but water. Grasses rarely became exhausted because people were constantly on the move with their herds of cattle. In the mid-twentieth century, the pasture land that formerly supported the rise of a specialised livestock husbandry declined and was replaced by bush-dominated vegetation. Shortly after the declaration of independence in 1963, Edmondson reported on the poor pasture conditions in East Pokot.

Grazing. There is nil grazing available in the bottom of the Rift [Valley]. Most of the fodder trees have been cut entirely. Much of the Olarabal (old scheme area) has been burnt, little or no grass has come up. (Visited 24th Sept 65). Churo is overgrazed. There remains remnants of the tougher grasses such as *cymbopogon*. (Edmondson, 1965a, p. 2)

N (northern) Baringo. There have been showers on Tiati [*sic*], Karossi [*sic*], & Paka Mountains, with consequent improvement in browse (i.e. mostly *acacia spp, indigofera spp*) for camels and goats. But grass lands at Churo ... Paka Mountain; Tiati Mountain are eaten down to ground level are completely overwhelmed by numbers of stock which eat off all grass before it can regenerate its roots and seeds. (Edmondson, 1966, p. 1)

From the perspective of a distant colonial observer, Edmondson describes the degradation of pasture land and the high numbers of livestock that he holds responsible for the decline. However, not only overstocking might lead to the disappearance of pastures but also under-management. Conant describes the same process of pasture land degradation in a later study. He focuses on the bush encroachment control of pastoral people and the consequences of abandoning land in times of conflict (Conant, 1982). He underlines how '[t]he combination of grazers and browsers is a technique for not only exploiting different kinds of plant cover, but also keeping the acacia thicket in check, and by doing so, helping to maintain the grassy cover' (Conant, 1982, p. 115). The results of an aerial photograph analysis from 1973 and 1978 show that over that period, bushland[5] increased from 24 per cent to 50 per cent of area coverage, and, at the same time, bush-grassland declined from 38 per cent to 13 per cent in areas that had been abandoned (Conant, 1982). As a result of the violent conflict, the border regions were largely avoided and remained unused, and this, in turn, contributed to their under-management. The consequences of this were a strong increase in bush vegetation and a decrease in areas still containing grass vegetation.

But the process of the savannah transformation towards more bushy vegetation was not limited exclusively to the border areas, as can be seen in the following with the help of several sources. As SALTLICK describes in the early 1990s, the grass cover was in a poor condition in the northern Baringo region.

Most of the vegetation in the area can be classified as Desert Grass-Bush verging on Desert Scrub in the drier more barren areas. The vegetation consists of a mixture of deciduous bushes and trees underneath which normally there are perennial grasses and shrubs. After the rains the area

---

5   Conant uses the categories 'bushland 'and 'grass-bushland' to illustrate the bush encroachment.

between the tufted perennials fills up with the rapid growth of annual grasses. It appears that this does not happen in most of the project area. Perennial grasses have virtually been grazed out in all except the most favoured areas and even after rain annual grasses flushes are limited, due to the fact that all annual grass seed has been germinated, eaten before it in turn is allowed to seed. (SALTLICK, 1991, p. 6)

In the late twentieth century, as SALTLICK reports, the bushes encroached on large parts of the Pokot area. However, some places with good pasture were still to be found, and these were also described by other researchers. In the late 1980s, Bollig wrote an interesting field note that gives a glimpse of the pasture land at Mt Paka.

We camped in Chepungus, about 1½ hours from the top; about 20 kilometres from Nginyang. After 11 kilometres the bush savannah turns into open grassland. A closed grass area with few acacia trees. On our way big herds of cattle. Towards the top of Paka exist excellent meadows; up into the crater. However, water points are dispersed widely; water for Chepungus is taken from Tapogh. (Bollig, 1988, p. 3)

Furthermore, Bollig differentiates between four types of vegetation zone in East Pokot. 'Bush savannah' and 'grass savannah' were the two dominant types of vegetation, each shaping approximately 40 per cent of the landscape in the late 1980s, whereas 'highland meadows' formed 15 per cent and 'gallery forests' along river beds constituted the remaining 5 per cent of the land cover (Bollig, 1992a). Although this is only an approximate estimate, it indicates two relevant aspects for Pokot pastoralists. On the one hand, even in the 1990s, large parts of East Pokot were still covered with grass vegetation that provided the basis for raising cattle. On the other hand, it is clear that the bush vegetation already played an equally important role in Bollig's assessment. Both types – bush savannah and grass savannah – represent the most important elements in the composition of the landscape. In 1990, two years after Bollig's fieldnote, Reckers indicates a similar situation:

The Paka provides a very good grass cover combined with a very good coverage percentage of 95 per cent. There are perennial grasses like *Enteropogon macrostachis* [*sic*], *Eragrostis suberba, Hyparrhenia rufa, Cymbopogon giganteus*, and *Chloris virgate*. The common trees are *Balanites aegipytiaca, Commiphora africana, Albizia amara, Sclerocarya birrea* and *Vachellia nilotica*, even *Vachellia xanthophloea*. The bush species diversity is low. (Reckers, 1990, p. 14)

Both scientists still detected reasonable grass coverage in East Pokot in the late 1980s, something also remembered by the elderly people of today. But the conditions for a livestock husbandry specialising in cattle were already inadequate, and the pastoral Pokot reorganised their herd structures with more emphasis on browsing species in the second half of the twentieth century. Oesterle (2008) identifies the end of the twentieth and beginning of the twenty-first centuries as the time when the diversification of herd structures was most evident. This involved small stock in the form of goats and sheep as well as camels. Although these species were also previously part of the pastoral economy, they had represented a considerably lower part of it. As he points out, small stock numbers were increasing rapidly at the beginning of the twenty-first century, and this led him to conclude that the formerly specialised cattle pastoralists of Pokot have reached a phase of diversification especially due to sedentarisation of livelihoods, the effects on herding of armed conflicts in the border areas, higher population numbers and declining cattle-to-person ratios. He also considers environmental change to be a major factor in explaining why livelihoods have diversified.

In the following, I examine the herders' perceptions in detail to gain a better understanding of these recent changes in the environment. In particular, I address how Pokot elders evaluate the changes and explain the availability of livestock forage in terms of the Pokot herders' perceptions of its quality and quantity.

Livestock forage rankings

Through everyday interaction with their environment, the pastoral community of East Pokot holds vast knowledge on plants, their uses and their forage quality for their livestock. In general, four livestock species can be identified that are herded on a daily basis. These are cattle, camels, goats and sheep.[6] In the following, I perform a comparative analysis of forage rankings for the most important three livestock species: cattle, camels and goats. My main interest in using this method is to determine how forage availability and quality have changed over time. The analysis must also consider that these animals are herded differently according to their specific needs. For instance, cattle herders walk long distances due to their cattle's dependence on grasses, whereas camels and goats can be herded in the homestead's vicinity. A variety of bushes and trees provide a forage basis for both species, and no herder ever mentioned difficulties in feeding these animals. However, goats are perceived as easily contracting infectious diseases such as contagious caprine pleuro-pneumonia. Camels are perceived of as performing well and being affected by few diseases – although herders mentioned that once camels are infected, diseases have a disastrous impact on them. Bollig claims that camels are

---

6   Donkeys are also part of Pokot pastoral economy, but are not herded actively.

especially prone to diseases in wet years (Bollig, 1992b). Cattle, in contrast, are seen as relatively resistant to disease.

In the following, I describe and discuss the local perspectives of herders. First, I illustrate ranking results to understand the herders' perception of the quality and quantity of forages. Then I compare these results to rankings reported by Bollig and Schulte (1999). In addition, I also let elderly Pokot give personal accounts of how they view environmental changes over the past four decades.

Free listing, ranking and pile sorting

First of all, I used free listing as a tool to elicit reasonable forage plants from herders and then rank these according to specific categories such as the quality or availability of forage. Herders often ranked the plants in categories such as 'these plants make the animals fat', 'if the animals eat these plants, they give a lot of milk' or just in terms of the opposition between 'sweet' (*anyin*) and 'tasteless' (*tadagh*). The lowly ranked plants species are often referred to as 'not preferably eaten', 'only eaten during the dry season' or 'the animals do not become fat'. In a second step, the herders were asked to rank the same plants again according to their prevalence in the area: this made the comparison of different plant species somewhat difficult in such a variable environment (Little et al., 2007b). The herders subsequently ranked the plants according to categories such as 'these plants grow abundantly when the rains come', 'you find this species in the whole area' or 'they grow very fast', in contrast to 'they are only found in the river beds', 'the grasses disappear completely after grazing, until the rains come back' or 'these trees grow very slowly'. Furthermore, the plant species were sorted into four predefined categories: 'increase', 'stable', 'decrease' and 'hardly seen'. These categories were used to compare my cattle rankings with the results published by Bollig and Schulte (1999) based on data obtained in the late 1980s and early 1990s.

In addition to the rankings described above, I conducted a historical ranking with 10 elders in Chepungus and related this to the perceived environmental changes between 1975 and 2015. I then analysed and illustrated the forage ranking data in a multidimensional scaling (Handwerker & Borgatti, 2014).

Ranking results

Figures 4–7 display the results of forage rankings for cattle, goats and camels. The ranking of cattle forage was the most variable of all rankings, especially in terms of availability. *Sehima nervosum* (*chaya*) is perceived as the best and most abundant grass species in the area followed by other grasses such as *Cynodon niemfuensis* (*seretion*), *Tetrapogon* spp. (*angoleyekion*) and *Enteropogon macrostachys* (*kipaupau*). *Eragrostis cilianensis* (*puyun*), *Triumfetta rhomboidea* (*koserinyan*), *Brachiaria deflexa* (*abrute*) and *ngilet*

1

Chaya

Amerkwoyon   Koserinyan

Puyun

Seretion   Churukechir   Arengreng

Kipaupau   Ngilet   Angoleyekion

Asukuruyon   Purteyon

Puresongolion   Pelesian Moikut

Aletetlete   Mukun

Tuyunwo   Sitat   Chesowoyö

Cheluwowes   Pekonion   Awawatian

Ngurumenwo   Kericheyan

Lotal   Kacheptilil   Kapengayan

Chepkaneroi

Ptaru   Makau   Aporpotoyon

Taran   Kowontö   Malumtich

Nyuswo

Atulayan

0

increase   stable   decrease   hardly seen

Relative decrease of forage plants

Relative quality of forage

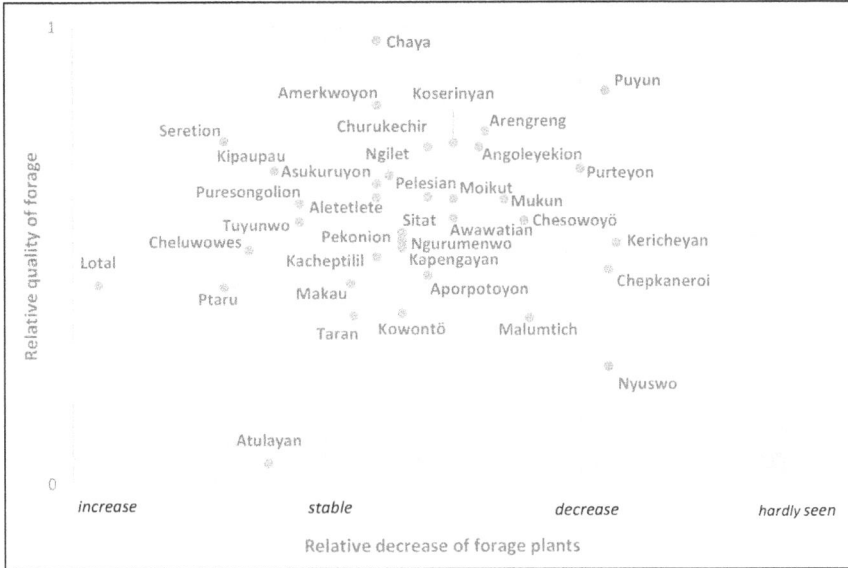

Fig. 4. Relative decrease in cattle forage, early 2000s–2015 (Hauke-Peter Vehrs).

(see Appendix) are also ranked high in forage quality, but the availability of these grasses is perceived to be low. Especially *Eragrostis cilianensis* (*puyun*) and *Brachiaria deflexa* (*abrute*) have been decreasing in the recent past (Figure 4).[7]

Only four grass species – *Cynodon niemfuensis* (*seretion*), *Enteropogon macrostachys* (*kipaupau*), *Aristida mutabilis* (*puresongolion*) and *Aristida adscensionis* (*cheluwowes*) – are seen as increasing, whereas almost 80 per cent of the plants covered in the ranking are perceived to have decreased in recent years Interestingly, the forage value of five tree species included in the ranking was low except during the dry season when grasses disappear and cattle browse on trees (Timberlake, 1987).

One possible reason for the cluster formation in Figure 4 might be that landscape changes are intra- and inter-annual. This is especially important with grasses, because they are the first plant to germinate and the first to die back. Additionally, cattle herders have the widest range of mobility in search of grasses. The cattle herders' experiences are thus far more diverse than those of herders who stay around homesteads.

---

7   The categories 'increase', 'stable', decrease' and 'hardly seen' were chosen in concordance with the categories used by Bollig and Schulte (1999) to make a comparison between the rankings possible.

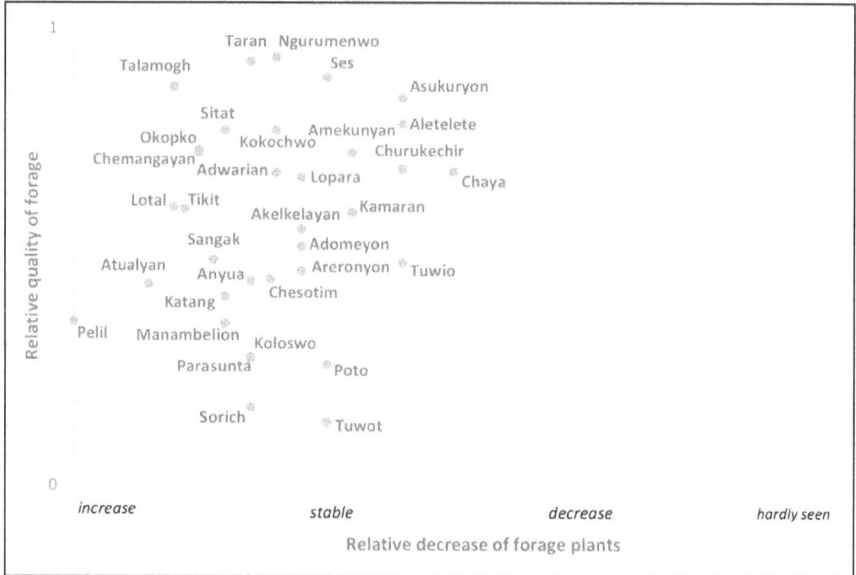

Fig. 5. Relative increase in small stock forage, early 2000s–2015 (Hauke-Peter Vehrs).

In contrast to the forage available for cattle, the herbs, bushes and trees goats use to browse on are dispersed abundantly in the area. *Digera muricata (ngurumenwo), Grewia tenax (taran), Vachellia tortilis (ses), Senegalia mellifera (talamogh), Tribulus spp. (asukuruyon), aletelete* (see Appendix), *Grewia bicolor (sitat)* and *Premna resinosa (kokochwo)* are recognised as high-quality forage plants. The cluster derived from the goat herders in Figure 5 is far less ambiguous than that in Figure 4, because goat herding takes place around the main homestead throughout the year. Hence, the reference area for goat herding is smaller and clearly defined.

The availability of plants varies widely, but only 20 per cent of those plants included in the ranking were perceived to be decreasing (Figure 5). Because the pods of acacia are perceived as a favourite feed for goats, three out of five acacia species were ranked highest, with four out of five perceived to be increasing rapidly in the area. In general, goat feed is highly diversified and forage is available all year round.

Camel forage displays a similar pattern to the goat ranking. The best forage plants are *Cyathula orthocantha (akelkelayan), Vachellia tortilis (ses), Vachellia nubica (pelil), Senegalia mellifera (talamogh), Vachellia nilotica (okopko), Salvadora persica (ashokonyon), Senegalia brevispica (ptaru), Cadaba farinosa (arerenyon)* and *Maerua crassifolia (tuwio).* These plants grow abundantly in the study area.

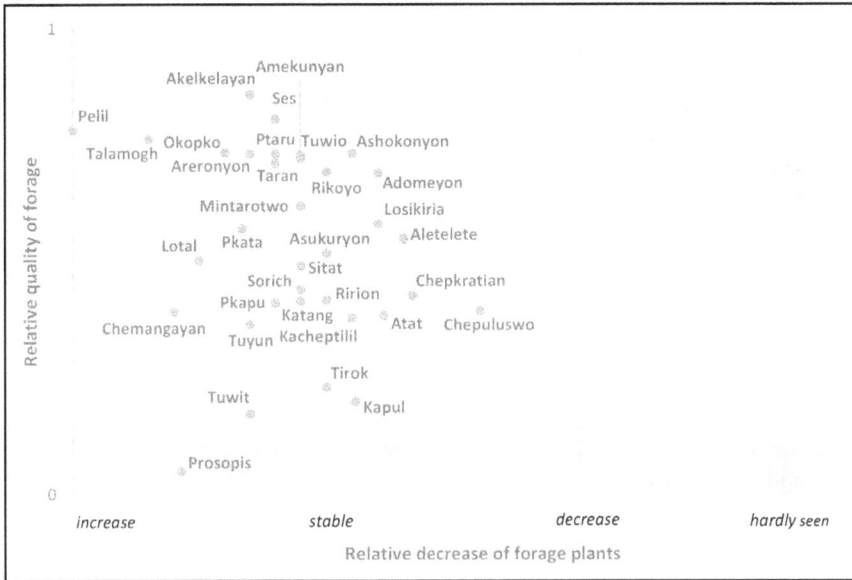

Fig. 6. Relative increase in camel forage, early 2000s–2015 (Hauke-Peter Vehrs).

Approximately 25 per cent of the plants discussed in the ranking are perceived as decreasing slightly, whereas only *Maerus spp.* (*chepuluswo*) is perceived as being in severe decline (although its forage value is markedly low, see Figure 6). *Vachellia nubica* (*pelil*) is seen as the highest 'increaser' throughout the camel and the goat rankings. Whereas goats browse only on its pods, camels prefer the leaves. This plant is severely encroaching on the landscape and is often found as the first intruder into cultivation areas in which its high-density stands form an impenetrable mass. However, camel forage is perceived as being abundant and of high quality in the lowlands and on the slopes of Mt Paka.

Bollig and Schulte (1999) described a similar scenario for forage availability. In their ranking, high-quality grasses such as *Sehima nervosum* (*chaya*), *Eragrostis cilianensis* (*puyun*), *Triumfetta rhomboidea* (*koserinyan*), *Eragrostis superba* (*churukechir*) and *kericheyan* (not specified) were ranked as strongly decreasing, whereas the unpalatable *Cymbopogon caesius* (*kowontö*) was spreading into degrading grasslands. Only five out of 26 plant species were assessed as increasing or stable, whereas the remaining grasses were all estimated to be decreasing.

Degradation involves a nearly complete replacement of perennial grasses by annual grasses and the widespread encroachment into grassland

communities of acacia thornbush (*acacia spp.*), a process frequently
dubbed 'green desertification'. (Bollig & Schulte, 1999, p. 498)

Grass availability appears to have been higher at the time of Bollig and
Schulte's study. The herders interviewed in my study were in their 20s and
30s. They perceive an enormous change in landscape over this period, typically
recalling that they were 'able to see far' when they were young, but now
bushes grow everywhere. Hence, the environmental changes reported from
the 1980s and early 1990s now appear more acute (Bollig & Schulte, 1999;
Timberlake, 1987).

Historical ranking

But not only does the young generation perceives a strong decline in grass
vegetation; their elders do as well. This section deals with memories of the
past and scientific accounts of the environment in East Pokot. In our historical
ranking for 1975, the Paka elders ranked quality and availability of the plant
species. Figure 7 shows the results and indicates a trend towards an incremental
decline of the grass cover from 1975 to 2015. The elders gave an account of
forage availability and quality in 1975 when the bush encroachment was not as
severe as today and grasses were still abundantly widespread. Figure 7 shows
the perception of forage decline. In particular, high-quality grasses such as

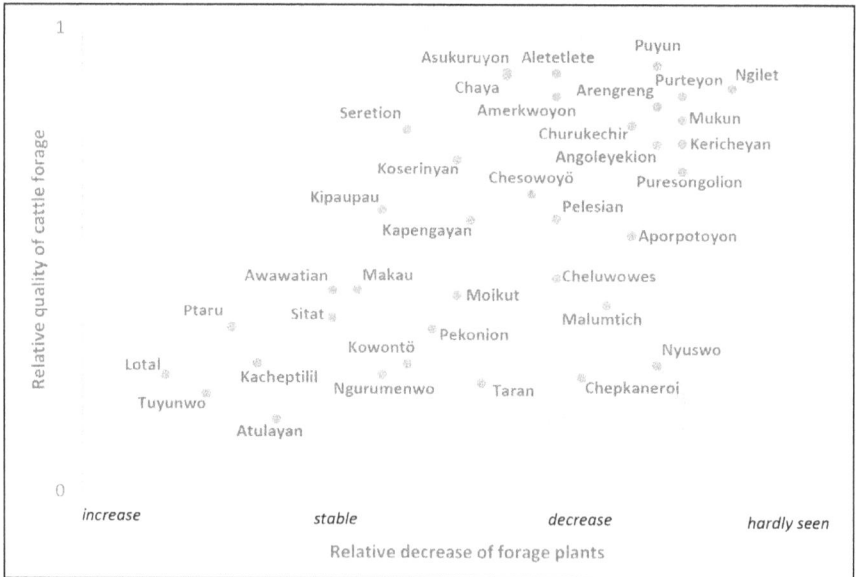

Fig. 7. Relative decrease in cattle forage, 1975–2015 (Hauke-Peter Vehrs).

Eragrostis cilianensis (*puyun*), *Brachiaria deflexa/Setaria homonyma* (*abrute*), *ngilet* (see Appendix), *Tragus berteronianus* (*arengreng*), *Dactyloctenium aegyptium* (*mukun*) and *Eragrostis superba* (*churukechir*) were perceived as declining tremendously.

The picture drawn by the elders is far more intense than that drawn by recent herders (see Figure 4), but the tendency is the same. Far less grass forage is available nowadays than in past decades. Only five plant species with very low forage quality for cattle were ranked as having increased since 1975, among them three tree species.

In a discussion over former descriptions of the environment, Bollig and Oesterle concluded that even these images of the past, described as pristine pastures with few trees, constitute a landscape that was already influenced heavily by humans and was to some extent overgrazed (Bollig & Oesterle, 2008). Grasses such as *Eragrostis cilianensis* (*puyun*) and *Aristida mutabilis* (*puresongolion*) are identified as indicators for this overgrazing, and thus support their conclusion that the environment in East Pokot cannot be viewed as stable. They further state:

> Environmental change is generally valued as negative both by outsiders and cultural insiders. The change from a grassland savannah to a bush savannah diminishes chances for cattle pastoralism significantly. However, both goats and camels (both browsers) profit from this expansion of bushland and indeed the increase of camel and goat herds may be encouraged by bush encroachment. (Bollig & Oesterle, 2008, p. 312)

Thus, the ranking results show clearly that changes towards an acacia-dominated bush savannah significantly favour browsing species such as goats and camels at the expense of cattle husbandry.

Internal reasoning over environmental changes

Whereas scientific accounts discuss population growth, land-use changes, high grazing pressure and changing weather conditions as the principal causes of landscape change in East Pokot, elders among the Pokot explain the causes from another perspective. Changes in land cover and environmental degradation are recounted by Pokot herders in detail, as the following statements of elderly people at Mt Paka indicate.

> *Nakan*: The land was good earlier [referring to 1975] and we had enough grasses. The rains were enough and we had peace [with the neighbouring groups]. In 1975, the land was good. There was grass; we had no trees like now; the land was open. You were able to see far – at Mt Paka and at Mt Silali and you can see zebras in the plains of Seronu when you stand at Mt Paka. Now you cannot see anything in Seronu [due to the high density of bushes and trees].

Tireng: The area was open all over the land. The area was good until 1984. ... The region was full of *seret* [grass species]. Many different grasses grew there.

Now the land is covered by *talamogh, pelil, anyua* and *kembirwo* [all tree species]. In 1975, the land was open and the plains were full of grasses like *amakwaratian, mukun, adwarian, amerkwoyon* and even *angoyelek*. It was prophesised before that the area will change. When the generation of Merkutwö comes, the land will not change much. But when Nyongi are circumcised, the past life will come again, the good one.

The hills were good this time during the second circumcision of Kaplelach [in 1996]. The first trees emerged in the hill sites, but we still had enough grass then. The plains like Naipacha were open, even the view from Mt Paka to Mt Korossi was open. There was a plain full of grass.

Riteluk: In my place [Tiaty] people were chased away by the war with Turkana. When the people returned after the war, they found the land overgrown with trees and the grass was interspersed with trees and the trees were replacing the grass for cattle.

Now, there is no place where you can see grasses – not at all! Just like the paths of the last season [the cattle tracks that people also used to walk], in the next year they are covered with trees. Cattle is becoming less and you cannot see them around here because grass is not available. The emergence of the war [with Turkana] brought the trees. Before, the rains were enough. The rains would start in March [*poykokwö*] and in April [*rikïsa*] the rains were enough. The girls were circumcised in May [*pirïwa*] or June [*melwon*].[8] Nowadays you cannot predict the rains, like before. (Group interview, 22 January 2015)

The three elders recall the higher grass availability three to four decades ago, the incremental expansion of tree species and the loss of wildlife species. They attribute the land-cover changes, on the one hand, to the unpredictability of rains and emphasise their perception of drier weather conditions in East Pokot during the past decades; on the other hand, to the Pokot–Turkana wars between 1969 and 1984 that caused a migration from the conflict-prone areas into the core zone of East Pokot around Mt Paka (Bollig, 1990b). Consequently, the grassland savannah that was already undergoing a gradual change experienced not only intense overstocking but also under-management (Conant,

---

[8]   Bollig (1992a) describes the months of the Pokot calendar and the time when the rains of the long rain period start in March or April. In *poykokwö*, the first rains appear and a certain plant (*kipsirioch/Scadoxus multiflorus*) starts to grow. In *rikïsa*, the rains continue.

1982). The ensuing scarcity of grasses, as explained by many elders, gave way to the encroachment of bushes. The bush encroachment was difficult to control, especially because management practices of burning were restricted by government legislation. These degradation processes gradually started in the early twentieth century and accelerated in the last quarter of the century when Pokot were confined to the area around Mt Paka due to the conflict with Turkana. This acceleration resulted in high-density bush coverage of *Senegalia mellifera*, *Vachellia nubica*, *Vachellia reficiens* and *Senegalia senegal*.

Another elder and the chief of the region, living in the lowlands east of Mt Paka, adds his perspective to the debate, emphasising other reasons, internal and external, for the degradation of pasture land.

> The area has changed a lot since I was young. For example, 200 metres around this place were no trees, only *ses* was found, few though. The area was open, no bush. There were few *anyua* bushes and the area was full of grasses, like the plain of Chepkoghio was full of grasses up to Adomeyon. The grasses that grew were *amerkwoyon, cheluwowes* – plenty! – *churukechir, abrute* – plenty! – up to Nginyang. Only small bushes grew and there were many *adome* trees that have disappeared today. There were many natural pan dams where animals could be watered. Nowadays they are all silted.

> There were a lot of wild animals here, leopards, lions, zebra, giraffes and all types of wild animals. Now they have gone completely. The area has become a bush, an increasing bush of *arekayan, talamogh, pelil* and *chemangoi*. So, the grasses cannot grow with the trees. *Tuwot* is the best tree for shade. *Pkapu* were also few by that time, but also good for shade. But the sun became hot and the area became a desert. Now, we find much *sesoi* and the area has changed completely compared to the past.

> The changes started in the 1970s up to now. Pokot people were very few during those days and were scattered over the land. You could find homesteads 1–2 kilometres apart. But now people are more.

> Another thing that has contributed to the increase of bushes is the absence of peace – the fight between Turkana and Pokot. Pokot people who lived in Silali were pushed up to Loruk and the land was left empty and was taken over by trees. The people use trees for the construction of huts and fences. The increase of livestock numbers is also important and the increase of people.

> Only the highlands are not affected so much by the changes. The lowlands are highly affected. The wild animals that were here have gone to the highlands [Laikipia County]. And there was no cultivation here before, like it is today. People cultivate the fertile land nowadays; before they did not do this. The animals have been affected by war, so they decided

to find another place – there is no grass here. Just like in Churo the area is full of *tabalak*[9] – no grasses. … There were many fruit trees in the area here, like *chemangoi, chepulus, tapoyo* and *kella*. Those trees are gone, so I see that the area has changed. It has come with poor rains. Everything depends on the rain, so these trees have to die. Sometimes we can spend even two years without rain. So these wild fruits have been affected by the [lack of] rains. Even honey was plenty here before, but is very little nowadays. These wild fruits were their [bees'] food. Before we had no sugar – and no chai tea – no *posho* [maize flour] and no drinks like *busaa* or *changaa*. The drink that was here, was *maratina* [honey beer] that was made for elderly people only. But now the younger generation is also drinking; everybody drinks *busaa* and this must be cursed. The respect [towards elders] is decreasing because everybody drinks alcohol. Nowadays the young generation is committing more adultery with the wives of the elderly people and those curse the young generation. So, the respect is gone with the consumption of alcohol. (Amos, 14 September 2014)

Amos recalls the vegetation of the past decades and describes the good pasture that was slowly replaced by bush and tree species. He also remembers the remnants of wildlife populations that still existed in the early second half of the twentieth century but quickly became extinct. He identifies the increase in human populations and livestock population numbers as one reason behind the land degradation, and mentions the use of farming as one reaction to the pressure on pastoral livelihoods. At the same time, he points to internal factors such as the increased alcohol production and its consumption by all members of the community. Before, consumption was restricted to elderly people, but the so-perceived 'misuse' of alcohol led to rude behaviour and an increase in adultery that then resulted in a curse on the land and its people by a generation of elders.

One of the elders at Mt Paka recapitualates the initiation of the past genera-tions – from Maina to Kaplelach generations – and identifies the Chumwŏ generation, which is senior to the Kaplelach generation set, as the one who cursed the land in reaction to the perception of the Koronkoro generation.

The elderly generation of Maina left Chumwŏ to take care of the land. The time Chumwŏ was in power there were no trees and the land was full of *seretion* [grass species]. The trees you can see now were not there. During the start of the raids [Pokot–Turkana war], the land was still open. Due to the raids, we fled from the region.

---

[9]   *Dodonaea viscosa* is a native plant species that has expanded rapidly in the highland areas around Churo. The spread of this plant, the relations between agriculture and the expansion and the effects on pastoral livelihoods are further examined in chapters 6 and 8.

In 1962, I lived in Chepchok and the land was still open. I can remember that a drought started during *Asis* [the eclipse of the sun in 1973]. I can say that Chumwö sent the drought to the land.

When the Koronkoro requested for *alim*,[10] many quarrels started among Chumwö men since they suspected some people among their generation to be favoured with gifts from the Koronkoro generation. Those [suspicious and jealous members of the Chumwö generation] sent the drought to the land. During the celebration of the *alim*, it stopped raining until November, because some Chumwö were annoyed. In the next year, it started to rain late and the drought never stops from that time until now.

Years later, when the people of the Kaplelach generation asked for their circumcision [which took place in 1988], the wild animals disappeared from the land. The Chumwö said we need to initiate Kaplelach because, if we stay with Koronkoro, it is not good. They called for a meeting of the elders with all the Chumwö people from Tiaty, and all over the land, they stopped the raids and it was peaceful for long. During this peaceful time, they circumcised Kaplelach and the rains were plenty. The land was full of grasses. When Kaplelach came out of their seclusion, the rains stopped and we experienced an outbreak of a disease [associated with flies – most likely trypanosomiasis] that killed the cattle in big numbers and the drought continued until now. I say Chumwö knows what they did to the land and they are the ones who cursed the grasses to vanish. (Tepakiang, 25 June 2015)

Tepakiang recalls the history of the past century and the different generation sets that have been initiated. After the second initiation of Koronkoro in 1949/59, the war with neighbouring Turkana people started and suppression followed until the end in 1984. Turkana drove Pokot people far south to the shores of Lake Baringo, and Pokot lost a lot of their territory during these fights. Only later, when Pokot were also armed with automatic guns, did they recapture the territory and push Turkana back north. During this time, bush encroachment increased tremendously and this encroachment is often perceived as a curse on the land and its people. In the former group interview, Tireng went so far as to say that the land would only recover with the initiation of the Nyongi generation, which will come after the Merkutwö generation that

---

[10] Bollig (1990a) describes the *alim* ceremony, paraphrased from the German: The younger generation, in this case the Koronkoro, ask the elderly Chumwö generation for permission to wear the black *alim* feathers and the white *ngaile* feathers. Furthermore, they get the right to cut the *amurö* meat, a highly valued piece of meat during ceremonies. The *alim* is the final ceremony in the whole promotion cycle and will hand over power to the next generation at a time when the older generation becomes weaker and many members have already died.

was initiated in 2016. As mentioned before, the generations recur cyclically, and with the initiation of a generation set such as the Nyongi perhaps around the year 2040, which was formerly associated with successful herders and good pastures, these conditions will also commence again.[11]

The conflictual relations between generation sets and age sets is not just an important topic among the pastoral Pokot, but can be found in the broader pastoral context of East Africa. For example Spencer presented the intra-ethnic conflicts in the gerontocratic acephalous political organisation in the context of the Samburu gerontocratic system (Spencer, 1965) or in relation to different Maasai groups (Spencer, 1976). Also conflicts in the Dassanetch pastoral group in the border region of Ethiopia and Kenya (Almagor, 1979), in Karimojong and related groups on the border with Kenya in north-eastern Uganda (Dyson-Hudson, 1966), and among the Turkana (Müller-Dempf, 1991, 2009, 2017) are well documented. Indeed, the conventional conflicts over the recognition of authority, the access to certain positions in society that are also associated with prestige and the distribution of responsibilities and opportunities is something that is common to many pastoral groups. As Bollig (1990a) demonstrates for the pastoral Pokot, initiation and graduation celebrations also comprise components of consolidation of the social organisation in which the elders retain their power and the initiators must submit to it, accept punishment and distribute gifts to the elderly generation. The fight for feathers and colours, as he terms it, has institutionalised elements as can be seen in the case of the *ametö* fights.

> The *ametö* fights between age groups that precede the graduation ceremonies can be seen in close connection with the ceremonies themselves. An *ametö* is usually ignited by the younger age groups wearing decorations that they are not (yet) entitled to. Stick fights often take place on the fringes of ceremonies or dances. The *ametö* is subject to strict rules. Only certain weapons may be used. ... Knives, bows and arrows, spears or even rifles are taboo in these fights. Men who resort to dangerous weapons in their rage (*woyogh*) in spite of the ban are collectively punished; but this happens rarely. (Bollig, 1990a, p. 265)[12]

The competition for authority and access to age groups is therefore not a new phenomenon, but part of the succession process in a gerontocratic system. Nevertheless, today's pastoral societies also face unique challenges, and new lines of conflict arise when young members strive for power and challenge the gerontocratic principle (Sortland, 2017). With today's opportunities to acquire financial resources and thus gain important positions in the rural

---

[11] This idea of periodical spaces is further explored in Chapter 7.
[12] Author translation of the original German text.

context, the power of the elders is being tested, as described, for example, for young Samburu who contest the established gerontocratic power relations (Meiu, 2015).

To return to the case of the Pokot and the oral accounts about the past, I want to outline two internal reasons from the perspective of pastoral Pokot that are highly important in explaining environmental changes. First, conflict and war are one cause of the changes described above. Second, the misbehaviour of younger generations towards elder generations greatly contributes to the bad conditions. As a result, the land is cursed and can be released from this course only if the young generation starts to behave. Elders are not confident about the current generation and rank the consequences of drinking on the same level as the consequences of war, saying: 'Drinking is the brother of war. Alcohol is a disease' (Tepakiang, 25 June 2015).

In the following, I shall examine the perceived decline of pasture land over the past decades from a distance. A GIS analysis of aerial photographs can indicate how the land surface has changed over the last 30 years and whether these changes match those in the accounts of Pokot elders.

Times-series analysis of land-use and land-cover change in East Pokot

Whereas the first two sections of this chapter dealt with a historical reconstruction of the landscape change on the basis of secondary literature as well as the oral history of the region's change from the perspective of the elders, in the following section, I use a GIS analysis of remote sensing data to provide a scientific perspective on the study of the landscape change in East Pokot over three decades from 1985 to 2015. In collaboration with the Centre for Remote Sensing of Land Surfaces (ZFL) in Bonn, land-cover changes were identified by analysing aerial photographs at five-year intervals. The analysis started by specifying the region under study. It consisted of the borders of the Tiaty Constituency and the southern Turkana County region, an area currently occupied by pastoral Pokot. Furthermore, a ground truthing took place, identifying five general types of ground cover shown in Photos 7–11. The details of the GIS analysis are described by Basukala et al. (2019a, 2019b) and selected time-series maps are displayed below. First, I describe land-cover changes for the pastoral region of Mt Paka, followed by an analysis of the complete study area. A third step focuses on the agro-pastoral region around Churo and the transition to farming in an agro-pastoral region.

Five categories were used to analyse the land surface: bare soil, open bush savannah, dense shrub and tree savannah, water and maize. The three categories bare soil, water bodies and maize cultivation are the easiest to distinguish. Bare soil, as shown in Photo 7, describes a nearly vegetationless type of area that can be found throughout the region, especially in the flatter regions or as gullies on the fringes of the Rift Valley. Water bodies are defined as all

7. Bare soil.

8. Open bush savannah.

9. Dense shrubs and trees.

10. Water (Lake Baringo).

Photos 7–11. Land-cover categories
(Hauke-Peter Vehrs).

11. Maize.

those areas that are covered by water. This is mainly Lake Baringo, which is located in the south of the study region, and about half of the total size of the lake is included in the analysis. In addition, there are dams in the region, but they make up a negligible part of the total area of the water bodies. The areas with maize cultivation are also included in the analysis, because especially in the highland regions of the Laikipia Plateau, the cultivation of maize and the changes in landscape use can be observed very clearly. The results of the increasing land surface under maize cultivation will be taken up in the next chapter when examining the social transformations towards agro-pastoral land use in the highlands more closely.

The variations between the other categories shrub savannah and dense shrub and tree savannah describe gradual differences in land cover rather than distinct land-cover types (such as water and bare soil). The dense shrub and tree savannah category is defined by the closed tree canopy. Because the bush encroachment processes in the region are perceived as increasing significantly, I chose this category to provide quantitative evidence for the picture presented by the elders of the region. The implementation of this category is therefore based both on observations made during fieldwork and the need to develop distinguishable categories for the GIS analysis. The shrub savannah category, on the other hand, is distinguished by the still-open character of the landscape as shown in Photos 7–11.

Land-cover changes at Mt Paka

The written and oral accounts and the ranking results all indicate heavy bush encroachment in East Pokot over the past decades. The transformation of former pasture land into an acacia-dominated savannah is narrated by Pokot elders and also observable in historical sources. Particularly interesting are the results of the historical forage ranking of the past four decades. Elders draw a picture of a rapidly changing environment that barely provides cattle forage.

Therefore, I focus first on the pastoral region around Mt Paka that was also the most important target of the elders. Map 3 displays the results of the time-series analysis of the former Kokore/Paka Ward for 1985, 2000 and 2015, and Figure 8 shows these changes in detail.[13]

In the pastoral region at Mt Paka, two processes dominate the land-cover changes. At first, and most importantly, a large part of the open savannah has changed into a dense shrub and tree savannah with a closed canopy. The time series indicates a manyfold increase of dense savannah stands from 4,000 hectares in 1985 to 15,000 hectares in 2015, while, at the same time, the open

---

[13] All remote sensing data have been analysed by Basukala et al. (2019a, 2019b). Maps 3–5 are based on the GIS analysis of both satellite images and ground truthing data.

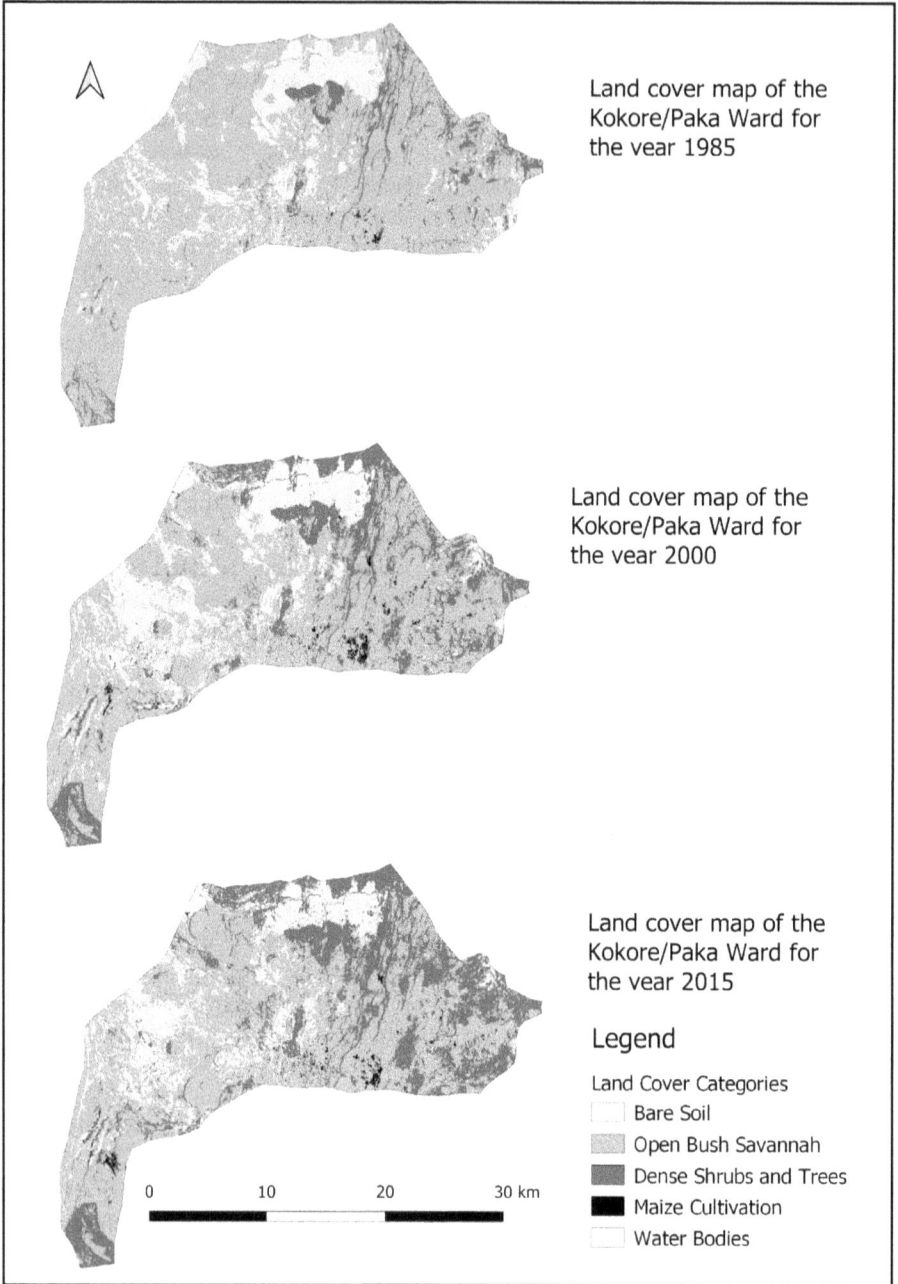

Land cover map of the
Kokore/Paka Ward for
the year 1985

Land cover map of the
Kokore/Paka Ward for
the year 2000

Land cover map of the
Kokore/Paka Ward for
the year 2015

Legend

Land Cover Categories

Bare Soil
Open Bush Savannah
Dense Shrubs and Trees
Maize Cultivation
Water Bodies

0   10   20   30 km

Map 3. Land-cover changes in the area round Mt Paka 1985, 2000 and 2015, showing the decrease of open grass savannah at the expense of dense shrub savannah (Hauke-Peter Vehrs; data source: Basukala et al. 2019a, 2019b).

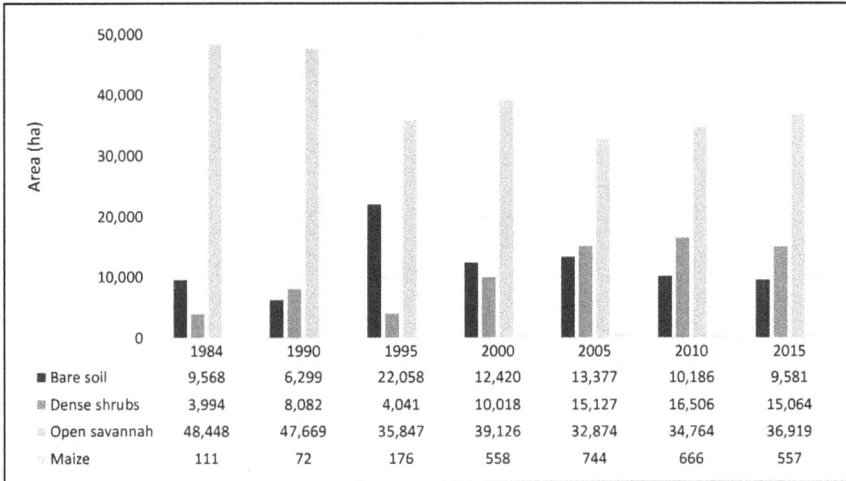

	1984	1990	1995	2000	2005	2010	2015
■ Bare soil	9,568	6,299	22,058	12,420	13,377	10,186	9,581
▨ Dense shrubs	3,994	8,082	4,041	10,018	15,127	16,506	15,064
▨ Open savannah	48,448	47,669	35,847	39,126	32,874	34,764	36,919
▨ Maize	111	72	176	558	744	666	557

Fig. 8. Land-cover changes (in hectares) for the former Kokore/Paka Ward, 1985–2015 (Hauke-Peter Vehrs).

savannah has been reduced by about 12,000 hectares, one quarter of the total open savannah area. These 12,000 hectares account for 19.3 per cent of the total ward area that turned almost completely into a closed canopy tree savannah.

Second, maize cultivation has taken place to an increasing degree. About 550 hectares of land were under maize cultivation in 2015. Although this accounts for merely 1 per cent of the total area, it is an increase of cultivation by a factor of five. The development of maize cultivation in the time-series analysis shows strong fluctuations in the area under cultivation due to the opportunistic character of farming attempts in pastoral livelihoods: in a year of higher precipitation, more people try to cultivate maize, whereas in years when the rainy season starts late or rainfall is merely erratic, fewer people start cultivation or succeed in rain-fed maize cultivation. Although the changes in the land cover are intense, most of the area of about 37,000 hectares is still classified as open savannah.

As can be seen in Map 3, most of the changes have happened north of Mt Paka around Naudo. There, at the southern foot of Mt Silale, dense bush populations occupy large parts of the land. Moreover, east of Mt Paka, bushes have increased strongly in the plains of Seronu. Both results, the encroachment of bushes around Naudo and that in Seronu, confirm the impressions and stories I was told during fieldwork. However, the Kokore/Paka Ward with its 620 km² covers only about 10 per cent of the total area analysed here. The following section deals with whether the bush encroachment process is also taking place on a larger scale.

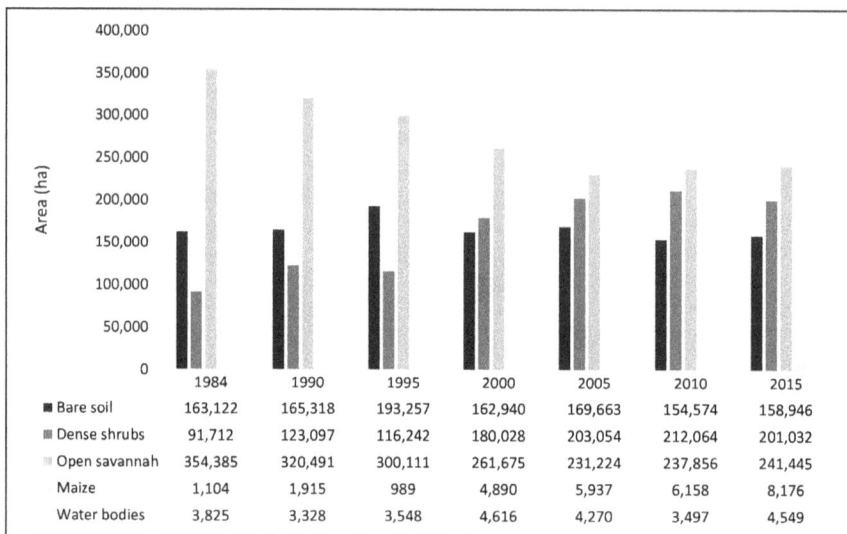

	1984	1990	1995	2000	2005	2010	2015
■ Bare soil	163,122	165,318	193,257	162,940	169,663	154,574	158,946
■ Dense shrubs	91,712	123,097	116,242	180,028	203,054	212,064	201,032
▩ Open savannah	354,385	320,491	300,111	261,675	231,224	237,856	241,445
Maize	1,104	1,915	989	4,890	5,937	6,158	8,176
Water bodies	3,825	3,328	3,548	4,616	4,270	3,497	4,549

Fig. 9. Land-cover changes (in hectares) for the total study area (Tiaty Constituency and former Nadume and Kapedo Wards in southern Turkana County), 1985–2015 (Hauke-Peter Vehrs).

Land-cover changes in East Pokot

The trend observed in the Mt Paka region has continued for the total study area of 6,142 km². Map 4 shows the land images in 1985 and in 2015. The most obvious increase is in the dense shrub category, which has increased by a factor of two from 900 km² to more than 2,000 km² – 32.7 per cent of the total area (see Figure 9). At the same time, the open savannah has decreased by about 1,130 km² to 2,410 km², constituting 39.3 per cent of the total area in 2015.[14] As Map 4 and Figure 9 show so strikingly, the dense shrub and tree savannah is expanding at the expense of the open savannah. These data confirm the accounts of the elders who described such a kind of bush encroachment, mentioning the 'open' character of the plains and the mountains sites where they were able 'to see far'. Nowadays, this is impossible, as elders have reported.

The general assumption of bush encroachment at the expense of the open savannah is confirmed in the total study area, and the processes observed are even more intense compared to Mt Paka. Over a period of 30 years, about 18 per cent of the total area has transformed into a bush forest with closed canopy.

---

[14] The fluctuations in all categories, especially the 'bare soil' category, can be explained by the closeness of this category to the open savannah category and the temporal effects of droughts on the vegetation cover.

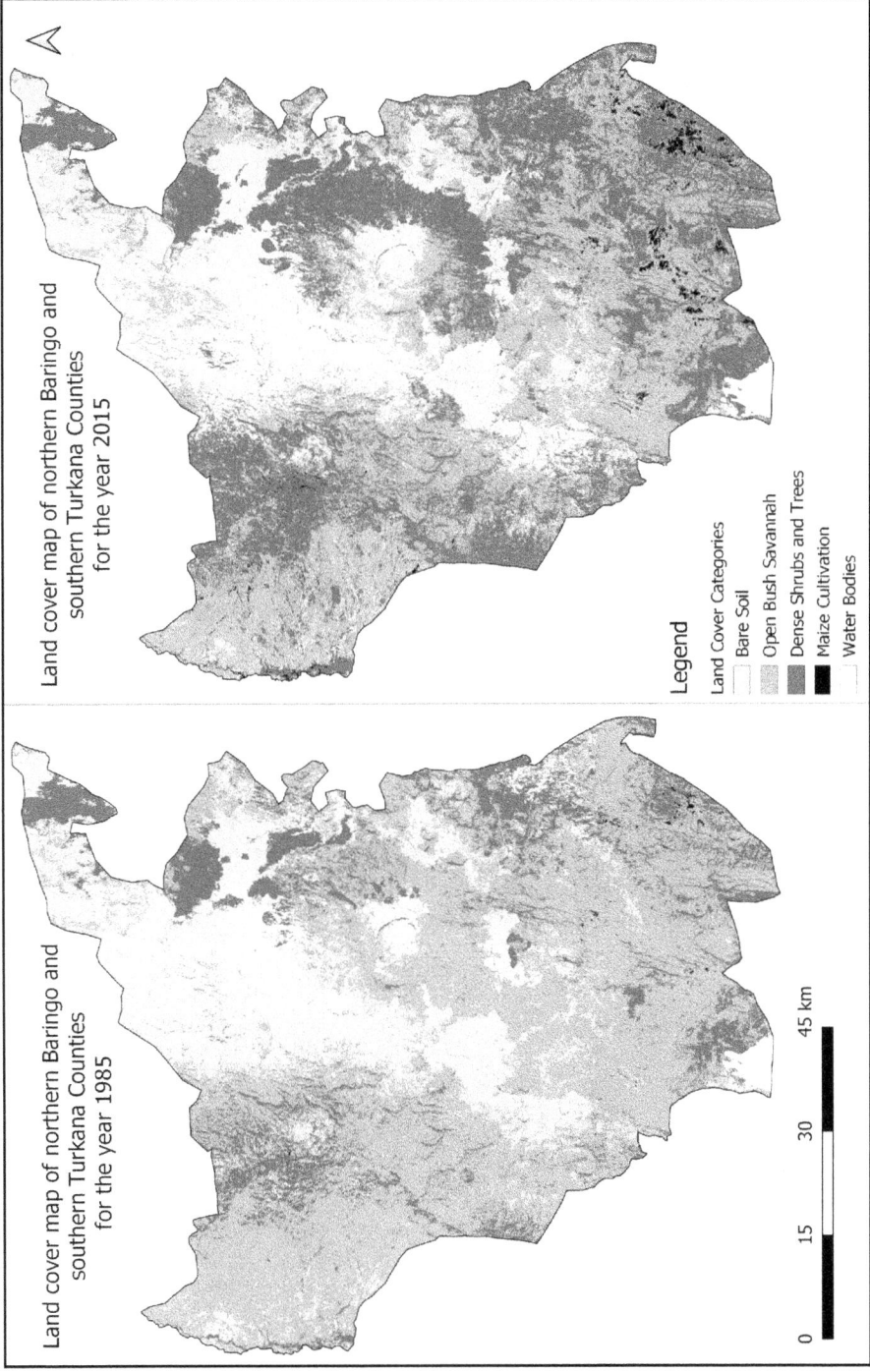

Land cover map of northern Baringo and
southern Turkana Counties
for the year 1985

Land cover map of northern Baringo and
southern Turkana Counties
for the year 2015

Legend

Land Cover Categories
Bare Soil
Open Bush Savannah
Dense Shrubs and Trees
Maize Cultivation
Water Bodies

0   15   30   45 km

Map 4. Land-cover changes in the area studied of northern Baringo and southern Turkana counties, 1985–2015 (Hauke-Peter Vehrs; data source: Basukala et al. 2019a, 2019b).

The rapidity of bush encroachment is astonishing and highly challenging for pastoral livelihoods.

Besides this overall process, the fast spread of agricultural practices describes another important trend. The black-coloured areas in Map 4 have increased strongly in the south-western and to some extent in the north-eastern parts of the study area. Maize cultivation in the region has also strongly increased by a factor of seven to a total of 7,000 hectares. In the Mt Paka region, however, farming has increased at a much slower pace. Therefore, the following focuses on the south-eastern region with the highest levels of maize cultivation.

Land-cover changes in the eastern highlands

The general trend of bush encroachment is also observable in the highland region around Churo. The open savannah declined by 27,200 hectares and the dense shrub and tree savannah increased by 25,700 hectares between 1985 and 2015 (Map 5 and Figure 10). Therefore, about one quarter of the land cover has transformed over the past 30 years. Against the general trend of acacia bush encroachment, the kind of bush encroachment observed here has a different character, because it is another plant that is mainly invading the landscape: *Dodonaea viscosa*. This variance in bush encroachment is also related to the different environmental conditions in this region that lies at the

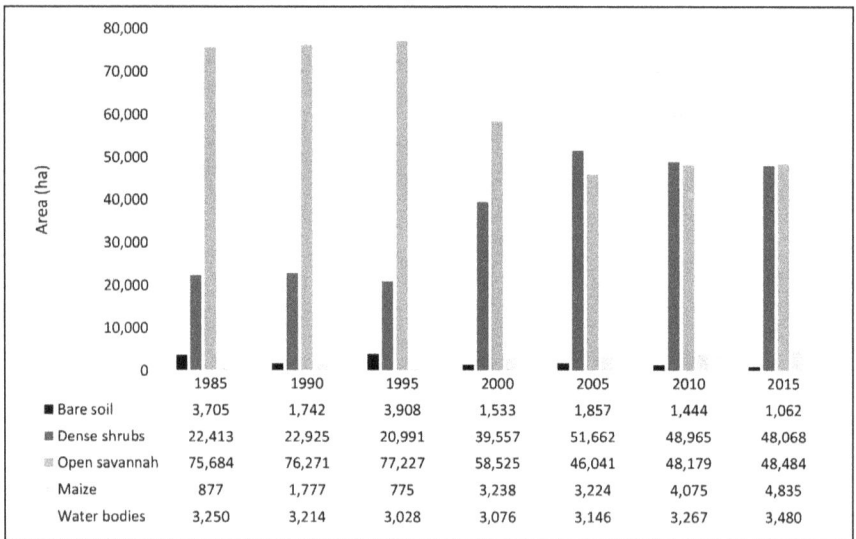

Area (ha)	1985	1990	1995	2000	2005	2010	2015
■ Bare soil	3,705	1,742	3,908	1,533	1,857	1,444	1,062
■ Dense shrubs	22,413	22,925	20,991	39,557	51,662	48,965	48,068
▨ Open savannah	75,684	76,271	77,227	58,525	46,041	48,179	48,484
Maize	877	1,777	775	3,238	3,224	4,075	4,835
Water bodies	3,250	3,214	3,028	3,076	3,146	3,267	3,480

Fig. 10. Land-cover changes (in hectares) for the agro-pastoral highlands, 1985–2015 (Hauke-Peter Vehrs).

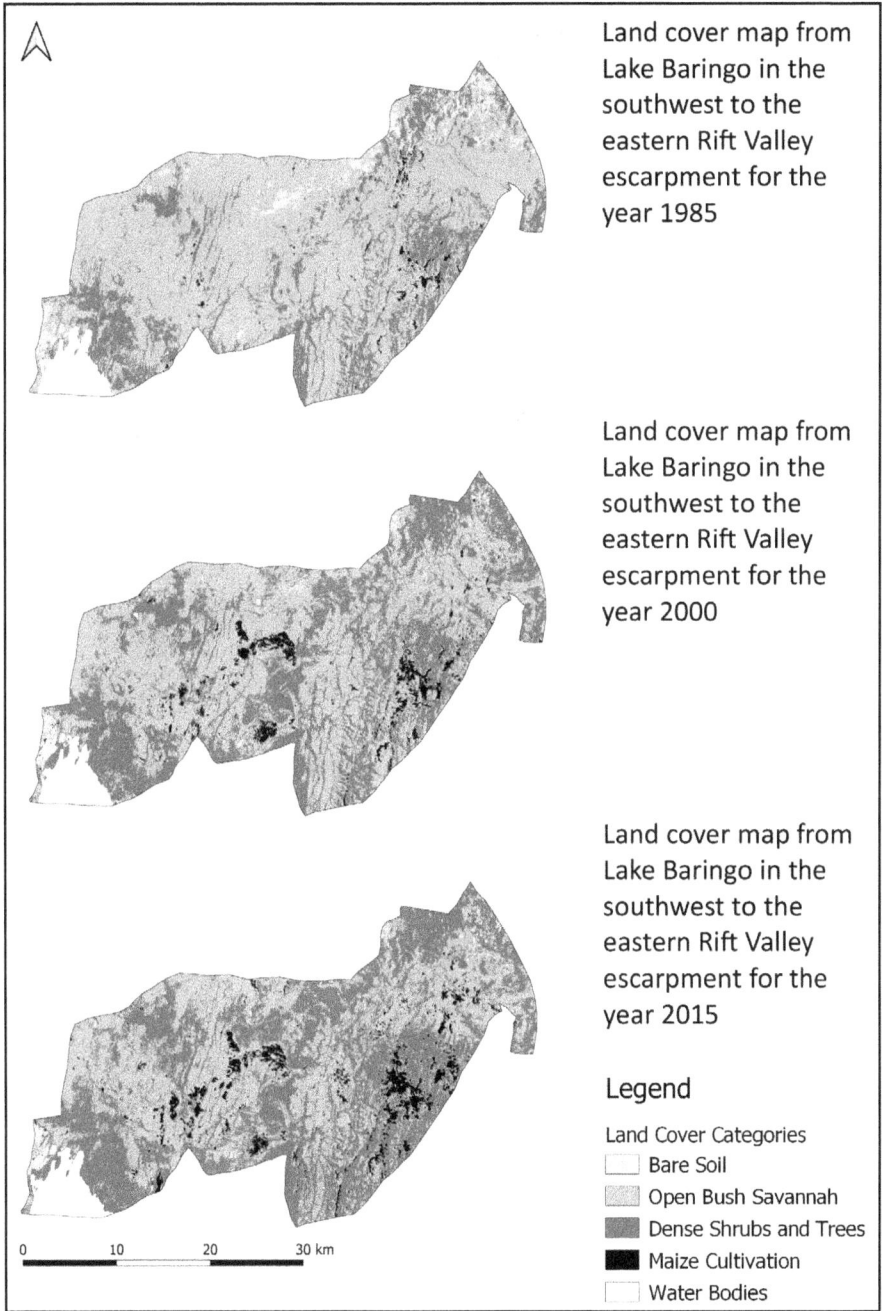

Land cover map from Lake Baringo in the southwest to the eastern Rift Valley escarpment for the year 1985

Land cover map from Lake Baringo in the southwest to the eastern Rift Valley escarpment for the year 2000

Land cover map from Lake Baringo in the southwest to the eastern Rift Valley escarpment for the year 2015

Legend

Land Cover Categories
- Bare Soil
- Open Bush Savannah
- Dense Shrubs and Trees
- Maize Cultivation
- Water Bodies

0   10   20   30 km

Map 5. Land-cover changes in the agro-pastoral highlands 1985–2015 (Hauke-Peter Vehrs; data source: Basukala et al. 2019a, 2019b).

Rift Valley escarpment and is higher in altitude. Furthermore, in contrast to the predominantly pastoral regions in East Pokot, land-use changes, especially maize cultivation, have also influenced the bush encroachment processes. The process of land-cover transformations and the drivers and effects of these changes are explored further in Chapter 7.

The time-series analysis of land-cover changes has brought to light tremendous land-cover changes in the highlands around Churo between 1985 and 2015. The area under cultivation increased by a factor of five between 1985 and 2015. Compared to the moderate increase in the total study area, developments in the eastern highlands show a new dimension of the trend towards the cultivation of maize in the region. Around Churo and Tangulbei, maize cultivation increased to 4.6 per cent of the land cover in 2015 compared to 0.9 per cent for the Mt Paka region and 1.3 per cent in general, and thus points to a new development in local livelihoods.

Table 8 summarises the two most important processes that were identified once again as the expansion of bushes and the increase of maize cultivation. Whereas in the Mt Paka region, the areas with dense scrubland increased to *only* 25 per cent, in the highland region around Churo almost 50 per cent of the area is covered with dense bushes. In the region as a whole, bush encroachment accounted for almost one third of the area's vegetation in 2015 compared with 15 per cent in 1985. Over time, the open areas in the study areas decreased to the same extent. Absolute figures suggest that the open savannah transformed almost entirely into a closed canopy savannah. In all three cases, open savannah has declined in total from 57.7 per cent to 39.3 per cent coverage of the total area between 1985 and 2015. At the same time, the dense shrub and tree savannah expansion doubled from 14.9 per cent to 32.7 per cent coverage between 1985 and 2015.

Table 8. Land-cover changes in East Pokot, 1985–2015.

	Mt Paka	Churo	Total study area
Total area km²	621	1,059	6,141
Open savannah			
Decrease (in km²) between 1985 and 2015	-115	-272	-1,129
Percentage of land cover in 1985	78	71.5	57.7
Percentage of land cover in 2015	59.5	45.8	39.3
Dense shrub and tree savannah			
Increase (in km²) between 1985 and 2015	111	257	1,090
Percentage of land cover in 1985	6.4	21.2	14.9
Percentage of land cover in 2015	24.3	45.4	32.7

Maize cultivation			
Increase (in km²) between 1985 and 2015	5.6	39.6	70.7
Percentage of land cover in 1985	0.2	0.8	0.2
Percentage of land cover in 2015	0.9	4.6	1.3

Sources: Basukala et al. (2019a, 2019b)

The results presented here also lead to the question why the expansion of maize cultivation is so clearly visible in the highland region but not to the same extent in the regions within the Rift Valley. Therefore, I want to take a closer look at the regions that have undergone the most extensive changes and represent the largest areas of land with maize cultivation today.

Two hotspots of maize cultivation can be identified in the GIS analysis and are both located in escarpment areas: Churo and Tangulbei at the eastern escarpment towards Laikipia County, and Mirigissi and Kolloa at the western escarpment towards West Pokot County (Basukala et al., 2019a, 2019b).

Seventy per cent of the land under cultivation – more than 5,600 hectares (total area 8,176 hectares in 2015) – is concentrated in these four wards in East Pokot. The question here is why maize cultivation is concentrated along the escarpment regions and is developing differently than in the other regions. I argue that farming intensifies in areas where precipitation is sufficient to establish maize cultivation, whereas, at the same time, opportunistic farming is employed in regions with less rainfall where people are now taking up the opportunity offered by hybrid maize species that can ripen within three months.

Developments in the highlands cannot be explained sufficiently by the mere fact that more precipitation is available there. External influences and social change, which have been present since the 1960s, also need to be taken into account in order to understand the current situation. Therefore, the next chapter focuses on the eastern highlands around Churo where pastoral land-use practices have changed and farming has become central to the subsistence practices of local livelihoods.

In the following, I concentrate on the transformation and diversification of local livelihoods in which land-use practices can best be described as agro-pastoral. However, bush encroachment is also observable in the highland areas, but to a different extent than that of the acacia encroachment in the lowland areas. The next chapter therefore compares the social transformations in the Churo highlands to the pastoral livelihoods at Mt Paka and links land-cover changes to the land-use changes of the past 50 years.

6

Socio-Ecological Transformations in the Agro-Pastoral Highlands

In the second half of the twentieth century the pastoralists in East Pokot diversified their livelihood assets over a relatively short time period, which is represented mainly by the modifications of livestock husbandry (Oesterle, 2008) and the increasing use of farming (Greiner et al., 2013; Greiner & Mwaka, 2016; Mwaka, 2014). One of the most important changes appears to be the emergence of agricultural practices in East Pokot. These range from pastoral farming in core pastoral zones with unfavourable conditions to intensive rain-fed farming in the more favourable highland areas towards the eastern and western escarpment regions.

In the eastern highlands towards Laikipia County, agriculture has evolved slowly since the mid-twentieth century, and the former dependence of livelihoods on livestock husbandry is no longer predominant. Greiner et al. (2013) describe land-use changes in the Churo highlands from pastoral modes of living towards crop cultivation and sedentarisation. In contrast to the picture of opportunistic pastoral farming in the pastoral areas, they reveal that agriculture is now the predominant mode of subsistence. Vast areas have been turned into cultivation grounds with regular fencing. Moreover, the region experienced an intensive increase in population numbers between 1979 and 2019. Agro-pastoral livelihoods have developed over time in the escarpment regions of East Pokot that still contain a few pastoral characteristics when it comes to livestock husbandry and the production and use of livestock products. However, the cultivation of maize and other crops for subsistence and revenue generation has become equally or even more important than keeping livestock.

In the following, I describe the emergence of farming and how it has developed over the past 70 years, discuss differences between agro-pastoral livelihoods in Churo and the pastoral livelihoods at Mt Paka and identify the drivers of this livelihood transformation. I conclude by looking at the relations between the land-use changes (especially related to farming) and land-cover changes in the Churo highlands against the background of the spread of *Dodonaea viscosa*.

Pastoral and agro-pastoral livelihoods

Ever since the formation of the pastoral Pokot in the eighteenth century, Pokot people have been differentiated by their occupation. The agro-pastoral Pokot from West Pokot County were named *pi'-pa-pagh* – the 'seed people' or 'agriculturalists' (*pagh* literally means 'corn' – see Beech, 1911, pp.15, 62). Those Pokot who migrated into the Baringo region and the Kerio Valley and started a pastoral life were called *pi'-pa-tich* – 'the owners of the cows' (see Beech, 1911, pp. 73, 145 and Barton, 1921, p. 82; the literal translation is 'the cow people'). In West Pokot, people are still mainly involved in agro-pastoral activities, whereas in northern Baringo, pastoral livelihoods dominate. However, the former shift from agro-pastoralism to pastoralism has reversed again over time, and pastoral livelihoods have turned into agro-pastoral livelihoods – at least in regions where agricultural practices are promising. In comparison to the intensive farming of West Pokot people, the farming attempts of East Pokot farmers are less intensive. Whereas Davies (2008) describes the elaborate irrigation farming in the West Pokot highlands, cultivation in the escarpment regions of East Pokot concentrates on rain-fed maize production and some staple food.

I differentiate between pastoral and agro-pastoral livelihoods here in order to describe the quality of change that has happened over time. Galaty (1996) describes how pastoral people are characterised by their dependence 'on domestic animals for subsistence, and that they are predominantly occupied with herding on natural pasture'. Agro-pastoralism is then distinguished by the aspect that 'cultivation supplements the pastoral diet ... and in densely populated agricultural areas, such as South Asia, animals are valued for milk, manure and traction, and as objects of strong cultural and religious emphasis' (Galaty, 1996, p. 415). If these definitions were to be applied to the Paka pastoral and Churo agro-pastoral people, both would be characterised as agro-pastoral communities, because 98 per cent of the households at Mt Paka also engage in irregular pastoral farming and 99 per cent of the households in Churo engage in regular maize cultivation. However, with reference to the initial definitions of pastoralism (see Chapter 3), I do not consider that the mere existence of cultivation practices can define agro-pastoral livelihoods. Instead, I consider the pastoral people at Mt Paka to be pastoral because their livelihoods are centred around livestock husbandry and not around farming. In contrast, the agro-pastoral livelihoods in Churo are centred around farming and are complemented by rearing livestock. These differences between pastoral and agro-pastoral livelihoods therefore represent two ends of a continuum, whose pure and stereotypical form – at least in East Pokot – can hardly be found today. Rather, the people representing the pastoral or agro-pastoral livelihoods move along this continuum. In the transition zone of this continuum, it is difficult to distinguish the different livelihoods from each other. However, I do not assume that moving on this continuum is a directed development from one livelihood system to another, but that the changes along the continuum can be made flexibly and opportunistically, also in order to be able to adapt to the changes in the environment already described. The differences between pastoral and agro-pastoral livelihoods are examined in more detail below.

In the study area of East Pokot, farming intensity varies greatly between the pastoral farming of those at Mt Paka and the maize cultivation of the agro-pastoral people in Churo. Differences are also observable in the way cultivation grounds are prepared and farming takes place. I understand pastoral farming as a practice executed on an irregular basis – for instance in years when the rainy season starts as expected. Cultivation grounds are fenced with acacia branches in an irregular, oval shape, and ploughing work is done predominantly manually with a hoe. To prepare a plot, beer is brewed and friends and neighbours are invited to work communally on the field. Therefore, in years when many households decide to prepare cultivation grounds, different 'ploughing parties' are held on an almost daily basis. Due to the sequence of ploughing activities, which start after the onset of the rainy season, the planting of maize seeds is often delayed, resulting in a shorter growing period. Because the regions with pastoral land use experience less precipitation than the highland areas and the period of rain is bimodal, the reduced growing period appears to be counterproductive. Consequently, cultivation plots are often located in places that gather water from a larger catchment area, and pastoralists favour hybrid maize seeds because some varieties grow and ripen within three months. Sometimes, women also separately cultivate small home gardens with cowpeas, mung beans and pumpkins. Very occasionally, farming plots are found that exceed all other farming attempts in terms of cultivation technique and crop variety. Nevertheless, with the rapid expansion of farming practices during the past decades, and the prospects of higher water availability in the pastoral region through the construction of geothermal wells and water pipelines from Lake Baringo, the potential for innovation seems to be given.

In contrast to pastoral farming, maize cultivation in the agro-pastoral highlands is more elaborated and protected with rectangular, close-meshed fencing. Manual ploughing labour is mainly substituted by tractor use, and average field sizes exceed the pastoral farming plots (0.6 hectares compared to 0.3 hectares in pastoral farming; Greiner et al., 2013).[1] Because the hybrid

---

[1]   Donkey ploughing was first introduced as an agricultural practice, but it has not established itself (Catholic Diocese of Nakuru, 1980). Whereas in the highlands, ploughing is mostly done with tractors, in the pastoral areas of the lowlands, a large number of people use the hoe to prepare fields for cultivation at 'ploughing parties'. As noted above, beer is brewed and the community members (men and women) are invited to come ploughing. After a previously determined part of the field is finished, a round of beer is served. Then another piece is prepared, and this continues until the field has reached the desired size.

maize variety used in the highlands often ripens within five to six months and achieves higher yields compared to the three-month variety, there is greater reliance on farming crops and less on livestock husbandry among the agro-pastoral livelihoods. In addition to maize cultivation, beans, colewort (Kiswahili: *sukuma wiki*), spinach, pumpkins, potatoes, millet, chillies, green grams, tomatoes, onions, sweet potatoes, cabbage, sorghum and a small variety of fruit trees (oranges and guava) are also cultivated, but to a lesser extent. This variety is in stark contrast to the practices in pastoral farming that rely mainly on maize and sometimes beans.

In general, farming attempts are increasing in the pastoral zone of East Pokot. Whereas Oesterle (2007) reports that 50 per cent of households conducted pastoral farming in the Paka/Kadingding area in 2007, in 2015, 98 per cent of the Paka people started maize cultivation. However, in drier years, this number can decrease significantly with household subsistence then still relying on herding livestock. In line with my differentiation, pastoral farming is conducted in those areas of East Pokot where livestock husbandry is still the dominant mode of subsistence, and farming is but one option among others by which to diversify livelihood assets. In contrast, agro-pastoral farming is characterised by the application of better techniques and the population's reliance on the farming output.

However, I do not intend to describe two entirely different or separate livelihoods. I strongly agree with Davies (2012) on the importance of linkages and networks between pastoral and agro-pastoral Pokot. These are maintained intentionally and are extremely important in times of crisis when either farming or livestock husbandry is under pressure. Therefore, farming activities in the East Pokot highlands cannot be thought of as being without pastoral ways of living or vice versa. In the following, I would like to take a brief look at the beginning of agricultural activities in Churo and the surrounding area and describe the influence of the external actors who have initiated changes. Furthermore, not only the land use itself has changed, but also the way of life of the agro-pastoralists. I describe this in more detail and also compare it with pastoral livelihoods.

The advent of farming in Churo

In the area around Churo, with an annual precipitation of 632 mm/m^2 and a monomodal growing period of 150 days, cultivation is more reliable than in the lowlands that are characterised by similar amounts of rainfall but a bimodal period of rains (Greiner et al., 2013). In contrast to the Pokot lowlands around Mt Paka and the mid-hill areas around Tangulbei, which are still characterised by pastoral modes of land use, highland areas towards the Laikipia Plateau are characterised by crop farming (Map 6).

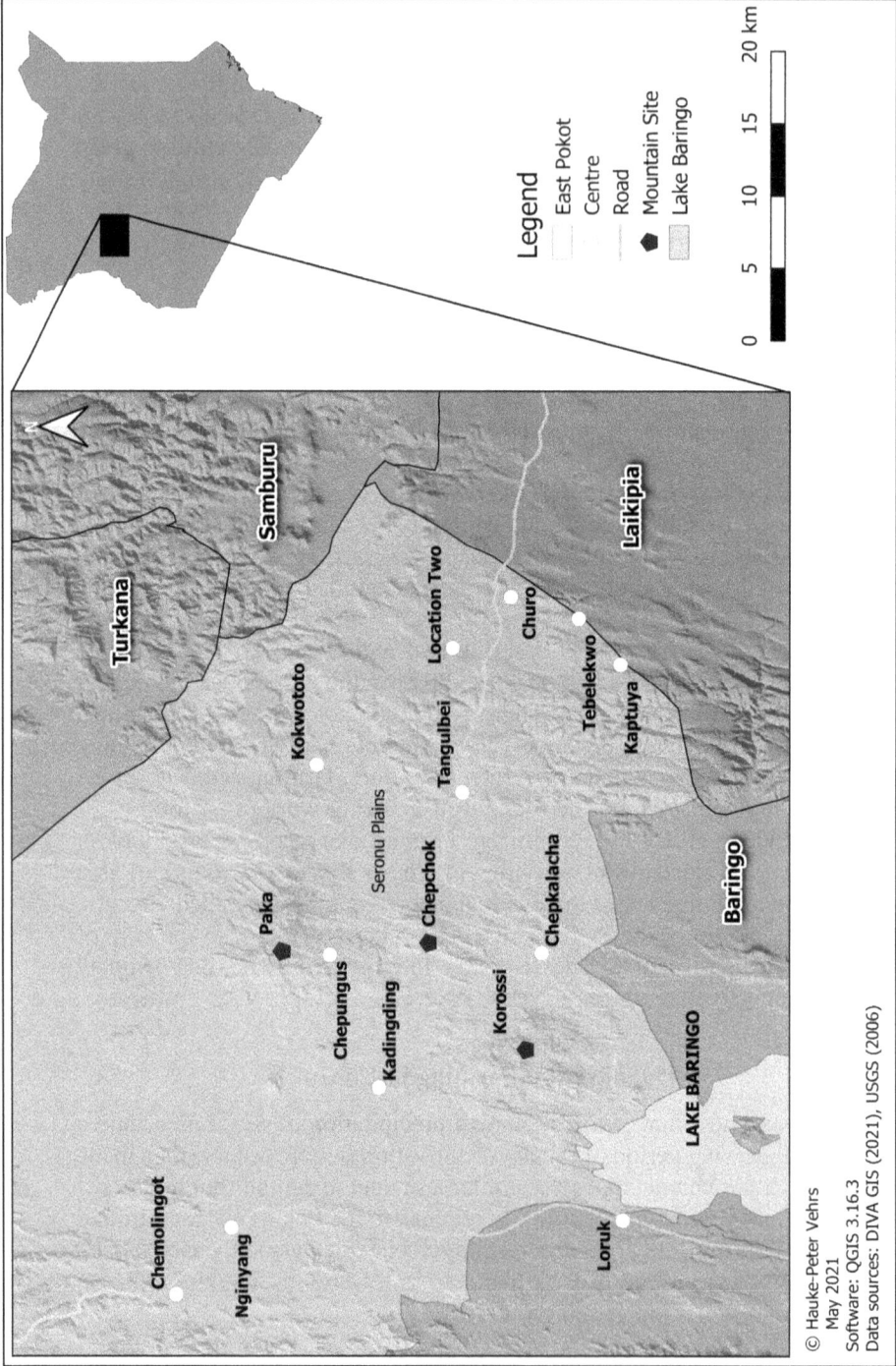

© Hauke-Peter Vehrs
May 2021
Software: QGIS 3.16.3
Data sources: DIVA GIS (2021), USGS (2006)

Map 6. The agro-pastoral highland area around Churo, 2015 (Hauke-Peter Vehrs).

Legend

East Pokot
Centre
Road
Mountain Site
Lake Baringo

0   5   10   15   20 km

Farming was introduced in the highlands in the 1960s and places were gradually occupied and pieces of land enclosed. The history of farming was recorded by SALTLICK.

> It appears that cropping was first attempted in the higher areas during the 1960s, and despite almost a 50% failure rate in most areas, continues to be tried. The original catalyst for cropping is not clear but appears likely to be due to influence from surrounding crop areas – Elgeyo Marakwet for the Kerio Valley areas, and Laikipia for the Churo area. There is also the influence from the availability of alternative foods (other than milk, meat and blood) first introduced in the famine relief supplies (1979–1982) and later freely available in the shops at trading centres. The Ministry of Agriculture now encourages cropping in suitable areas combined with some water harvesting techniques and suitable varieties selected and bred for low rainfall conditions. (SALTLICK, 1991, p. 39)

The implementation of farming techniques took place at a time when pastoralism, which was also the dominant mode of subsistence in the highlands at that time, came under pressure. The initial pastoral farming attempts were modified over time, and plot sizes, ploughing techniques and seed quality advanced. According to Oesterle (2007), the Kenya Freedom from Hunger Council and the German Agro Action strongly contributed to the establishment of intensive farming practices in the Churo highlands in the 1980s and 1990s.[2] One man who lives around Churo stills recalls the events of the 1960s and the advent of the farming project.

> The first people who knew how maize is planted are from Kaptuya [a region west of Churo] in 1960. Kaptuya was the first place, followed by others, and people had cultivated gardens just like animal kraals.

> These people farmed until 1979, when a project started here. It was started by an NGO called 'Freedom from Hunger' [Kenya Freedom from Hunger Council] through the Ministry of Agriculture. They sent an agricultural officer ... through the AIC [Africa Inland Church] to start a project. You were given five by five metres demonstration plots. The agriculture office educated people on how to grow maize. ...

---

[2] Different stakeholders have been involved in the history of promoting agricultural activities in the highlands. These are, most importantly, the Catholic Diocese of Nakuru, the Baringo Pilot Semi-Arid Areas Project and the Kenya Freedom from Hunger Council. This last seems to have had the strongest impact – at least from retrospective accounts given by the current generation of highland farmers – and it is highlighted repeatedly as having been the initiator of agricultural activities.

The cultivation of maize picked up quickly. The project just came at the right time, when people were suffering from an outbreak of East Coast Fever that affected their cattle and there was no medication. So, in a home like this there, not even a single cow was found anymore. So, the project came when the area had problems, animals died of East Coast Fever. (Interview 10 March 2015, anonymous)

However, implementing and providing education in farming techniques alone do not sufficiently explain the triumphant advance in the following decades. It was the situation in the eastern highlands around Churo – a crisis in pastoralism and the construction of schools and churches – that contributed to the successful story of maize cultivation. From the perspective of an elderly person belonging to the Koronkoro generation set who grew up in the Churo highlands, the transition to farming was accompanied by other changes that have occurred in the past 40 years.

In those old days of our fathers, people were very few. Five homesteads were found in Tebelekwo; in Naminito up to Riwo, you found five homesteads … Location Two was called '*Mot pö soo*' [Kipokot – head of the buffalo] by then and only had three homesteads.

You can imagine, it was raining almost all the season, it can only stop for two months, the grass is still enough, the cattle of these few homesteads never finished the grass of the entire area. What I am saying is that there was no drought. The rains were like this: it rained in the entire area, but nobody reached everywhere [i.e. the few people did not need to roam in many places in search of cattle forage], so you found grass everywhere because there were no animals to graze over all the land.

In 1975, there were grasses like *ngiriamatian, nyuswo*, other places *ngawian*. So, this area here up to Naminito and Amaya was full of *ngiri-amatian* and also *amakwaratian*. These hills here were full of *ngawian*.

In 1975, I was an old man already, I had a family. That time we lost cattle. We lost them through a disease, not drought. … We learned to cultivate after we lost our animals in 1975. We started farming very much, we did farming until we saw the benefit of it, we fed our children with the harvest. People from Nginyang, even people from Tangulbei, they came here and also started cultivation. … Schools also started in 1975. The first school here was in Kasilangwa. … By the year 1984 there were schools all over. (Ngolekow, 6 March 2015)

From Ngolekow's perspective, consecutive changes had enhanced agro-pastoral land-use practices in the past. The degradation of pasture land and the emergence of the East Coast Fever put pastoral land-use practices under pressure. The external intervention of the 'Kenya Freedom from Hunger' project gave an incentive to farm in a time when pastoralism was unable to sustain all local livelihoods. Furthermore, the construction of schools led to the education of youth – something that is still not part of pastoral livelihoods at Mt Paka.

In the following, I describe the stabilisation of agro-pastoral livelihoods in Churo and compare the agro-pastoral livelihoods with the livelihoods of pastoral people from Mt Paka. This comparison aims to understand the socio-ecological transformation process that agro-pastoral livelihoods underwent in the past; and, furthermore, it evaluates the potential for change to pastoral livelihoods at Mt Paka.

Comparison of pastoral and agro-pastoral livelihoods

The lowlands, where Mt Paka is located, are entirely different to the region around Churo. On the escarpment towards the Laikipia Plateau, pastoral liveli-hoods used to dominate the picture some decades ago. Between 1,630 and 1,960 metres above sea level, the vegetation differs widely from that of the lowlands (780–1,000 metres above sea level) and the preconditions for both cattle husbandry and farming are different. In the Churo highlands, cattle are prone to trypanosomiasis (sleeping sickness), the rainy period is unimodal and, compared to the lowlands, longer; and the soils are more suitable for farming. Furthermore, the population has increased rapidly since the 1980s, when the population numbers per square kilometre were still comparable to those at Mt Paka in 2015. Table 9 illustrates the population growth of both regions between 1979 and 2019.

For the highland region, it is noticeable that large areas were already fenced in and permanent settlement structures were built when Pokot from other parts of East Pokot settled here over time. For the administrative unit of Churo Centre alone, the official population figure from the 2019 census is estimated to be 6,846 people (in an area of 66.9 km²) (Republic of Kenya 2019), which would even mean a population density of 102.3 people per square kilometre. Those who know the region are aware that these figures do not depict reality. The same difficulties in data collection and projection also apply to Mt Paka. In my opinion, both estimates are too high (discussed in detail in Chapter 3). At this point, I want to emphasise that the population dynamics in both pastoral and agro-pastoral areas nonetheless reflect a strongly increasing trend. Although moderate levels of population density still prevail in pastoral areas, the highland areas around Churo reveal how natural population development and intra- and trans-regional migration have resulted in a settlement with a high population density.

Table 9. Population growth in the pastoral and agro-pastoral regions of East Pokot, 1979–2019.[3]

Region	Churo Region (Agro-pastoral)		Mt Paka Region (Pastoral)	
Year (census)	1979	2019	1979	2019
Population number	2,337	17,936	1,095	3,513
Area (km²)[4]	107	279.9	270	134.8
Population density (people/km²)	21.8	64.1	4.1	26.1

Notes: District boundaries of the administrative units have changed over time. As discussed previously, official population figures must be viewed with caution, although they probably do indicate rapid population growth. In the case of Churo, however, it is necessary to consider the possibility that population growth in this region may also have been impacted by intra-regional migration.

Sources: Republic of Kenya (1981, p. 98; 2019, pp. 157–89)

In the agro-pastoral setting, the population density was about 22 people/km² in 1979 and has – according to official numbers – almost tripled within 40 years. In the pastoral region around Mt Paka, a six-fold increase in population numbers is observable between 1979 and 2019, and the recent population density of 26.1 people/km² is comparable to the population density of Churo in 1979. Even assuming that the official population figures are overestimates, it must be noted that population figures have risen substantially in both contexts, but have reached a level in the highlands that is far higher than the pastoral lowlands.

Compared to the attempts at pastoral farming in the lowlands, highland farming is more efficient (yield/ha and revenue/ha), cultivation was adopted earlier (1960s) and it is carried out more frequently (mainly annually). Furthermore, sowing takes places earlier in the year, tractors are mainly used for tilling, herbicides are sometimes applied, production also targets local markets and the conditions for farming (water availability and nutrients) are better, according to Greiner et al. (2013), who calculate the average farming plot size to be 0.3 hectares and the return per hectare as 335 Euro in the pastoral lowlands, compared to a size of 0.6 hectares and 503 Euro return per hectare in the agro-pastoral highlands. But apart from purely agricultural aspects, other elements also characterise agro-pastoral livelihoods: the sedentariness

---

[3] As discussed previously, official population figures must be viewed with caution. In the case of Churo, however, it is necessary to consider the possibility that population growth in this region may also have been impacted by intra-regional migration.

[4] Differences in the extent of administrative units between 1979 and 2019 can be explained by the fact that district boundaries have changed over time.

of households, the smaller numbers of livestock and the presence of governmental and non-governmental agents such as churches and schools. Pastoral livelihoods, in contrast, have a larger livestock on which they depend. Table 10 illustrates the lower livestock numbers in the agro-pastoral households that are almost half those (in TLU) of pastoral livelihoods at Mt Paka.

Table 10. Comparison of average livestock herds between pastoral and agro-pastoral households in East Pokot.

	Cattle	Small stock	Camel	Donkey	Chicken	Total
Households owning livestock (Churo) in per cent	78.4	88.7	5.2	3.1	73.2	
Households owning livestock (Mt Paka) in per cent	98.1	100	27.8	n.a.	29.6	
Average animal numbers per household (Churo)	23.7	57.8	0.6	0.2	7	
Average animal numbers per household (Mt Paka)	37.8	140.3	1.6	n.a.	3.1	
TLU per household (average; in Churo)	23.7	7.2	0.8			31.7
TLU per household (average; Mt Paka)	37.7	17.5	2.1			57.3

Source: Author research

As can be seen in both contexts, most households have substantial numbers of livestock, albeit at a lower percentage in agro-pastoral households than in pastoral ones. Although the number of cattle with an average of 37.8 (pastoral) versus 23.7 (agro-pastoral) already mark a clear distinction, differences are even more pronounced for small stock. With 140.3 shoats per household, the pastoralists have more than twice as much small stock as the agro-pastoralists with an average of 57.8 shoats. The trend towards more small stock, which Oesterle already described, can be seen clearly here. With a TLU of 57.3 per household, the average is almost twice as high as that in agro-pastoral households that have a TLU per household of only 31.7.

Paradoxically, although the average animal numbers decrease strongly in the agro-pastoral households, the bridewealth payments are still on a high level and comparable to those at Mt Paka (as discussed in Chapter 4).[5] One

---

[5] The calculation of bridewealth payments only contains those cases in which bridewealth agreements were made. In some cases in the agro-pastoral highlands, bridewealth is no longer negotiated, and many people mentioned during interviews that especially young people decide on their future partner themselves. Marriage is

reason why these numbers resemble each other might be that men in the Churo region often marry women from the pastoral lowlands and must agree to a bridewealth payment similar to those made under pastoral conditions. People from the agro-pastoral highlands seem to value the pastoral wealth of livestock and might also wish to be associated with a more pastoral status. However, it is not clear whether marriages between partners from different backgrounds (pastoral or agro-pastoral) influence the spread of agricultural knowledge. This has been reported from other places in East Africa; for instance, in extremely difficult times (e.g. the period known as Emutai when the rinderpest broke out in the late nineteenth century and largely diminished cattle herds), Maasai men married women from other ethnic groups who then introduced agricultural knowledge to the 'pastoral system' (McCabe et al., 2010). However, this has not been observed for pastoral livelihoods in East Pokot so far.

When looking at pastoral and agro-pastoral livelihoods, I did not just want to compare those aspects that represent the obvious changes regarding livestock and farming. I also selected four additional categories that I believe can give a further impression on how the transformation of a pastoral society, at least in some respects, can take place. One of the interviewees accurately illustrated the social change that goes hand in hand with the transformation of livelihoods: 'Here (in Churo), education has changed people. You will also see here some people are engaged in church so much. Also, people have intermingled with other people, those of Laikipia. So, they lost their cultural values' (Interview 9 March 2015, anonymous). The interviewee identifies four categories – education, religion, ethnic diversity and cultural values – that have informed the social transformation over time. In the following, I compare the pastoral and agro-pastoral livelihoods in terms of these categories and demonstrate the social dimension of change.

To start with education, I compare the percentage of households that have (or had) at least one child at school. In the pastoral context, less than one third of the households have (or had) a child at school; and if a child did attend a school, it was always limited to primary education. In 2015, only 25 per cent of households had at least one child at school, whereby 67 per cent of the children were male (14 out of 21 schoolchildren) and 33 per cent were female. Out of 451 children, 4.7 per cent attended primary school in 2015 (21 pupils).

---

organised along several principles. If a man decides to enter bridewealth negotiations, he must ensure that the proposed woman is the daughter of a man who does not belong to the same generation set as the proposer. Furthermore, clan exogamy is a necessary precondition, not only for the clan of the proposer but also to exclude all those clans of his previous wives. However, in the agro-pastoral context, these rules are increasingly diluted, which shows the independence of the adolescent generation on the one hand, but also arouses the resentment and incomprehension of the elders on the other hand.

In agro-pastoral households the situation is completely different. Almost every household had a child at school: generally, more than one child and often all children attended school, and education was not limited to primary school. Secondary school education is also available in Churo and some children also get higher education. In 2015, a total of 91.7 per cent of households had at least one child at school, 3.1 per cent had had children at school in the past, whereas 5.2 per cent have or had no child at school (five households out of 97). In all of the five households, there were either no children at all or none had reached schooling age. In general, 37.6 per cent of all children were schooling in 2015 (313 pupils out of 832 children).

The percentage of schoolchildren in the agro-pastoral context is clearly much higher than in the pastoral context. This is due partly to the availability of primary schools in the immediate vicinity and partly to the possibility of earning the necessary money to send a child to secondary school at a later stage. Furthermore, positive experiences with school education in the agro-pastoral context of Churo have already stabilised over several decades, and the education of children has attained a certain standard. This is in stark contrast to pastoral households in which household work, especially that with livestock, is very time-consuming and intensive. This is especially true during the phase when young families are breaking away from the parental household and setting up their own homestead. Help from children even in their early years is regarded as normal. Furthermore, in 2015, even the distance to a primary school was still very great, so that the incentives for children from pastoral households to be sent to school were not very strong.

However, differences in educational background are not just observable between the children of the pastoral and agro-pastoral context but also between household members. At Mt Paka less than 5 per cent of all respondents had an educational background, limited to primary school education, which often ended before Grade 8.

Furthermore, at 8 per cent, more men had access to school education compared to only 3 per cent of women. Four men out of 52 visited the primary school. Two men finished Standard Eight, one man reached Standard Seven, one man finished Standard Two. On the women's side, three out of 98 women visited primary school, whereby all of them dropped out before reaching Standard Eight. One woman reached Standard Two, one woman Standard Three and one woman Standard Five. None of the pastoral people at Mt Paka attended secondary school. In contrast, almost 45 per cent of the respondents in the agro-pastoral context had an educational background, and for 20 per cent (of all respondents), this was even at secondary school level or higher. One consequence of school education is also the acquisition of Kiswahili as a second language, which serves as a lingua franca in East Africa. Without this skill, communication beyond ethnic boundaries is more difficult.

Next, I look at the ethnic diversity of the pastoral and agro-pastoral regions. Although it is often assumed that the ethnic composition of the community might be more diverse in the agro-pastoral area with its better access to roads and higher mobility, this does not apply in the agro-pastoral highlands around Churo.

In both cases – the pastoral lowlands and the agro-pastoral highlands – the percentage of respondents with two Pokot parents is around 84 per cent, whereas the percentage with one or more parent with another ethnic affiliation is around 16 per cent. The only observable difference is that, in the agro-pastoral context, apart from Turkana and Somali ethnic affiliations, there are also Tugen, Kikuyu, Maasai, Sabaot, Luhya, Meru, Il Chamus and Rendille affiliations. Therefore, I note that the ethnic composition of the people in the regions has not necessarily changed during the course of the transformation towards agro-pastoralism. Although there have been interventions from outside, as described earlier using the example of the Kenya Freedom from Hunger Council initiative, it can be assumed that the social transformation was accomplished largely by Pokot people who live in the region.

Beyond that, one of the most distinctive characteristic differences between the pastoral and agro-pastoral contexts, and perhaps as important as school education in the transformation process, is the religious affiliation. In the following discussion, I examine only the differences in the affiliation to Christianity[6] and to the ancestral beliefs of pastoral Pokot in Tororot, Ilat and Asis.[7]

Christian beliefs have reached the remote pastoral region at Mt Paka, although neither church services nor any other Christian practices are performed independently. Instead, a few church members organise sporadic meetings at Mt Paka and a US missionary has established a borehole at the foot of the mountain. In the agro-pastoral context, the picture is completely different. Although one third of the respondents claimed not to have a Christian religious affiliation, the presence and impact of churches is omnipresent. Oesterle describes the emergence and rise of Christian religious practices and institutions in East Pokot and locates their success in the centres of East Pokot that were not in the pastoral zone (Oesterle, 2007). An interviewee

---

[6] The following churches are contained in the category Christian churches: the African Inland Church (AIC), the Anglican Church of Kenya (ACK), the Pentecostal Assemblies of God (PAG), the Full Gospel Churches of Kenya (FGCK), the Seventh-day Adventist Church (SDA), the Mafuta Pole movement, the Winners Chapel and the Desert Rose Ministries.

[7] Tororot is the most important deity in the belief system of the pastoral Pokot. Asis is his younger brother, whereas Ilat is the son of Tororot, as described in detail by Mutsotso et al. (2014).

(male, educated, married and Christian) with an agro-pastoral background describes the situation in the highlands as follows:

> Churches changed people to become Christians and they [the people] started to believe [in God]. ... Education is boosted by the church and people go to school, get educated and get jobs and they are able to feed their families through their salaries. Everybody is able to help himself, his family and can even buy his own animals from the money they get. Other people went to business. ... When people here started to go to churches, it helped them mostly to leave cultural practices. So, what changed Pokot here was mostly the church, not education so much. When you are educated and not [a God] believer, you do all these cultural practices, you do the *sapana* [the initiation ceremony for men], even *kilokat* [home-based healing ceremony], everything. So, when you see all these homesteads around, they do not practice all these cultural practices because they are Christians. (Interview 10 March 2015, anonymous)

The emergence and establishment of missionaries and churches in the agro-pastoral highland has been an important driving force of change. As the interviewee states, the missionaries also supported school education and encouraged the hitherto pastoral people to adopt a different lifestyle. The first missionary base was established in the border zone of Baringo and Laikipia in 1938 (Du Plessis, 2005).

However, the beginning of the Christian mission in East Pokot was difficult. Oesterle (2007) describes the opposition to the African Inland Mission (AIM – which became the African Inland Church in 1952) and the 'burial of the pen' in Chemolingot in the late 1940s as a sign of resistance to the initial missionary and educational efforts. Nonetheless, this first phase of resistance was followed by the adoption of Christian religious practices. One might well wonder how the rejection turned into acceptance, at least in the small centres in East Pokot. Du Plessis (2005) recalls the story of a miracle that happened in the 1950s when a missionary, by the name Mr Collins, 'resurrected' a boy from the dead. The author traced the story back and interviewed the cousin of Mr Collins, who confirmed the healing of a mortally sick person whose father was an outstandingly rich and influential person among the elders of that time (Du Plessis, 2005). The exceptional healing of the boy must have had an immense impact on the pastoral people, because the story is still being narrated. This could have been a starting point for the acceptance and expansion of missionary services beyond the centres in East Pokot.

In the lowland area at Mt Paka, however, missionaries and other church members arrived only a few years ago, and the first church on Mt Paka was established in 2016. The initial scepticism of the local people towards outsiders was overcome with material incentives (food, a borehole and a flour mill in Adomeyon, 50 audio bibles) and mediated by the local chiefs (Desert Rose

Ministries, 2018a). One of the members of the otherwise competing churches reported a similar miracle at Mt Paka in 2016 to that in the agro-pastoral highlands in the 1950s.

Miracle on Mt Paka

Ok, I was told I needed to write this and post it. This happens all the time and I don't think to post it. Miracles should be expected and be such a natural part of our lives. We shouldn't be shocked if we pray and see something change. Instead, we should be shocked if it doesn't happen. I expect to see healing when I pray for someone. I just don't hope and wish for someone to be healed. I expect them to be healed! Isn't that what the Bible tells us? So, anyway, here is what happened on Mt. Paka last week.

They told me there is someone sick over there and needs me. I got my first aid kit and went to see what I could do. When I got there, there was someone under a blanket, covered up completely from head to toe and I couldn't see them. But, the blanket was shaking very violently! Actually, it was so violent, I was a little scared of what was under it. I even ask[ed], 'Who or what was under the blanket?' They told me it was a man. I asked if I could remove the blanket and see him. They said I could. I pulled the blanket and there was a young man, lying on the ground shaking very violently. I touched his forehead. He was burning up!!! I got my digital thermometer out and put it under his arm. It registered 103.6 [39.8°C]!! You add a degree if taken under the armpit, so his temp was 104.6 [40.3°C]. I just guessed he had malaria or typhoid or both. I didn't have any medications for either. All I had was some Tylenol and gave him two and left him with several. I told everyone who was standing around him that we had to pray for healing right now and everyone lay hands on him and believe he is healed. I lead them in prayer, took authority over his sickness in Jesus' name and cursed it and believed he is healed by the blood of Jesus! I knew that's all I could do for him, we left him and I walked away. In 5–10 mins at the most, people started calling me. Mama! Mama!! Come and see! He is here!! I said who?? The young man is healed!! I turned around and here he comes walking toward me with a BIG smile on his face!! He tells me Jesus has healed me!!! I even know this young man. He is in his 20's, but he was so sick that I didn't even recognize him when we were praying for him! I touched his forehead and he was normal. We hugged and gave Jesus all the praise!!! Yes, Jesus still heals! Yes, I gave him 2 Tylenol, but you know it doesn't work that fast and doesn't cure. No, Jesus healed this man. Just a normal thing for me here in Kenya and it should be for you too, wherever you are. (Desert Rose Ministries, 2018b, 13 October, 2016)

The direct link between a miracle and the acceptance of missionaries and churches seems comprehensible in the case of the pastoral Pokot, who also follow the advice of their powerful diviners. However, the process towards establishing a religious community at Mt Paka cannot take place overnight and will have further impacts on pastoral life as it currently stands.

One indicator of this process might be the decline in customary ceremonies in the Churo highlands. These are still commonplace in the pastoral liveli-hoods at Mt Paka and constitute the background for the dense social network there (as described in Chapter 4). The Paka community conducts different ceremonies such as *sapana, kirket, tapa, kolat, kanyan* and *pution*. In the agro-pastoral highlands, however, the performance of customary ceremonies is declining. Figure 11 shows the proportion of households (in the agro-pastoral context) still performing these ceremonies. The figure clearly illustrates that almost 70 per cent of respondents still exchange livestock between households. Most of these households exchange animals for bridewealth payments or for the redistribution of bridewealth among kinsmen (*kanyan*). Furthermore, the *tapa* healing ceremony is still performed in which a goat is slaughtered in the homestead and the meat consumed with special herbs. However, another healing ceremony, *kolat*, is no longer performed as often. This change could be a result of a slayer having to be involved in the ceremony and the practice not conforming to Christian religious beliefs. The same holds true for the *sapana* in which young men must kill an animal with a spear and the *pution*

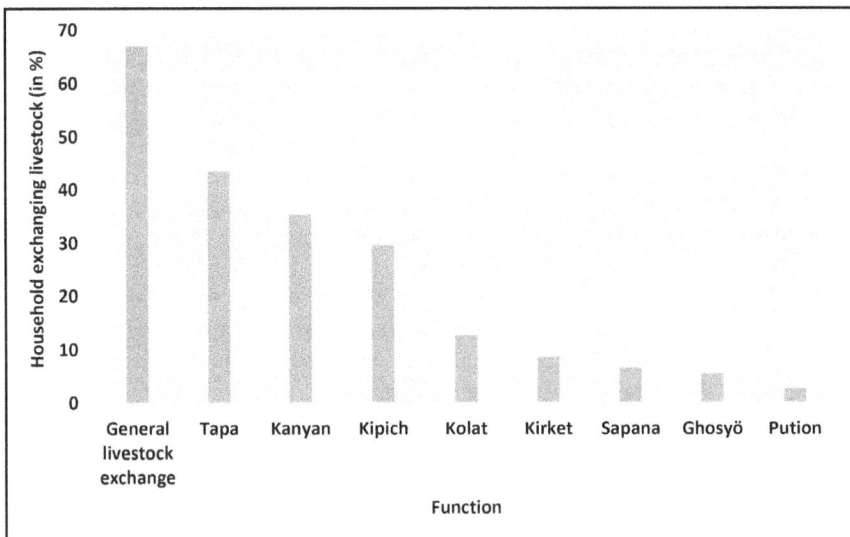

Fig. 11. Percentage of surveyed households performing ceremonies in the agro-pastoral context, 2015 (Hauke-Peter Vehrs).

that relies on the dreams of the prophet and includes killing animals with a spear. Therefore, animal exchange for ritual reasons has declined more in the agro-pastoral context than in the pastoral context, and there are thus few return reciprocal gifts (*ghosyö*). Only the unproblematic ceremony of *tapa* and the exchange of livestock from brother to sister (*kipich*) is easy to sustain in the context of a rising Christian influence on agro-pastoral livelihoods.

The reduction in ceremonies is an important development in the agro-pastoral setting. In the following, I look at how two interviewees commented on it. The first impression is given by a man (educated, employed and Christian) from the Kaplelach generation set.

> Those old practices were for those days when no clinics were available. In those days without clinics, people did *kolat*. About the *kirket* [half-circle of men during a ceremony], nobody will give out his goat for free, someone must pay 7,000 KSh. The elders of Sowö or Koronkoro [generations] cannot be feared anymore. The majority of people belong to Kaplelach – people act the way they want. *Pution* is only done when the enemy is approaching. But there is no enemy here, so people go and pray in this place [referring to the church]. (Interview 9 March, 2015, anonymous)

Second, an elder (pastoralist, no formal education and no affiliation to Christian beliefs) from the Koronkoro generation set explains how he sees the developments and compares the highland agro-pastoral Pokot to the lowland pastoral Pokot.

> *Sapana* is still in place, it never reduced here; *lapan* is still there but only few homesteads because there is quarrel with the government on girls' circumcision. It is prohibited, so when you circumcise your daughter and do *lapan*, maybe the government will hear it. So, *lapan* is there but not exposed so much and not frequently done also. These practices are reduced here, but in the lowland it is still rampant. (Interview 6 March 2015, anonymous)

Although perspectives on the performance of ceremonies differ between respondents, the trend towards a reduction in customary ceremonies is obvious. Bearing these results in mind, I want to return to the initial theme of this chapter: the differentiation between agro-pastoral and pastoral livelihoods. I hope to have shown the differences between the two livelihood approaches in the lowlands and the highlands, both inhabited mainly by Pokot people. The Paka pastoral people dwell in the lowlands on the slopes of the Paka mountain and live a life corresponding to the description of pastoral livelihoods by Fratkin and Smith (1994; see Chapter 3). Moreover, the changes that occurred in the escarpment region towards the Laikipia Plateau may have led to land-use practices that are best described as agro-pastoral. These can be seen most clearly in the cultivation practices that shape the landscape in ways that cannot be observed to this extent in the pastoral lowlands. In addition to the implementation of farming and the reduction of livestock numbers, I have emphasised the important role of schools and churches here in order to show the transformation process from different angles.

The picture of changing livelihoods – from pastoralism to agro-pastoralism – is to some extent surprising against the often-repeated statement that the pastoral Pokot are reluctant as far as changes are concerned (Davidson, 1984; Schneider, 1953). The pastoral life was always said to be highly valued, and even during the formation of the pastoral Pokot in the eighteenth century, the agro-pastoral Pokot from West Pokot aspired to become pastoralists (Beech, 1911). Schneider (1953, p. 225) also mentions that 'most Pakot [*sic*], if they had sufficient herds, would certainly abandon agriculture, not because they dislike it but because they would not have time enough to herd and cultivate'.

However, the situation in East Pokot has changed, and as a result of a strongly increasing population, the reduction in livestock numbers per person and the otherwise high total numbers of livestock in a limited Pokot territory, the basis for exclusively pastoral livelihoods is no longer given. Therefore, the specialised cattle pastoralism – as narrated by past generations – can no longer sustain all Pokot people in East Pokot. One consequence of this is an intensification of agricultural practices in places where farming is suitable. From the perspective of an agro-pastoralist, the future is no longer dependent on livestock husbandry.

> I can see in future, this area will not have any space [remaining]. The children born in 20 years to come will all live in settlements. You see every valley, every slope of the hills is all already occupied. ... Like I am living here, everything up to there is my territory, nobody will touch it. After my fence, next, is somebody's home. So, space to live is limited now.

> Even the animals we have will have to go somewhere because there is no space to graze. These animals will be reduced to only few, which are enough to be grazed around your compound. People will have five goats or one cow only. ... What is increasing so much is education because new schools are being opened. Those days when the [government] project started and churches came, the schools were few.[8] Now, there are many primary schools and even two secondary schools around here. Education is growing and herding is decreasing. (Interview 10 March 2015, anonymous)

[8] The interviewee dates the events back to the 1960s and 1970s when farming was first established in the region.

The interviewee emphasises the reduction in pastoral activities and the increase in alternative ways of living. Education and religion are two characteristics that contribute to the alternative livelihood approaches that I have discussed in this section. I have also illustrated the importance and extent of farming activities. However, these social transformation processes and changing land-use practices have strong influences not only on social life, as described above, but also on the environment. In the following, I shall examine the impacts of agricultural land-use change in terms of the unprecedentedly rapid expansion of a native plant species.

The expansion of *Dodonaea viscosa*

As described above, since the 1960s, the former focus on subsistence herding has been slowly substituted by farming practices in the Churo highlands. These, in turn, have had a huge impact on the environment. Becker et al. (2016) observed the main spread of the plant species *Dodonaea viscosa* in the highlands around Churo over the past decades and considered this bush encroachment to be linked to land-use changes such as farming and sustained overgrazing.

From a scientific perspective, *Dodonaea viscosa* (L.) Jacq. – the hopbush – is a small shrub belonging to the Sapindaceae family. It can reach a height of seven metres and grows even under difficult habitat conditions such as on rocky and sandy soils or under drought conditions (Rani et al., 2009). It is not browsed by animals, because the foliage is inedible due to the high concentration of saponins (Ludwig, 1985).[9] Therefore, it is not valued by the pastoral Pokot as a forage plant, because it competes with other forage plants and has recently formed thick stands of impenetrable bush in the highland area around Churo.

The spread of *Dodonaea viscosa* can be traced back over a few decades. Being native to Kenya, this plant has its natural habitat on steep rocky outcrops. In Churo, it grows way beyond its habitat and is taking over bare ground as a first successor in an estimated area of more than 200 km². For instance, cultivated grounds become overgrown with *Dodonaea viscosa* after the cultivation period or in a fallow period. Furthermore, its seeds are fire-resistant and germinate easily after slash and burn practices are applied to new cultivation grounds. This is because germination occurs after disruption or dislodgement of the impermeable seed coat layer (Baskin et al., 2000).

Dodonaea viscosa is used mostly to construct houses and fences (resistant to termite infestations), as firewood and for selling purposes. It also has some medicinal usages. More negative effects are reported as being due to

---

[9] Depending on their concentration, saponins can have strong antiprotozoal effects due to changes in the rumen flora.

its allergenic characteristics,[10] the infestation of former grassland, the diffi-culties in herding livestock in the thick stands of *Dodonaea viscosa* and the low soil fertility it indicates. Many people consider that the soil fertility is low in farms where it grows. They observe a link between the infestation of *Dodonaea viscosa* and low yields of their maize harvest. Although the link between low soil fertility seems reasonable, the argument can be inverted. Rather than *Dodonaea viscosa* being the cause of low soil fertility, it can also be an indicator for monocropping and a lack of crop rotation. Maize is the staple food and is used mainly for cooking *ugali*, the local maize meal or for selling. Because *Dodonaea viscosa* advances beyond its natural habitat, it may actually be a successor plant on highly degraded soils. Furthermore, the dense stands create spaces for wild animals such as lions, hyenas and wild dogs to move into the area from the Laikipia Plateau and kill livestock.

In general, the plant cannot be ascribed a solely negative impact on local livelihoods. Instead, the rapid expansion of *Dodonaea viscosa* [Kipokot: *Tabalak*] is viewed positively in some aspects and negatively in others, as the following statement illustrates:

> In terms of its usages, it helps so much because it is used for construction. So, we hate and we love it. Some people say that it is a medicine used to treat ringworms. In terms of farming, *tabalak* makes the soil infertile. Whenever you see a lot of *tabalak*, the soil is not very good. When you burn *tabalak*, its seedlings grow rapidly. So, burning is like putting fertiliser. The problem is that it kills grass. Cattle do not even browse on *tabalak*. (Interview 9 May 2015, anonymous)

More generally, during the course of changing land-use strategies, land was cleared, the use of fire for land management changed and the native plant *Dodonaea viscosa* appears to have been extremely successful in taking over formerly cultivated or cleared grounds. From a scientific perspective, its encroachment must be characterised as a succession of bare grounds. It has formed monocultures in some places and dominates the landscape vegetation in others.

For most farmers, the spread of *Dodonaea viscosa* is a clear sign of low ground fertility, but the removal of the plant is unproblematic. When preparing fields, the plant is easily removed with a disc plough. The expansion of *Dodonaea viscosa* and the infestation of cultivated grounds creates the impression that land-use and land-cover changes are closely linked. At a time when highland Pokot started their first attempts at farming, *Dodonaea viscosa* remained in its niche, expanding only slowly into the newly created areas.

---

[10] Singh and Kumar (2002) also identify the allergenic potential of *Dodonaea viscosa*, among other plant species, in their study in India.

The resistance to fire and the easy seed dispersal by wind perfectly match the newly implemented farming practices. Therefore, the spread of *Dodonaea viscosa* and the transformation from a cattle-based to an agriculture-based mode of living went hand in hand.

Some elders explain that *Dodonaea viscosa* was already present in the region during their adolescence and started to spread in the 1960s and 1970s. However, the initial phase of encroachment appears to be rather slow compared to later developments. After the long drought in the beginning of the 1980s, the expansion experienced another push and it started to infest larger areas. There may have been two reasons for the expansion. The prolonged drought might have triggered the encroachment to the extent that the region's forage was completely exhausted and grass cover declined. Furthermore, people started to turn towards agriculture and cleared plots for farming in the 1960s. In the course of sedentarisation and the implementation of agricultural practices, the use of fire also changed. The extensive use of fires by pastoral people to regenerate pastures disappeared, giving way to the use of small-scale fires to eliminate plant remnants on the farms. In the late 1980s, when the expansion accelerated, a place south of Churo was renamed 'Tebelekwo' because of the high prevalence of *Dodonaea viscosa*, as the following sequence shows: 'The region was called Kangonis. When tabalak emerged, the name changed to Tebelekwo. This was in 1984, when it started to grow there' (Ngolekow, 6 March, 2015).

Thus, *Dodonaea viscosa* first captured new areas slowly and steadily before spreading more rapidly in the late 1980s. Then, it established and expanded its stands before a third wave of expansion led it to dominate the landscape. In the mid-twentieth century, Churo highlands were still dominated by pastoral land use. Large herds of cattle moved to the highland areas when forage and water became scarce in the lowlands. At this time, trees and bushes did not dominate the landscape as they do today. Extensive meadows and limited water access constituted the face of the region and even forced pastoral nomads to leave pastures behind before they were exhausted in their search for water.

Local people distinguish positive and negative effects on local livelihoods through the spread and impact of *Dodonaea viscosa*. Agro-pastoral people can come to terms with the effects of bush encroachment more easily than pastoral people who tend to evade affected areas and move into already occupied areas, such as the Laikipia Plateau and the region east of Lake Baringo, in their search for pastures. This movement has also led to violent conflicts[11] in border zones in the recent past.

---

[11] During the dry season, the pastoral Pokot can rarely fall back on grass forage storage since most sites are depleted. This constantly leads to violent clashes with neighbouring groups in the border zones, as documented in the headlines of the *Daily Nation* national newspaper: 'Cutting bullet supply key to draining swamps in the

The case of the expansion of *Dodonaea viscosa* differs from the acacia bush encroachment to be found all over East Pokot. Whereas in the first case, land-use practices are the foremost driver of change, the incremental transition from a grass to a bush savannah is not linked directly to changing human land use. In the following chapter, I shall describe different explanations for the general land-cover change from both a scientific and a pastoral perspective before comparing two cases of acacia bush encroachment and *Dodonaea viscosa* expansion in Chapter 8.

North Rift of lawlessness' (Kagwanja 2014); 'Bandit raids push 10,000 out of school in Baringo' (Kipsang 2015); 'Baringo County conflicts. Why peace remains a pipe dream' (Kariuki 2015); 'Police seem overwhelmed by insecurity in Baringo' (Lomorita 2017); 'Bandit attacks force hundreds to flee homes in Baringo' (Koech 2017b).

7

Ecological Change and Local Livelihoods:
Scientific and Pokot Perspectives

Shifts in the East African savannah ecosystem occur on different levels and according to different time scales. Whereas the dry periods lead to a landscape dominated by dried-up vegetation and – from a pastoral view – the ongoing search for water and pasture, the rainy periods often turn the landscape abruptly green. From the short-term perspective, landscape changes occur regularly – for instance during drought periods – and pastoralists deal with these changes by applying versatile mobile strategies such as seasonal migration to those regions that, at a given time, provide the best basis for maintaining their herds. In the long term, spanning decades and centuries, pastoralists have also adapted to bush encroachment and pasture degradation by diversifying their livelihoods. However, the question arises why the environment is changing – sometimes slowly, sometimes rapidly. The latter was already mentioned in the last chapter when highlighting relations between land-use change and land-cover change in the highlands. This clearly revealed the connection between the spread of agricultural activities and the rapid expansion of *Dodonaea viscosa*.

In this chapter, I want to discuss the background to the long-term ecological changes and bush encroachment in East Pokot and scrutinise the formerly common explanation based on pastoral degradation narratives. In the following, I reflect on the land-use and land-cover changes from a scientific perspective, with an emphasis on several landscape agents. Two of these are rarely found in East Pokot nowadays: *wildlife*, and *fire*, which was used for pasture management. Their absence has had a tremendous impact on the environment and thus on local livelihoods.

Furthermore, I complement natural science accounts with the perceptions of the Pokot pastoralists, because the emic evaluations are also relevant and not just the scientific findings. In contrast to the science perspectives, the pastoral Pokot do not assume that processes and changes in the environment are linear. On the contrary, their prevailing assumption is that the cyclical generation classes recur over a period of more than 200 years. This return of older generation classes will not only re-establish characteristics of these generations such as their achievements in cattle herding, their effective defence against enemies or the raiding of neighbouring groups, but also lead to the reappearance of certain components of the environment. The changes in the environment are therefore not traced back to ecological factors, but – in the eyes of the senior generation – particularly to the misconduct of the younger generation classes that puts a curse on the land. This cyclical reoccurrence of the past in the future is also reproduced when prophets engage in divinations.

In the following, I want to present and combine these two very different perspectives – the scientific and the local. The presentation of the latter perspective in this work is by no means intended to serve a monolithic representation of a local community, but rather to not only add a local perspective to the scholarly contributions in many respects in order to include them in the discussion but also to scrutinise them in other respects and provide alternative interpretations. In doing so, one is at risk of overly conflating the 'emic' and 'etic' perspectives and thus evoking a unity that does not actually exist on this level. In such a case, both perspectives are an abstraction from scholarly and respectively local discourses and represent internally heterogeneous and contested positions. Both focus on very different explanatory patterns and thus imply very different ways of dealing with environmental challenges. In science, the focus is on the restoration of the landscape and active intervention 'from outside'. The Pokot, on the other hand, trust in the immanent change that will take place through the initiation of new generation sets – something that does not require a proactive role on the part of the pastoralists.

Fire as a savannah landscape constructor

The effects of fire on the formation and maintenance of the East African savannah ecosystems are much discussed in the scientific literature, and fire is recognised as one of the most important agents in the sustenance of open savannah landscapes. Although its general contribution to the construction and maintenance of open savannah landscapes is acknowledged, the dynamics and interactions with other ecological factors are much debated. These include the difficulties in understanding the complexities of different types of fire (high-intensity, low-intensity, duration, frequency, etc.) under various ecological conditions and their possible effects on a large variety of different plant species in the ecosystem (Smit et al., 2010). The exact effects of fire on the savannah ecosystem and the effects of rangeland management practices based on fire use are difficult to generalise and must always be considered in the specific research context.

The role of fire in the formation of savannah ecosystems is acknowledged. For instance, Dublin et al. (1990) suggest that the Serengeti–Mara woodlands have turned into grassland through the impact of fire. They investigate woodland decline in the Serengeti–Mara woodlands in the twentieth century and identify two elements of change that have had a major impact on the decline of woodland and the transformation towards grassland. Both elephants and fire were important agents of the landscape change. Fire was identified as being 'the perturbation which changed the vegetation state' whereas 'elephants were able to keep the vegetation in the grassland state' (Dublin et al., 1990, p. 1158). Furthermore, the authors assume that in the late nineteenth century, the region was in a grassland state and that woodland vegetation also increased as a result of the massive decline in elephant populations due to hunting, the expansion of human settlements and the concentration of elephants in protected areas. In their article the authors discuss the transformation of vegetation cover from grassland to woodland, and vice versa. In the East Pokot case, the transformation is taking one direction: grassland has changed into woodland and, due to the lack of agents such as elephants and fire, a reversal of the process is currently not likely without external interventions.

Boonman (1993) also highlights that East African savannahs have formed under the influence of unintended and intended outbreaks of fire. Fires with varying intensities and frequencies contribute significantly to the limitation of woody vegetation in an open savannah landscape. For example, fires influence the establishment rate of young trees and also weaken those trees that have already established themselves. High-intensity fires can retard the growth of trees and influence tree-grass competition in favour of the latter. The occurrence of such fires is determined by the availability of grasses as combustible material and particularly strongly by the amount of combustible material.[1]

Fire-herbivore interaction, furthermore, can also lead to the weakening of trees – for instance when elephants strip off the bark, making trees more susceptible to fire damage (Levick et al., 2015). The effects of wildlife defaunation and rangeland management, which will be discussed later, are certainly important factors in the transformation of the landscape. In order to gain an impression of the extent to which fire was an element of the open savannah in the nineteenth and early twentieth centuries in East Pokot, it is necessary to trace it through archival data. I describe these briefly below and relate them to the broader Baringo region in order to understand how fires might have had an effect on rangelands in the region.

The early explorers give some accounts of fire outbreaks in the broader region around East Pokot in the late nineteenth and early twentieth centuries, as the following descriptions by Thomson and Gregory depict:

> [W]e set off [from Lake Baringo], going east to the base of the Lykipia [*sic*] mountains. We then ascended three steps, which were clearly formed

---

[1]   Whereas, the impact of fire on woody vegetation in the savannah ecosystems of eastern and southern Africa is undisputed, it must be acknowledged that different types of fires differ in their impact on the given vegetation (Smit et al., 2010). Marchant (2010) also shows the complexity of savannah ecosystems and the influence of a variety of factors including fire and human interventions.

by as many lines of fault running parallel to the principal direction of the escarpment. The grass had been only recently burnt off, leaving the country under a perfectly black pall, unrelieved by green or yellow. (Thomson, 1887, p. 318)

On reaching the summit of the last pass over the chain of Subugu, to the south-east of Baringo, we saw in the distance the smoke of great prairie fires, which my men said were lighted by the Wanderobbo [*sic*]. (Gregory, 1896, p. 328)

Furthermore, it is not just the occurrence of fires that plays a role: the intensity of these fires also has an important impact on the formation of the landscape. Peters, who also admits that their expedition caused the fire outbreak that burnt down extensive parts of the grass savannah, describes the intensity of fires and their longevity.

So it was not until January 5th that we quitted the gorge of the Guaso Tien, a river which reaches to the south-west angle of Lake Baringo, to turn our steps, in a westward course on the edge of the declivity, directly across the plain of Njemps. ... On this day I had the camp pitched below the Dongo Gelesha, by a little affluent of the Guaso Tien. While this was being done one of the porters let a burning brand fall into the tinderlike grass. It caught fire at once; and with express-train speed the conflagration spread, happily in a direction away from the camp, over the slopes and the grassy steppe. This occurrence fortunately occasioned me to seek a camping-place that had already been burnt bare, and consequently presented no danger of fire. I say 'fortunately', for in the evening the wind veered round, and now all at once the fire, which at noon had rushed forth across the steppe, came back upon us by a circuitous route, and, indeed, with a speed which, if we had been among the masses of grass, would have rendered flight almost impracticable. With difficulty we succeeded in getting the donkeys and the ammunition into the centre of the little bare camping-place I had selected. Herr von Tiedemann, who had set up his tent on the edge of the grassy steppe – indeed, in the steppe itself – was obliged to rush out, unclothed, in headlong flight, to escape the danger of being burnt alive in it. (Peters, 1891, p. 266)

However, fire was not only a danger for the people in the region but also a constant threat to the goods that were kept there. This applies, for example, to elephant tusks that had to be be protected from burning. Von Hoehnel describes the risks of fire for the trading caravans that were looking for ivory and had to find a way to protect their valuable goods from a fire outbreak.

Our tent was pitched in the midst of the camp of a trading caravan some 170 strong, as it was the only dry place to be had. These traders had come from Leikipia [*sic*], and had already been waiting here two months for

another caravan, which had gone to Ngaboto, a district on the north of
Lake Baringo. They had collected a lot of ivory, and, as they expressed
it, done a *biaschera ku*, or good business. They had buried their treasures
to protect them from fire. (von Hoehnel, 1894, p. 165)

All these examples show that fire, in both its intensity and its occurrence,
was an element that occurred in the region. However, none of the sources
demonstrates fire being used for forage regeneration by the pastoral Pokot
themselves during the nineteenth century, although oral accounts of elderly
Pokot people refer to it. Only Conant (1982) and Bollig (1992a) briefly mention
the use of fire for rangeland management by the pastoral Pokot. It can be
assumed that the grassland savannah in northern Baringo, like other pastoral
grassland areas in Kenya and broader East Africa, emerged under the influence
of fire and herbivory. However, during the twentieth century, large-scale fires
were no longer occurring or were hardly used to manage pasture regeneration.

During my research in East Pokot, small-scale fires occurred only twice.
First, a boy had started a fire unintentionally when he harvested honey and
tried to smoke the bees out of the beehive. Second, in the Churo highlands,
a small fire broke out on an unpopulated hill. This was interpreted by local
farmers as an intentional fire by a herder to enforce the regeneration of grasses.
However, fire-based pasture management can hardly be applied nowadays,
because people populate most places and fire could cause damage that would
have to be compensated within Pokot society. Furthermore, combustible
substances, such as dry grasses and undergrowth, are lacking in most places.

Officially, the use of fire in public places in Kenya is restricted by the
Grass Fires Act of 1972 (Republic of Kenya, 1972). Whereas Reckers (1989)
and Bollig and Oesterle (2013) report that fire continues to be used for bush
and tick control in some areas, Boonman identifies the absence of fire, along
with high grazing pressure, as major causes for land-cover change.

> A more general problem is bush encroachment due to overgrazing and
> absence of fire. In Pokot and similar semi-arid areas, the grass cover
> has been reduced to the point of denudation. For a large part of the
> year the soil is bare and hard, partly due to treading and hoof impact
> … so that rain does not infiltrate, while run-off is not checked by grass
> vegetation. … Not enough grass can accumulate because of the high
> grazing pressure, low soil-moisture and bush encroachment; conversely,
> bush growth increases since there is not enough grass to provide a burn
> in the dry season. (Boonman, 1993, p. 54)

The correlations between fire and other factors such as vegetation cover,
water run-off and negative feedback loops in the availability of combustible
material still need further investigations, and more research is also needed
to understand synergy effects between (over)grazing, livestock composition

changes, grass species diversity, water storage capacity, soil erosion and the impact of fire on the vegetation cover.[2] As Midgley and Bond have observed, acacia bush encroachment may seem to be caused by a 'bewildering diversity of factors' (2001, p. 871). Generally, in many in-depth studies in pastoral landscapes, the assumption that pastoralists are the main drivers of negative impacts on their environment due to overstocking, overgrazing and degradation has been largely superseded (e.g. Anderson, 2002; or more recently Boles et al., 2019). However, certain conceptions that the relationship between humans and the environment is fragile continue to persist, and an increase in human activity is considered negative per se – especially in the conservation discourse on the management of protected areas (e.g. Veldhuis et al., 2019).

As indicated above, fire is not the only important factor in the creation and maintenance of a grass-dominated ecosystem. Rather, 'fire is a a key determinant of woody vegetation structure in savanna ecosystems, acting both independently and synergistically through interactions with herbivores' (Levick et al., 2015, p. 131). Therefore, I elaborate on the effects of wildlife and livestock, their browsing and grazing habits and their interaction with the ecosystem in the next sections.

Effects of defaunation processes in Baringo

In this section, I deal more generally with the importance of herbivores for the conservation of grasslands. An evaluation of individual species is not feasible at this point, because the range of interactions between different species is simply too complex to be presented here. This becomes evident when one acknowledges that even the interactions over time between the pastoral Pokot and their environment already have so many facets that it is difficult to describe them in particularity and precision while also paying attention to the linkages between them (e.g. the challenges for the gerontocratic political system, the changes in rangeland management and herding structures, the responses to bush encroachment and forage species composition changes, alteration of fire regimes, the emergence of external development companies, among many other factors).

A historical perspective cannot be accurate in terms of specific wildlife–environment interactions and any evaluation of the effects arising from the loss of most wildlife species. However, I want to emphasise that, with the disappearance of wildlife species, important sustainers of the grassland savannah

---

[2] For instance, Roques et al. (2001) have discussed the interactions between grazing, fires, browsing and rainfall variability in bringing about bush encroachment in Swaziland where they detect a strong link between grazing pressure and the occurrence of fires in the savannah and the prevalence of bushes at the study site.

have vanished – a matter that has not been prominent in many analyses of pastoral landscape change and deserves more attention.

The defaunation concept has been addressed most prominently in small-scale natural science studies as well as in discussions of global trends such as the Anthropocene defaunation as a component of the sixth mass extinction event (Dirzo et al., 2014; Young et al., 2016). The potential risks of defaunation for local ecosystems are widely acknowledged in terms of both human expansion into previously unaffected habitats (see, e.g., Tregidgo et al., 2017) and an increasing domestic animal population such as the spread of cattle across the African continent at the expense of wildlife populations (Hempson et al., 2017). However, there is hardly any discussion of the historical and often colonially shaped roots of many defaunation processes and their effects. Although the processes and the impact of colonial hunting on wildlife populations are well documented (as outlined for the case of elephant hunting by, e.g., Somerville 2016) and can be traced throughout the accounts of the so-called early explorers and 'sports hunters', little attention has been paid to the retrospective view of animal–human history, to how defaunation processes have shaped today's landscape, or to the local perspectives on these processes (see, e.g., Fernández-Llamazares et al., 2016). More focus is placed on present and future perspectives and what drives defaunation processes, what are the effects of increasing human activities, and how could conservation and restoration (Seddon et al., 2014) halt or reverse such trends.

My focus, however, is on the defaunation processes in northern Baringo and its impact on today's bush-dominated savannah in the region around Lake Baringo. I would like to draw attention to the fact that the massive defaunation in Baringo most probably made a major contribution to those past landscape transformations that have shaped the present landscape and the present livelihoods of Pokot pastoralists. As described in Chapter 5, the pastoral landscape of the nineteenth and early twentieth centuries was home to extensive wildlife herds such as elephants, rhinoceroses and ungulates. Whereas on the one hand, the defaunation itself already represents a loss, on the other hand, it continues to have a lasting effect on the landscape in general.

As research has shown, large herbivores play an important role in the maintenance of grassland savannahs in East Africa. For instance, ungulates are described as 'engineers of habitat structure' (Pringle et al., 2010, p. 43). However, the effects of the various wildlife species on the ecosystem cannot be generalised, because the effects of browsing or grazing sometimes take different directions. For instance, browsing ungulates might have a negative effect on acacia tree establishment, but at the same time, grazing cattle may also influence the tree-grass competition in the other direction, favouring seedling establishment (Goheen et al., 2010; Pringle et al., 2010). For the Laikipia highlands, Kimuyu et al. (2017) emphasise the complexity of interactions between different animals species (browsing and grazing) at different times of the year (dry and wet): grass cover correlated positively with some species (zebra and oryx), whereas forb cover correlated positively with other species (e.g. eland).

Therefore, the removal of one wildlife species from the ecosystem has adverse, long-lasting effects on the land cover vegetation in one direction or another. But, in this case, we are not dealing with the loss of only one wildlife species in an otherwise highly diverse ecosystem. At the end of the nineteenth century and in the first half of the twentieth century, almost all larger wildlife in the region disappeared and, with very few exceptions, have not returned to the region. These are, for instance, large herbivores such as elephants, rhinoceroses, antelopes, buffaloes and zebras that were found in the grass–savannah ecosystem at Lake Baringo.

An example of a keystone species with a significant influence on the surface vegetation of the savannah is the elephant. Although not the only driver of woodland change, elephants are held responsible for keeping the grassland savannah in a more or less stable state (Dublin et al., 1990). In a meta-analysis, Guldemond and van Aarde (2008) conclude that elephants always have a negative impact on woody vegetation in arid savannahs and are therefore important sustainers of an open savannah landscape. Furthermore, Kusimba (2011) stresses the importance of human–wildlife interactions in a case study in south-east Kenya, and identifies the decline of the elephant population as a major driver of change leading to the development of dense forests in wetter areas and bush encroachment in drier areas. These developments have been followed by an increase of tsetse flies (*Glossina morsitans*) and conse-quently more cases of trypanosomiasis. He concludes that the reduction of grass forage and the increase of domestic animal infections have led to these areas being abandoned by pastoralists who were unable to reverse the process of environmental change. Kusimba states that the 'increase in bushland would have discouraged pastoralists' use of these areas; although cattle-keepers are known to use fire and grazing to maintain high-quality browse growth in many areas, they doubtless depend on similar results from elephant foraging' (2011, p. 147; see also Lankester & Davis, 2016). In line with these findings, I assume that the presence of elephants and other wildlife species contributed strongly to the maintenance of the grass-dominated savannah at Lake Baringo and the northern plains. But also, the distribution of elephants matters: Western and Maitumo (2004) discuss the impact of elephants and of pastoral land use in the Amboseli National Park since 1950 and compare the strong impacts of the two factors on the ecosystem in relation to the delimited territories of the national park.

> Inside parks, high elephant densities are creating open grassland conditions, dominated by grazing ungulates. Outside, high livestock densities are creating dense woodlands favoured by browsing ungulates

(Western, 1989). … The new habitat configuration in Amboseli is mirrored regionally across eastern Africa. Here a fivefold differential in elephant densities in and outside parks due to human disturbance is promoting grasslands inside protected areas and woody invasion outside. (Western & Maitumo, 2004, p. 120)

The loss of elephants and other wildlife in northern Baringo County must have had a tremendous impact on the landscape and supported the growth and expansion of woody vegetation. The rapid extinction of elephants can probably be attributed to two processes: Hakansson (2004) distinguishes direct effects of wildlife hunting and indirect effects of the ivory trade. He outlines the example of Lake Baringo and the coincidence of two factors. First, pastoralists from northern Kenya were integrated into trade networks from the coast at an early stage and the wildlife-rich region became the destination of trading caravans. Second, Hakansson (2004) argues that the severe rinderpest in the late nineteenth century urged pastoralists to intensify their hunting and restock their herds with the revenues from the ivory trade.

So far, I have outlined the impact that the absence of larger wildlife herbivores can have on the grass and bush vegetation, as well as the impact of fire and its absence on savannah ecosystems. In the following, I shall return to pastoral land use and discuss how pastoralist land management is organised and how the fragmentation of the pastoral landscape contributes to pastoral livelihoods coming increasingly under pressure. Therefore, I explain the rangeland management of the pastoral Pokot and ask how far the degradation of the rangeland might have been influenced by the (over) grazing of cattle.

Rangeland management in a non-equilibrium ecosystem

In the following, I address the debates on rangeland degradation, habitat loss and local rangeland management practices while focusing on East Pokot rangelands. This is a difficult matter, as already often remarked, in the sense that savannah ecosystems are highly complex systems that cannot be explained by or reduced to a few factors without losing important insights. For this reason, the focus here will be particularly on the perspective of rangeland fragmentation and how this process is perceived from a scientific perspective. Furthermore, I describe the Pokot rangeland management system that is not characterised by intensive pasture management. Instead, the constraints of scarce forage resources and water availability are met mainly through higher mobility.

Reid et al. (2004) reflect on the terminology used in the debate about rangeland habitat loss and degradation and differentiate between habitat modification and habitat loss (or conversion). Whereas habitat modification refers to 'a change in quality of the habitat so that it is no longer entirely suitable for the user', the loss or conversion of a habitat describes 'a direct change in the composition of the elements of a rangeland landscape, which changes a suitable habitat so that it is entirely unsuitable for the original user' (Reid et al., 2004, p. 172). Both processes can be observed in East Pokot.

In the case of the pastoral lowlands, I would argue that a rangeland modification has taken place over the past two centuries. Today, pastoral land uses are still dominant; and over the years, pastoralists have adopted to comprehensive land-cover changes with an increasing focus on rearing browsing species instead of grazing ones. In the agro-pastoral highlands, however, both changing land-use practices and the invasive bush encroachment processes of *Dodonaea viscosa* have contributed to rangeland loss and conversion. Whereas in the 1960s, the rangeland became more fragmented with increasing maize cultivation and the establishment of small-size enclosures, the rapid expansion of *Dodonaea viscosa* especially since the 1990s can best be described as a conversion and loss of rangeland. As these two cases already show, the modification and conversion of rangeland can take place on different temporal levels and – depending on the particular land-use situation – can also lead to different results.

Concerning the temporality of such processes, Little et al. (2007a) distinguish three types of environmental fluctuation that differ on temporal levels and on – what they call – scales of drought: (1) seasonal or annual drought, (2) medium-term drought and (3) long-term climatic trends. They argue that Turkana pastoralists in northern Kenya react to different kinds of changes in various ways, often by increasing their mobility and following the strategy of opportunistic grazing of accessible vegetation. Similar to the Turkana pastoralists, Pokot also respond to seasonal changes and drought conditions with increased mobility and the exploitation of distant and contested resources. Medium-term changes, such as the encroachment of *Dodonaea viscosa* in the Churo highlands, are responded to by permanent avoidance and the migration and use of other grazing areas. Climatic variations are more difficult to assess. With reference to Lake Baringo's history, a plausible explanation is that the desiccation of the lake led pastoral and non-pastoral groups to withdraw from the region and not return until the conditions for pastoral livelihoods were restored. Nowadays, in contrast to these eras, it is possible to influence fluctuating environmental conditions technically, as can be seen in the recent construction of community and livestock water points by the Geothermal Development Company (GDC). To what extent this is causing fundamental changes of livelihoods that have so far relied on pastoral strategies is not predictable. But the pastoralists themselves are convinced that it will influence their mobility – leading to even more sedentarised livelihood structures and overgrazing and overstocking in the vicinity of water points. The pastoral future of the community is being examined internally and both a pastoral future and other, non-pastoral possibilities are being considered as reasonable options.

However, environmental changes alone are not a sufficient condition with which to explain social transformations of the pastoral Pokot, because social and ecological transformation processes always interact. Although it has often been argued that pastoral groups have adapted to environmental changes, as can be seen in, for instance, the case of changing herd structures (from cattle to goats), it was also human interventions such as big-game hunting that had an immense impact on the agents of landscape change. Ascribing a negative influence on the landscape to the pastoralists and to the rangeland system per se is not a sufficient explanation. Although processes such as overstocking, overgrazing, a decline in above-ground vegetation, the emergence and expansion of bare ground patches that can lead to increased erosion and the loss of grazing forage potential (Homewood, 2008; with reference to Lamprey, 1983) are also evident in East Pokot, pastoralists have also been very successful over a long period in establishing their livelihoods and managing their resources in this semi-arid environment and disequilibrium system. Disequilibrium systems are characterised by large and unpredictable intra- and inter-annual fluctuations that result in strong fluctuations in the primary production of vegetation (Homewood, 2008, with reference to Oba et al., 2000). Pastoralists must therefore follow the unpredictable vegetation patterns in order to feed their livestock opportunistically. It is water availability that is more relevant here, because it limits the range in which pastoralists can graze their cattle, and it is rainfall rather than grazing that determines vegetation growth (Brockington & Homewood, 1996). These opportunistic mobile strategies and flexible, common management systems are therefore essential for a successful livelihood.

The land-management system of the pastoral Pokot has not changed fundamentally in recent decades. Barrow (1988) depicts the pastoral Pokot grazing system in the late 1980s as follows: little agriculture was practised during that time, but the trend towards agricultural practices in some regions was already visible. He describes the seasonal migration with cattle up to 50 kilometres distant from the homestead, whereas other livestock species such as camels, goats and sheep were kept more in the vicinity of the main homestead; and he argues that East Pokot were achieving an optimisation of livestock production without rangeland depletion. However, he also observes that, although the access to grazing resources is common, stock ownership and management are organised on an individual level and this 'can lead to the maximisation of individual herds, at the expense of the communal graze and browse which is one of the biggest problems of successful range management' (Barrow, 1988, p. 2).[3] For the 1980s, he also describes the extent of grazing reserves as being 'many thousands of hectares' according to Pokot elders (Barrow, 1988, p. 2).

---

[3]   Barrow's original intention was to understand both Turkana and Pokot grazing systems in order to make practical suggestions for their development. In the Pokot

Not much has changed to date, with the exception of the organisation of grazing reserves. Today, these are much smaller in extent compared to the 1980s and 1990s, and often, while having been declared formally, no longer offer much benefit in practice. On one hand, this is related to the fact that the vegetation of the grazing reserves has changed completely, as can be seen in the example of Moruase Hill that used to be a calf grazing reserve for the dry season and is now completely overgrown by acacia bushes. On the other hand, the elders of the region can no longer enforce compliance with their decisions because (at least in 2014–15) the grazing grounds were already so much depleted towards the end of the rainy season that many pastoralists ignored the closure of the montane grazing areas. Because some elders themselves also ignored the decision to close the grazing reserves, the restrictions were ultimately not enforced. But although the elders insisted repeatedly that the younger generations would no longer listen to the elderly generation set, they also emphasised that in times of better rainfall and better availability of forage, the decisions of the council of elders would be respected again. However, these are also problems that all elderly generations stress repeatedly and that already existed in the 1980s.

Barrow (1986) also described the erosion of the gerontocratic system and perceived the future of the pastoral Pokot as being rather difficult. He states that increasing access to veterinary services and livestock medication might lead to increasing herds and rising population numbers that would put more pressure on natural resources that are already near their 'maximum subsistence potential' (1986, p. 480). He suggests that any improvements in water supply must consider grazing patterns to avoid overgrazing and degradation in the vicinities, and that rangelands are gradually being turned into agricultural land (Barrow, 1986). However, he highlights the positive aspects of the Pokot rangeland management in contrast to the problematic perception of the future of pastoralists in the region.

> Few people perceive the use of their land-use strategies as a soil and water conservation benefit, yet in preserving their land and vegetation this is exactly what it is. Likewise, in many cases planners in soil and water conservation do not see the value of such strategies, preferring the use of structures to cure the problem rather than preventing the disease. (Barrow, 1986, p. 471)

Thus he also contradicts the rather prominent narrative that the degradation of the environment is the result of overpopulation by people and livestock. Similarly, Homewood identifies the processes of privatising former rangeland

---

case, he suggested that the current grazing patterns could be used to form group ranches in East Pokot (Barrow, 1988).

and the conversion to commercial monoculture as main drivers of rangeland fragmentation in the Serengeti–Mara conservation areas (including the buffer zone), whereas other factors, such as population growth and agro-pastoral land-use practices are not critical (Homewood, 2004). Thus, she also offers new explanatory possibilities that are contrary to earlier assumptions that it is mainly the pastoral groups themselves who are the most prominent drivers of rangeland degradation (see, e.g., Talbot, 1986) and contribute to Hardin's 'tragedy of the commons' and generally act destructively towards their environment (Warren, 1995).

From a social perspective, it is still necessary to ask what are the effects of rangeland conversion and the loss of local livelihoods and who are the winners and losers of the land-cover changes, because pastoralists and agro-pastoralists deal differently with changing conditions. On the one hand, the pastoralists, who definitely have less high-quality rangeland for cattle grazing available, have lost the flexibility to choose different grazing grounds. Not only have the bush-encroached areas in the lowlands reduced their grazing quality (rangeland modification), but especially the highland areas, which were used extensively until the late twentieth century, are now completely useless due to rangeland conservation and no longer offer any potential for cattle husbandry. Because of this, the pastoralists have to move to other regions outside the Pokot territory during the dry season in order to find enough feed for their cattle, which – as already described – leads repeatedly to violent conflicts in the border zones. But even the recognition of environmental changes by the pastoral Pokot does not lead to countermeasures being applied. Neither temporary grazing bans nor active measures such as clearing bush-encroached areas or felling expanding species (such as *Senegalia mellifera*) are implemented. Only the formal declaration of Mt Paka as a dry-season forage storage is still maintained by the elders, although even some of the elders themselves violate this regulation without sanctions.

The agro-pastoralists in the highlands, on the other hand, are affected far less by the change in the landscape and the reduction of the rangelands, because they are not dependent on livestock farming. By focusing on maize cultivation, they are able to cultivate a small area very intensively. However, through the agricultural use of the region and the de facto privatisation of land, they have contributed substantially to the fragmentation of the rangelands in the past, and agro-pastoral land use has also facilitated the rapid spread of the *Dodonaea viscosa* that makes it impossible for pastoralists to graze cattle in these regions. In their historical accounts of the region, the highland pastures are still remembered vividly by elderly Pokot, but nowadays pastoralists have to migrate beyond the escarpment region to find sufficient grazing grounds on the Laikipia Plateau. There, however, the ownership of the land is largely regulated, and this leads regularly to violent conflicts between pastoralists and residents (Gravesen, 2021; Gravesen & Kioko, 2019).

Therefore, both processes – the fragmentation of the pastoral rangelands and bush encroachment in the highlands and the lowlands – increase the pressure on the remaining pasture resources. Together with growing human populations and high livestock numbers, the reduction of grazing ground amplifies the transition from an 'extensive [use of] grazing lands' (with less than 20 people per km^2) to the 'intensive [use of] grazing lands' (more than 20 people per km^2) (Reid et al., 2008, p. 2). Against the background that 91 per cent of total rangeland area was considered to be 'extensive' and 9 per cent as being 'intensive' (Reid et al., 2008), the transition towards more intensive land use also exemplifies the transition of pastoral land-use strategies being complemented by other strategies such as agro-pastoral land use.

In contrast to this scientific view, the perception of a pastoral future from the view of the elders also allows other ways of interpreting recent trends. Whereas the description of the historical developments and the current emphasis on challenging situations for pastoralists always point towards a future beyond the actual pastoral activities, at least some elders believe that the future could also look quite different.

Periodical spaces: the renewal of pastoralism

In 1959, Harold K. Schneider published an article entitled 'Pakot Resistance to Change', in which he describes the groups of agro-pastoral and pastoral Pokot in north-western Kenya and demonstrates his view of their reluctance to include external changes into their way of living. He emphasises the peoples' strong attachment to a pastoral way of life and summarises that 'their herding life provides all they need and all they want, and they have found almost nothing in Euro-American culture that will entice them to abandon their old ways' (Schneider, 1959, p. 160). But, merely from an etic view, it seems as if Pokot would insist on the pastoral life against the introduction of alternative modes of life. In the following, I approach the explanation of the land-cover changes from the perspective of elderly Pokot men and how they evaluate these changes. Therefore, I refer to the generation-set system – as described in Chapter 3 – and the idea that life does not follow a linear path but is connected to a continual iterative past. In the case of Pokot pastoralists, the past re-establishes itself when the generation sets that already existed in the past are re-initiated.

As noted in Chapter 3 in Pokot cosmology, life is understood as a cyclical recurrence of seven Pokot generations. Every generation set is endowed with its own characteristics regarding the type of people and the specific landscape settings (*kor*).[4] The landscape of the Koronkoro generation set, for example,

---

[4]   Schneider (1953) translates the term *kor* as 'country'. In my understanding, the term *kor* implies different meanings. It could describe a specific place, such as

is quite different from that of the following Kaplelach generation set. When Merkutwö was initiated in 2016, yet another landscape had to commence. The decline of the grasses and the increase of bushy vegetation over the last century is also perceived as coinciding with the initiation of the generation sets of Koronkoro and Kaplelach.

Figure 12 displays the periodical recurrence of generation sets among the pastoral Pokot. A generation set is based on male circumcision and covers a period of about 25–35 years. All men who are circumcised in one generation-set period belong to the same generation set.

In the past 200 years, the following generation sets were initiated: Kaplelach, circumcised around the year 1815; Merkutwö, around 1840; Nyongi, around 1865; Maina, around 1890; Chumwö, in 1916 and 1920; Koronkoro, in 1949 and 1959; Kaplelach, again, in 1988 and 1996; and now Merkutwö, in 2016. Currently, members of three generation sets are living in East Pokot: Koronkoro, the oldest generation, followed by Kaplelach and the newly initiated generation of Merkutwö.

In East Pokot, the previous Merkutwö generation, circumcised around 1840, is often associated with successful warriors, green pastures and prosperous livestock herding. In the same sense, the new generation of Merkutwö, circum-cised in 2016, is perceived as performing similarly in terms of successful resistance to enemies and successful livestock herding even though the conditions for cattle herding have changed tremendously over the past 200 years. From the perspective of the older Koronkoro generation, the latest period of bush encroachment is often attributed to the initiation of the younger Kaplelach generation. Members of the Koronkoro generation blame the Kaplelach generation for misbehaviour and disrespect that has led to the disappearance of grasses.

With the initiation of a new generation set in 2016, the elders say that the area and the people must change again. The forecast of the future is the task of a prophet (*werkoyon*), who dreams about the future and conducts forecasts in times when a community is under pressure.[5] When a prophet is asked for advice, several actors are involved: the elders, highly respected in the neigh-bourhood councils (*kokwö*); the prophet himself; and the community leaders, who also act in place of the elders.

---

korpowuw – the place of the dense stands of bushes – or the broader landscape, with all its characteristics and inhabitants such as people, animals, but also roads, schools, vegetation or generation sets. For instance, the *kor* of the past also incorporates the remembrances of the people from the past, such as the Nyongi generation set – one of the most successful Pokot generations in the view of current generations.

[5]   The role of the prophet in the communities is highly important, because he forecasts the future in his dreams – also described earlier by Schneider (1953).

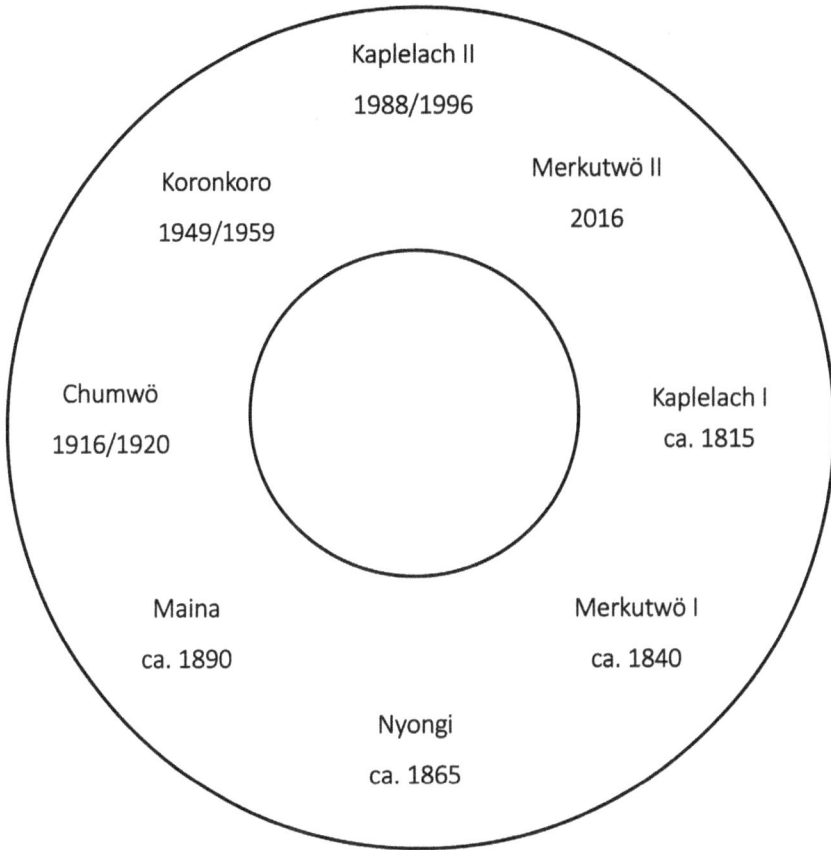

Fig. 12. Cyclical recurrence of generation sets in East Pokot pastoral society, early 1800s –2016 (Hauke-Peter Vehrs).

Generally, in the divination procedure, the community identifies a problem and the community leaders visit their prophet and describe their concern. The prophet does not always provide a concrete answer to the question raised. He often simply dreams of the future. Depending on his dreams, he gives explicit advice in many different cases – for instance the prevention of a disaster through the performance of a certain ritual. Nevertheless, the prophet's advice must still be interpreted by the elders.

According to the forecast for the newly initiated Merkutwö generation, there is one important prophecy based on situations and revelations from the past. At the end of the nineteenth century, members of the Maina generation set misbehaved and disrespected the elders of the Nyongi generation. For the current situation of perceived disrespect and misbehaviour, past and present are compared.

> When I was growing up, the land was beautiful. I first lived near the river Nginyang. In those days no disease affected the stock of goats, camels and even cattle. There were droughts, but not such long droughts like nowadays.

> In case adultery happened, the culprit was punished and had to kill his big bull among his stock and the elders ate it. Then he had to take one gallon of honey and tobacco to the husband of the woman. The culprit was cleansed with milk. In those days, there was no *sitasita*,[6] like it is happening now. And there were no fights with Turkana in the past.

> *Sapana* has been there since, but then only few elders attended the ceremony; only old women and men were blessing the opening of the ceremony and local brew [*busaa* and *kipketin*] was only given to elders. It was made in small quantities. Also, there were no quarrels during the ceremony.

> During the onset of the fights in Silali [with Turkana], the area changed. People were even moving to Nginyang and back again for water, but the area was full of grasses. By that time the trees started to grow, like *panyarit* [several acacia species] emerged.

> With the emergence of bushes, livestock diseases appeared. Humans also fell sick with typhoid, brucellosis[7] and diseases such as dehydration or the shortage of blood. Again, a disease appeared called *yomöt*[8] and the hands are being paralysed and you immediately die. Also cholera started.

> The fights with Turkana continued and guns came to the area. When we went for a raid the roads were open, but became bushes, and the places that were full of grasses became bushes. These areas were full of grasses, such as *churukechir* and *cheluwowes*. The land was open from Monti,

6   '*Sita*' means 'six' in Kiswahili and '*sitasita*' refers to a recent punishment of giving six cows and six goats in adultery cases.
7   Typhoid and brucellosis were named with their English terms.
8   *Yomöt* is a disease that has not occurred before and took many lives in the middle of the twentieth century. It is called *Yomöt* (Kipokot; 'air'), because it spreads through contact with infected people. Bianco (1996) describes it as a disease that paralyses the legs and could be caused by witchcraft, after elders are abused: 'Like hunger, sickness may "follow" unethical conduct. ... *Yomöt* sufferers feel coldness in the limbs; within a day or two they are unable to walk. Ilat "can get annoyed and send this disease if a person has said an abuse," explained an elderly Pokot man. But, he continued, *yomöt* can also start from witchcraft' (Bianco 1996, p. 29).

Paka and Kasakaram up to Kapogh. Now it is *panyarit* all over. Even other areas where grasses like *seretion* were growing, the herb *atulayan* came out of it. Even places like Napokoriatom and Moruase were open places, but now it is a bush. Even Mt Paka was open and full of grasses. The area of Tilam was full of *makäny* trees, but now is even impassable and full of bushes. Tilam was also full of grass, like *seretion*.

Humans caused all these changes. People have all kinds of bad behaviour, adultery cases, aggressiveness and young men moving with old women. I can see the elders cursed the people and the land.

In the past there was an outbreak of a disease called *Molmoloy* with the reduction of the population in big numbers. What has happened before the disease was that young men [of the Maina generation] mistrusted the elders and were beating them for no reason and forcing them to kill parts of their stock for the young warriors to eat. This group of warriors did the same repeatedly up to Tiaty. They met a very old man of the Nyongi generation and his daughter who were moving with the animals. The warriors asked him to kill his big oxen, which the old man used for the transportation of millet. The old man was beaten and the warriors slaughtered the animal and left only the head for him. The rest they ate. The next day the warriors went to raid in Turkana land. All of them were killed with only two remaining to pass the message of failure. Several raids followed this and wherever the young Maina generation attempted to raid they were killed in numbers.

Peace came again and the Nyongi generation was left with very few Maina. Nyongi added the members of the generation of Maina, which was cursed before, to the generation of Chumwö. So, the remaining few Maina joined the Chumwö generation and were blessed for the generation to come. This is how the land was and I believe soon this will repeat after the generation of Merkutwö or next one coming because the signs of the past are repeating themselves.[9] You can see now, the young generation are starting to steal from the old, like cases of camels and goats being stolen[10] and sold by young men. ...

It was a prophecy for a long time that a disease will come, animals will be affected and human beings also will die of diseases. You will only see the fire of human dwellings in Mt Tiaty. Nobody will remain in the

[9]   The reference to 'after Merkutwö' refers to the generation set that is going to be circumcised after Merkutwö, probably in 25–35 years after the first Merkutwö initiation (2040–50).

[10]   In Kipokot a distinction is made between stealing (from other Pokot) and raiding animals (from other ethnic groups). Whereas the former is punished by disciplinary measures and compensation payments, the latter is associated with prestige.

plains. Later the land will burn until you can see clearly. Then, heavy
rains will start all over the land and grass will be all over the land. The
few people left will start to move from the hills. So, it is said by the clan
Katumewio and this has to come. (Riteluk, 4 September, 2014)

According to Riteluk, environmental changes are linked to social transformations. In the past, the occurrence of diseases and the failure of raids were
attributed to the bad behaviour of youths. When the Maina generation behaved
badly towards the older Nyongi generation, the elders cursed the members of
the younger generation, who were then annihilated almost completely during
their raids. The curse first affected the generation of Maina but also influenced
the people and the land when a fatal disease broke out, called Molmoloy.
Mariner and Paskin (2000) refer the term Molmoloy to the rinderpest, but this
cannot be confirmed entirely. Bollig notes that the rinderpest is called *Kiplok*
in Kipokot (Bollig 1995). Considering that the interviewee refers to great
losses in human populations through the disease called Molmoloy, he could
also be referring to the smallpox epidemic that occurred in 1902 right after the
massive reduction of cattle populations through the rinderpest in the end of
the nineteenth century (Bollig 2006) The Maina generation was circumcised
around 1890, and therefore the two disasters that happened after the initiation
of this generation set could time-wise be related to their misbehaviour, at
least from the point of view of the elderly Nyongi generation, as both the
rinderpest and the smallpox outbreak fell into their time. In the prophecy,
it was only after the Maina generation was decimated and their remaining
members absorbed by the Chumwö generation that the elders blessed them
and the land and the people recovered.

In the present situation, many Pokot believe that the war with the Turkana
and the aberrant behaviour of their youths are signs of a new curse. Bush
encroachment and the occurrence of different diseases are the outcome of this
curse. It is said that finally a great fire will roll from north to south sweeping
the land clean. Only then will the survivors re-establish a pastoral way of life
once the bushes have been burnt away and the grasses restored. The elders
date the revival of livestock husbandry to the initiation of the Merkutwö
generation or the following Nyongi generation set.

From the perspective of elderly Pokot belonging to the Koronkoro
generation set, the bushes started to infest the region after the first circumcision
of the Kaplelach generation (1988).[11] Following the notion of intergenerational
change, the circumcision of the next generation set (Merkutwö) must bring
with it the return of yet another environment. The existence of generation sets

---

[11] Bollig recalls that during his research in the late 1980s, it was not the Kaplelach
generation that was blamed for the emergence of bushes but the Koronkoro generation
initiated in 1949 and 1959.

and the divination of the future are still important in everyday life. However, the resistance to change, as described by Schneider (1953) earlier, can no longer be taken as true. Instead, the pastoral Pokot integrate several other income-generating activities into their livelihoods. A big challenge for the next decades is the elders' struggle for their position in their communities due to the rise of young men who successfully engage in businesses. The Geothermal Development Company (GDC) is bringing rapid changes to the region such as the construction of roads and the provision of water (Greiner, 2020). These changes are being followed by hitherto unknown opportunities and are challenging existing social organisation structures.

Concluding remarks

Whereas both the scientific explanations of land-cover change and the memories of the pastoral Pokot refer to the incremental decline of pastures, it does not suffice to assess land-cover change on the basis of one single aspect. Currently, environmental conditions in East Pokot do not favour cattle herding, and new ways of herding are already emerging with an emphasis on goats and camels. As Little notes, this shift is marked by a move away from a specialised cattle pastoralism towards flexible pastoral livelihoods that are not wholly dependent on livestock. 'With reduced lands, especially those that support perennial grasses, and restricted mobility, herders are keeping hardier, browse-dependent goats and camels, as well as innovating in other ways' (Little, 2013, p. 248).

The pastoral Pokot refer to the decline of grass cover without over-emphasising the negative over the positive effects. Although grass is perceived to be scarce, the abundance of bushy vegetation is also acknowledged. The evaluation of land-cover change therefore also depends on the context of land degradation (Warren, 2002), whereas perceptions of degradation vary with changing subsistence patterns (Roba & Oba, 2009). For instance, the value placed upon grazing grounds might change when browsing species complement cattle herding, or when livelihood transitions occur such as the adoption of new agricultural practices or increased market orientation of livestock production, as described by Oesterle (2007) and Greiner et al. (2013).

In contrast to the long-standing narrative linking pastoral land use to land degradation (Lamprey, 1983; Mainguet, 1994), the scientific accounts indicate that not only 'the pastoralists' have degraded the land. For East Pokot, the defaunation and removal of main landscape agents has mainly led to the land cover being transformed. However, the explanations offered by science and by pastoralists diverge. For instance, Bollig and Schulte (1999) found obvious signs of degradation in their study in the 1990s, but the herders interviewed in 2014 and 2015 collectively remember the abundance of grasses at that time. The elderly Pokot tend to refer to internal reasons that have caused the pasture land degradation. Koronkoro elders currently blame the Kaplelach generation for causing these changes, whereas some decades ago, Chumwö elders blamed the generation of Koronkoro. However, the bush encroachment is not seen as purely negative; its positive aspects are also described. Browsing species are often favoured: bush branches can be taken for garden fences, acacia honey can be harvested (Mwaka, 2014), firewood is greatly valued and local handicrafts benefit from the availability of wood. Whereas cattle are often seen as losers in these environmental changes, goats and camels are favoured. Herders of these browsing animals do not emphasise the negative aspects of bush encroachment.

To summarise the most important processes that are part of the socio-ecological transformation in East Pokot, Table 11 lists the variety of factors discussed so far – from the scientific and the pastoral perspectives.

Table 11. Changing pastoral livelihoods in East Pokot.

Field	Processes	Comment
Environment	Large-scale bush encroachment has occurred in East Pokot, accelerating in the twentieth century. Different processes are identifiable over time and on different spatial scales. Changes include the incremental acacia bush encroachment and the rapid expansion of *Dodonaea viscosa*.	The formation of pastoral Pokot and the transformation processes discussed in this contribution (200–250 years) cover a relatively short time span in the history of East African landscapes. Marchant et al. (2018) discuss the land-use and land-cover changes in the region from 6,000 BP to present.
Wildlife	Large herbivore and carnivore populations existed in the Lake Baringo region in the eighteenth and nineteenth centuries and were hunted to local extinction in the mid-twentieth century.	The effects of defaunation can vary enormously depending on the species considered, how they interact with other species or with the ecosystem, and the extent to which their presence or absence influences other ecological processes.
Rangeland	Rangeland has decreased and the quality of the remaining pasture has declined.	During the rainy season, Pokot pastoralists graze their cattle in Pokot territory; during the dry season, they migrate to the border zones and frequently engage in combat with neighbouring groups or the Kenyan police and defence forces.

Field	Processes	Comment
Precipitation	Elderly Pokot report a decline of rainfall over the past decades and more erratic conditions.	Long-term decline of total rainfall amounts is also recorded for other regions in Kenya such as central Marsabit between 1961 and 2010 (Dabasso & Okomoli, 2015).
Livestock	Herd structures diversified from a specialised cattle-centred pastoralism in the nineteenth and early twentieth century towards an emphasis on small stock and camels.	In contrast to earlier assumptions that an end to pastoral ways of life was to be expected, pastoralists in many regions in East Africa have shown that they can respond to changing conditions (Bollig, 1992a; Oesterle, 2007).
Social organisation	The gerontocratic system in the acephalous Pokot society is gradually eroding. Younger generations are less dependent on elder generations because they engage in new income-generating activities.	In other cases, the erosion of the social political system becomes even more important, resulting in intra-generational conflict, as shown in the case of Samburu 'beach boys' illustrated by Meiu (2017).
Infrastructure	In the pastoral hinterlands of East Pokot, the construction of schools, churches, roads, geothermal wells and water pipelines are planned in process.	The construction of infrastructure (roads, pipelines etc.) for geothermal energy production is already very advanced (Greiner, 2016a; Greiner et al., 2021; Klagge et al., 2020). Other projects, however, which were once planned to run through East Pokot, have been relocated (see, e.g., the LAPSSET project).
Politics	Pokot politicians from East Pokot are often sidelined in politics and county positions are highly contested.	Two members of the County Assembly and a parliamentary aspirant were killed in 2017. The member of parliament from the Tiaty Constituency was accused of being involved in one of the cases and was voted out of his seat in 2017. [12]

[12] The MCA of Loyamork Ward, Fredrick Kibet Cheretei and the parliamentary aspirant Symon Kitambaa were assassinated in Marigat in February 2017 (Koech, 2017a) and the MCA of Churo-Amaya, Thomas Minito, was killed in May 2017 (Koech, 2017c).

Table 11 continued.

Field	Processes	Comment
Conflicts	Some pastoralists cause violent conflicts in the border zones of East Pokot during the dry-season migration. They violently occupy regions with pasture and access to water and displace former residents. In the media, pastoral Pokot are often displayed as brutal culprits in recent conflicts over land in southern Baringo County and Laikipia County.	The conflicts over access to pastureland and water frequently heightens during the dry seasons, as can be seen again in 2021. The reaction of the Kenyan government often is the intervention with the Kenyan Defence Forces in Baringo and the application of the 'shoot to kill' order.[13]
Mobility and sedentarisation	Pokot livelihoods are nowadays highly sedentarised compared to the mobile cattle-centred pastoralism of the nineteenth century. The earlier migration patterns have changed towards a short-term migration of a few household members and their livestock beyond the borders of East Pokot during the dry season.	The availability of water through the construction of small dams in the region as well as the establishment of water points by GDC has ensured that the shortage of water in the dry season is no longer a major reason for household migration. In addition, the conversion of herd structures towards browsing species has given households the opportunity to keep a part of the herd in the homestead so that only the cattle are taken for the temporary migration.
Markets	Through the establishment of weekly markets in many centres and several 'bush markets' in East Pokot, the marketisation of livestock increased over the second half of the twentieth century (Oesterle, 2007).	Livestock trade was initially condemned by the community and some traders were even accused of witchcraft during that time (Bollig 1992a). Nowadays, trade in cattle at the various small and large cattle markets in the region is absolutely normal and animals are often bought by middlemen in the hinterland and sold to external traders on market days at the large markets in Nginyang and Tangulbei.

[13] 'William Ruto orders police to shoot, kill bandits on sight' (Koech, 2017b).

Field	Processes	Comment
Agriculture	The cultivation of maize has become more important for pastoral and agro-pastoral livelihoods in East Pokot.	Pastoral farming, intensive maize cultivation and mixed farming are found to varying degrees in different parts of the region (Greiner et al., 2013).
Land tenure	In the process of devolution, land rights in East Pokot have also changed. Previously, they were characterised by open access to resources and land, but with the demarcation of agricultural land, the de facto privatisation of enclosures, and the Community Land Act, the land tenure system is set to change profoundly in the future.	Due to the ongoing privatisation process as well as increasing bush encroachment resulting in rangeland modification and conversion, pastoral landscapes have become increasingly fragmented, forcing pastoralists to resort to exploring resources beyond their own territory.
Rangeland management	The management of dry-season forage storages has collapsed. Until the second half of the twentieth century, pasture management was conducted successfully and mountain sites were reserved for cattle. This management is currently conducted only in a rudimentary way.	The enforcement of this practice by the elders has eroded over time. Nowadays, people even live in the protected areas of the mountain sites and ignore the advice of the elders.
Wage labour	The introduction of the large-scale geothermal projects created some temporary opportunities for wage labour that are highly valued, e.g. road construction or security jobs, and revenues from labour are perceived as contributing to the growth of the livestock wealth of households.	Although most pastoral Pokot still emphasise livestock production, the increasing importance of money to purchase food and goods makes labour an important source of income.
Livestock diseases	Livestock diseases are still perceived to have a huge impact on livestock herds. East coast fever in cattle and contagious caprine pleuropneumonia in goats are reported to have disastrous effects on herds.	On the other hand, many pastoralists are also making use of the increasing availability of medication and vaccinations for livestock. These are also often applied – for instance regular spraying of cattle against ticks.

Table 11 continued.

Field	Processes	Comment
Trade	Trading of food and goods is still marginal in the pastoral hinterlands, but a few pastoralists engage in trade and offer their goods occasionally near the drinking places and during the celebration of ceremonies. The prices for the goods leave hardly any profit margin for the trader after subtracting the purchase price and transport costs to the hinterlands.	The construction of roads and the busy traffic through GDC offer many possibilities to transport ordinary goods to the hinterland as well as to import new products.
Bee-keeping	The production of honey for sale or the production of honey beer (*maratina*) has increased and is an important income opportunity (Greiner & Mwaka, 2016).	This is one of the positive side effects of bush encroachment, because the many acacia species in the region are well suited to both hanging beehives and producing high-quality honey from the flowers.
Alcohol production	Alcohol is produced locally by women. Both *busaa* (beer) and *changaa* (spirits) are produced daily and consumed by both women and men.	The brewing of alcohol is an opportunity for women to generate their own income that they can use to purchase goods and food for the household.
Alcohol consumption	The consumption of alcohol has increased in the views of elderly people. Whereas the consumption of honey beer was a privilege of elders in the past, in the last decades, the cheap production of *busaa* and *changaa* has made such beverages affordable to all members of society.	Both production and consumption also have negative impacts on pastoral livelihoods (Becker, 2014). Elders also connect the misbehaviour of younger generations to the increasing consumption of alcohol.
Exiting pastoralism	Pastoral livelihoods in East Pokot are constantly under pressure from several sources. Recent conflicts, droughts, livestock diseases, bush encroachment and pasture losses force some pastoralists to abandon livestock husbandry.	Impoverished pastoralists seek alternative income opportunities in the small centres in East Pokot.

Source: Hauke-Peter Vehrs

As Table 11 shows, the transformation processes in East Pokot are informed by a number of different factors that are interrelated in many different ways. A simple explanation for the socio-ecological transformations is not possible. What can be recorded clearly is a decrease in the quality and quantity of rangeland, which impacts particularly on the keeping of cattle. Close grass cover has disappeared from the plains to be replaced by several acacia species. On the other hand, browsing species are experiencing a continuing boost, and Pokot pastoralists are once again revealing how they can deal with difficult medium-term changes to the environment. Absurdly, water is now more widely available, often provided by boreholes; huge pipelines are planned from Lake Baringo to Mt Korossi, Mt Paka and Mt Silali to provide water for both geothermal projects and community use. The change in natural plant composition is accompanied by other significant economic and social developments that will have major impacts on the livelihoods of pastoral communities in this area.

Whereas many elders also perceive the future as pastoral, many members of younger generation sets are breaking new ground and taking advantage of the many opportunities available to them. This goes beyond the general use of maize cultivation or honey production or the making and selling of alcohol. Rather, it is the income opportunities provided by the Geothermal Development Company that enable them to generate a monetary income to pay for everyday consumer goods and, at the same time, to increase their own herds – whether by avoiding selling their own animals or by purchasing new ones.

In the following chapter, I take up the already described ecological transformation processes in the highlands again and discuss them against the background of their invasiveness. For pastoral livelihoods, this type of transformation poses a new challenge, because rangeland conversion has occurred in a very short period, leaving pastoralists only with the choice to abandon these areas. Therefore, the chapter will describe and compare different invasion processes and their effects and it will discuss the use of the 'invasion' terminology for rapid socio-ecological transformation processes.

8

Ecological Invasions:
Agents of Socio-Ecological Transformation

This chapter takes up the notion of inherently changing pastoral landscapes more generally. My understanding of the transformations of pastoral landscapes in the past centuries is based on the awareness that multiple agents are involved in an ongoing process of land-use and land-cover changes. These changes are not unusual, and I would assert that pastoral landscapes are continually exposed to changes on different levels. Scientific works on other pastoral groups and their changing environments have paid much attention to the actions of pastoral groups and their impact on their environments, ranging from allegations of landscape degradation and desertification (Hare et al., 1977) to lauding their position as pastoral stewards of the environment (Heine, 2015). Both these perspectives focus on the strategies of pastoral groups, but hardly on the other landscape agents involved in forming and maintaining pastoral landscapes. The perspective towards the landscape and other agents of land-use and land-cover changes to be found beneath the pastoralist level is often neglected, and few scientific accounts focus directly on pastoral landscapes and their transition processes.

Nonetheless, one good example is the great work of Reid et al. (2005) who describe and compare the grasslands in East Africa taking the examples of Sudan, Eritrea, Djibouti, Ethiopia, Somalia, Uganda, Kenya, Rwanda, Burundi and Tanzania. For their study on changing pastoral landscapes, they took various factors into account such as population and livestock densities, ecological vegetation zones, wildlife population densities, non-pastoral land-use strategies and different grassland zones with varying grass species compositions (Reid et al., 2005). The authors also identify trends towards bush encroachment, the fragmentation of pasture land, the implementation of farming, changing fire regimes, conflicts with wildlife populations, the spread of animal diseases, the competition with non-pastoral land uses such as farming and the difficult situation for pastoral groups when dealing with the rapid changes of the recent past. They mention that under these conditions, 'pastoral success depends largely on tracking patchy resources through time' (Reid et al., 2005, p. 46) and that pastoralists must maintain both their access to key resources and their high mobility to ensure the success of their livelihoods.

This need also implies that pastoral groups must respond to externally driven transformation processes such as development projects that operate in their regions or the designation of conservation areas for wildlife protection and tourism. In a later work, Reid (2012) challenges the notion of a conservation approach that excludes pastoralists from a conservation area. She recalls the mutual use of the savannah ecosystem by both wildlife and pastoral people over millennia, and combines different perspectives on pastoral people, domestic animals, wildlife, degradation processes and conservation efforts, farming, land tenure, conflicts and demographic change. Her book *Savannas of Our Birth* can be read as a history of pastoral groups in East Africa and the complex history of pastoral landscapes, constructing a positive image of co-existence between wildlife and pastoralists.

In the following section, I discuss the land-cover changes described so far in relation to the notion of ecological invasion. Not only from the perspective of an outsider but, strikingly, also that of an insider, invasions are crucial to understanding the dynamics of pastoral savannah landscapes.

Invasions and 'evasions' in East Pokot

So far, I have tried to capture the landscape changes and social transformations in East Pokot over the past 200 to 250 years, and the results presented here go far beyond my initial expectations about the extent of changing environments in pastoral landscapes. The changes in the recent past, especially in forage composition (Bollig & Schulte, 1999; Vehrs, 2016) and the profound social transformations (Greiner et al., 2013; Oesterle, 2007) are well documented. However, developments over past centuries and their gradual and, at times, also rapid shifts along with the contemporary scale of landscape-level changes are less well understood. As shown in the previous chapters, the profound bush encroachment process has a huge impact on local livelihoods and constitutes an enormous challenge to current land-use practices. But not everything that has had a far-reaching impact on local livelihoods can be detected easily – some elements simply no longer exist. Whereas the invasive processes focus on species that enter and occupy a new space over short periods of time, a reverse process that could also be identified and termed 'evasion' (Lat.: *evadere* – to evade, escape or avoid)[1], for instance in the case of defaunation and the use of fire for land management. The evasion of a landscape agent

---

[1]   As outlined before, big-game species have completely vanished from the region north of Lake Baringo (a process that could also to some extent be explained with the concept of avoidance). However, the idea of 'evasion' is rather an attempt to point out that it is not just invasive processes that have an enormous impact. It is also necessary to consider evasive processes in the sense that, when landscape agents are no longer present, they impact on the ecosystem with their absence.

therefore describes the retreat of a species, or another agent, such as fire, whereupon the landscape changes due to the missing effects of these agents.

This section critically discusses the temporality of the ecological encroachment processes – especially the ecological invasions – and the pastoralists' abilities to respond to them.[2] The results of the environmental changes described in Chapter 5 cannot be viewed as a mere shift from one state to another – for instance, from a grassland savannah to a bushland savannah. It is more the case that the pastoral landscape has changed several times in both the composition of species and forage quality as well as in its extent and fragmentation.

Before the pastoral Pokot formed in the mid-eighteenth century, Lake Baringo had been desiccated for a couple of decades and conditions were unsuitable for pastoralism. With the appearance of a wetter climatic period and the re-emergence of the lake, pastoral groups migrated to the region in northern Baringo and started to inhabit the lake sites and their surroundings. The following time was characterised not only by the increase in number of the pastoralists and the contestation of access to land and resources between various ethnic groups, but also by an open savannah landscape and the co-existence of people and wildlife. In the nineteenth century, the Baringo plains were home to huge wildlife populations, with large herds of elephants and other herbivore and carnivore species roaming the wetlands around the lake and the savannahs beyond. Their former appearance in East Pokot is still observable in many ways – for instance in the naming of different places (e.g. the place of the elephants) or during ceremonies when leopard or lion skins are worn by some elders or giraffe tails are used. In oral history, both the existence and the extinction of wildlife is remembered, and the latter can be dated back to the mid-twentieth century. The defaunation, at least from a scientific point of view, had a strong impact on the environment and initiated the acacia bush encroachment process.

The extinction of elephants, however, cannot be explained by the limited elephant hunting by pastoral and agro-pastoral Pokot. Instead, it was the international demand for ivory and the desire for wildlife hunts in the late nineteenth and early twentieth century that triggered the defaunation process. As described in Chapter 5, wildlife hunters visited Lake Baringo frequently, publishing their 'successes' in *The Wide World Magazine*. Together with the customary hunts for wildlife and the European hunting and exploration expeditions, the demand for ivory put the elephant populations under pressure. But

---

[2]   My theoretical discussion focuses especially on the invasions of plant species. However, to highlight the variability of land-cover changes and the interdependences of land-use and land-cover changes, I also consider other invasive processes such as animal diseases or conflicts.

even beyond the elephant populations, Europeans have drastically depleted wildlife populations almost to a point of local extinction.

The results of the nearly complete removal of wildlife from the Pokot territory are still omnipresent. The incremental acacia bush encroachment can be referred to as a consequence of the missing 'sustainers' of the savannah. Also the changing grazing and browsing patterns of other herbivores and the demise of a significant spectrum of browsers shifted the grass–bush competition in the savannah landscape, fostering the establishment of the bush savannah at the expense of the grass savannah. This biotic change, coupled with stern colonial measures, also disadvantaged fire as a key mechanism and tool in maintaining a grass savannah.

The gradual cessation of the use of fire for pasture management had a strong impact on the landscape composition, with two factors playing a major role in this process. First, the slow reduction in the amount of combustible material led to fires being less intensive, which possibly had a positive impact on the establishment of shrub and tree species. Second, over time, the increase of human populations prohibited large-scale, high-intensity fires because damage to humans and livestock could no longer be avoided. As Pokot elders narrate, a few decades ago, grass cover was extensive and grasses still grew waist high, providing both forage for cattle and fuel for fires. The dry grasses in the plains were burnt regularly at the end of the dry season to stimulate the growth of fresh grasses. These large-scale, high-intensity fires also had a second effect beyond the restoration of grass forage. The heat of the fires retarded the growth of small bushes and shifted competition between bushes and grasses in favour of the latter. Therefore, the landscape agents – wildlife and fire – had a strong impact on creating and maintaining the savannah ecosystem in East Pokot and still influence it by their absence. The slow and incremental bush encroachment through acacia species is the main outcome of their 'evasion'.

Besides this slow process of landscape change, I address a much more rapid change in the following: the ecological invasion. I already mentioned one example in Chapter 6 when describing the spread of the native plant species of *Dodonaea viscosa*. In the following, I further illustrate the rapid expansions of plant species using the examples of the alien species *Prosopis juliflora* and *Opuntia stricta*, and use this to question the common understanding of the 'invasion' term and promote a more holistic understanding that includes changes *of* and *in* the environment.

Prosopis juliflora *at Lake Baringo*

Prosopis juliflora is an evergreen tree belonging to the *Fabaceae* family. It was introduced to Kenya in 1973 (Choge et al., 2009) and to Baringo in the 1980s in response to the deforestation and degradation of the lake site around Lake Baringo (Mwangi & Swallow, 2008). The tree has nitrogen-fixing properties and is drought resistant. It can provide local livelihoods with several goods and ecosystem services such as firewood, forage for browsing species, timber, the resources for charcoal production or honey production and the rehabilitation of the soil (Mwangi & Swallow, 2008). Becker et al. (2016) mention that *Prosopis juliflora* is highly competitive against other tree species at Lake Baringo such as *Balanites aegiyptiaca* and *Vachellia tortilis*; and, furthermore, it impedes the growth of ground cover and grasses. The current state of tree expansion covers the southern and western shores of Lake Baringo, the southern region of the Njemps flats towards Lake Bogoria, and a few patches in the north-east and in the north-west of Lake Baringo (Mwangi & Swallow, 2005). The rapid expansion is often termed an invasion (Becker et al., 2016; Maundu et al., 2009; Mwangi & Swallow, 2005, 2008; Mworia et al., 2011), whereby Mwangi and Swallow (2008) state that the characteristics of the expansion also depend on how it is perceived by local people.

In a study at different *Prosopis juliflora* sites in Kenya, the most important impacts of the tree expansion were identified as the encroachment of pastureland and farmland and its growth in homesteads (Maundu et al., 2009). Whereas officials and scientists are still discussing the positive and negative impacts of *Prosopis juliflora* (greening of degraded land vs invasion of farming and pasture land), two thirds of the respondents in the case study at Lake Baringo state that 'life would be better without Prosopis' (Maundu et al., 2009, p. 33). Another study from South Africa indicates that although the expansion of *Prosopis juliflora* into pastureland reduced the rangeland grazing capacity in the Nama Karoo, grazing capacity improved after the clearance of the trees even under conditions of heavy grazing (Ndhlovu et al., 2011). Furthermore, biological control of the *Prosopis juliflora* expansion started in the 1980s and 1990s in South Africa with the introduction of the seed beetles *Algarobius prosopis* (1987) and *Neltumius arizonensis* (1993) that infest and damage the seeds of the plant (Klein, 2002). The implementation of biological pest control through *Algarobius prosopis* (seed beetle) is also being discussed in Kenya, but has not yet been implemented (Ogutu et al., 2008; van Klinken et al., 2009). Moreover, the damaging effect of the conchuela bug (*Chlorochroa ligata*) has been known since the 1970s (Smith & Ueckert, 1974). Even other animal species such as livestock, on the other hand, can have a detrimental effect. Whereas the damage of livestock browsing on the seeds is rather limited, this browsing actually contributes to the seed dispersal of the *Prosopis* species (Alvarez et al., 2016; Bovey, 2016).

The spread of *Prosopis juliflora* at Lake Baringo occurred within a few decades since the 1980s, and it has created many new challenges and some opportunities for the population living at the lake. However, its further potential spread of *Prosopis juliflora* is limited spatially (Alvarez et al., 2019).[3]

Opuntia *in Northern Baringo and Laikipia County*

Other invasive plant species introduced to Kenya in the mid-twentieth century (exact dates are not verified) belong to the *Cactaceae* family. At Lake Baringo, for instance, *Opuntia stricta* grows in association with *Opuntia elatior* (Muniappan et al., 2009; Shackleton et al., 2017; Zimmermann et al., 2009) and forms thick stands in some places around the lake. The *Opuntia* species are well adapted to arid environments, are able to reproduce sexually and asexually, and can outcompete native plant species (Zimmermann et al., 2009).

On the Laikipia Plateau, at a short distance from East Pokot but at higher elevations, the expansion of *Opuntia stricta* took place rapidly. It encroached on several regions and had a strong negative impact on pastoral land use (Strum et al., 2015). The pastoralists in Laikipia started to avoid the area of the *Opuntia stricta* invasion, and, as a result, the population density of pastoralists increased in other areas that were not yet highly affected by the plant's encroachment. The avoidance of affected areas is one strategy with which to deal with the negative outcomes of the expansion of the plant. Another way to respond to the increasing *Opuntia* population is to invent innovative strategies such as producing juice or wine from its fruits (Sitole, 2016).

Similar to the *Prosopis* situation, biological control of the expansion of *Opuntia* species is also possible with the scale insect *Dactylopius opuntiae* (Denoth et al., 2002; Foxcroft & Hoffmann, 2000). Furthermore, regular fires seem to curtail its expansion and the distance to water sources (> 1km) also confines its growth (Foxcroft et al., 2004).

Although the expansion of the two plant species *Prosopis juliflora* and *Opuntia* species is characterised *per definitionem* as an invasive process, Pokot pastoralists do not care much about either.[4] In the case of *Prosopis juliflora*

---

[3]   The access to ground water is an important factor, as are the soil properties. The Marigat plains in the southern part of Lake Baringo are alluvial plains offering special soil properties that also influence the expansion of *Prosopis juliflora*. The dynamics of the expansion and its effects on a possible future spread are therefore more complex than presented here.

[4]   The perception of the impact of this ecological invasion on the local population depends heavily on who is being considered. Whereas Pokot pastoralists have not experienced major constraints as a result of this invasive spread, Il Chamus agropastoralists on the riparian areas of the Lake Baringo are highly constrained by it. Little (2019) outlines the spread of *Prosopis juliflora* in their region and illustrates these descriptions with comparative photographs from the 1980s and early 2000s. Whereas mobile Pokot pastoralists can avoid infested regions, more sedentary Il Chamus are heavily impacted by the expansion, because pasture and croplands are overgrown, thorn

at Lake Baringo, the north and western shores are still uninfested, and pastoralists' access to fresh water is not adversely affected. Occasionally, herders mention that the poisonous thorns of *Prosopis juliflora*[5] cause some problems, but, overall, neither the tree species' introduction nor its expansion have had a direct impact on pastoral livelihoods so far.[6] The pastoral Pokot are also still not much concerned about the expansion of the *Opuntia* species. In contrast to other regions in Kenya (e.g. the Laikipia highlands), the spread of the plant in East Pokot is not yet infesting former grasslands to any large extent. The species is found mostly in the town centres of the region and occasionally in remote areas such as dam sites or former homesteads where *Opuntia* species was used to demarcate land boundaries.

The rapid expansion of Dodonaea viscosa *in the absence of human influence*

The invasion process of *Dodonaea viscosa* was described in Chapter 6, where I related its rapid spread mainly due to current land-use changes in the agropastoral highlands. However, the expansion cannot be reduced to the anthropogenic land-cover changes alone, but must also be understood with all its inconsistencies. For instance, in other mountain regions above 1,250 metres above sea level, such as Mt Chepchok and Mt Korossi, *Dodonaea viscosa* is expanding rapidly, and the oral histories of both places indicate a trend similar to that depicted in the Churo highlands. In past decades, *Dodonaea viscosa* populations have increased from a few individuals to a population that dominates whole regions. In the case of Mt Korossi, both farming attempts and burning are very limited for two reasons. First, the mountain site is less suitable for inhabitation, because fresh water sources are limited, and the

---

injuries cause serious infections in some cases, and the sweet seed pods of *Prosopis juliflora* exert a strong negative impact on their goats' dental health (Maundu et al., 2009).

[5] In Pokot language, it is also known as 'Prosopis' or the Kiswahili term '*mathenge*'.

[6] Apart from at Lake Baringo, *Prosopis juliflora* grows abundantly mainly in the town centres where it was introduced by outsiders, as in the case in Nginyang, Chemolingot and Loruk – sometimes just with few individual trees as in Chepkalacha and Kadingding. In Nginyang and Chemolingot, the tree is spreading in the town centres and along the river Nginyang where it can draw on ground water. In Chepkalacha, however, the tree is not spreading due to the limited access to ground water. But, at some distance from the centre of Chepkalacha, a small wetland area is located that is used currently for grazing because grasses still grow abundantly after the water has drained off and evaporated. In this wetland, one exemplar of *Prosopis juliflora* has become established and might change the face of this wetland over the next few years.

closest reliable water sources are to be found at Lake Baringo in the south or at Tuwö Dam in the north. Moreover, the higher elevations of the mountain site are officially restricted to dry-season grazing (as is the case at Mt Paka). One elderly person reported that in 1975, the top of Mt Korossi was plain and overgrown with grasses, and no trees, not even *Dodonaea viscosa*, were to be found.

> In 1975 we lived here at Mt Korossi and only few other people lived around here. There were fewer trees, and *Dodonaea viscosa*, the plant that is dominant now, was not growing here, not even this plant called *chepkamatian*[7] [not identified]. Here in Chepelion there was a very nice plain full of grasses. The hills around here were also full of grasses – no trees, no *Dodonaea viscosa*. (Musa Akortepa, 19 July 2015)

At Mt Chepchok, the situation is slightly different, but also exemplifies the complexity of the *Dodonaea viscosa* invasion. Here, no homesteads were constructed until 2015 and no farming took place. Whether fire was used for land management in the past is unknown, but it is reasonable to assume so because the use of fire for pasture regeneration is not prohibited by the elders (with the exception of Mt Paka). Although land-cover changes through farming are not observable, the population of *Dodonaea viscosa* has spread on top of the mountain and is competing with the grass vegetation. The expansion of *Dodonaea viscosa* – from the view of the pastoralists – suppresses the establishment of grasses and does not contribute in a positive way to livestock herding because neither grazing nor browsing species profit from its growth.

However, to a large extent, the expansion of *Dodonaea viscosa* in the Churo highlands can be attributed to the land-use changes of the past in which land was cleared constantly and sometimes burnt for farming. This land-use and land-cover change opened a 'plant invasion window' (Johnstone, 1986, p. 382) or, as it was later called, a 'transient window of opportunity' (Pyšek et al., 2004, p. 106; taken from Valéry et al., 2008, p. 1349). The rapid expansion of *Dodonaea viscosa* can therefore be attributed to a 'successive invasion' (Shigesada & Kawasaki, 1997, p. 4): the plant colonises bare ground left by the clearing of fields. The plant itself probably did not invade the pastures of

---

[7]   This plant is most likely to be *Hypoestes forskaolii* ssp. *hildebrandtii* (Lindau) I. Darbysh. (in personal communication with Dr Miguel Alvarez from the University of Bonn). It might be an indicator of overgrazing in the lower mountainous region of Mt Paka where the increased availability of water in recent years has resulted in more intensive grazing by cattle, goats, camels and sheep. First evidence of this can be found in studies in the central rift valley of Ethiopia where the observed dissimilarity of species compositions such as *Hypoestes forskaolii* is related to heavy grazing (Yadeta et al., 2018). However, the exact ecological processes observed in the Mt Paka region have yet to be investigated further.

the Churo highlands before the implementation of farming in the region in the mid-twentieth century. Oral accounts (reported in Chapter 6) indicate that *Dodonaea viscosa* was not a dominant species in the highland environment until it started its unprecedented expansion a few decades ago.

In the following section, the three cases mentioned here will be considered as ecological invasions, and I discuss different scientific notions of the invasion term. Then I use these cases to illustrate a more general understanding of invasions beyond the hitherto focus on plant species.

The terminology of ecological invasions

The terminology for biological invasions has yet to be finally determined, and alternative terms attributed to 'biological invasions' or 'invasive species' are manifold such as alien, allochthonous, exotic, non-indigenous, imported, non-native, immigrant, coloniser or naturalised (Valéry et al., 2008, who refer to Elton, 1958). Since the mid-twentieth century, when the debate about invasions started, the term has not been defined clearly, and many attempts and interpretations have followed. A short, geographical definition is given by Vermeij (1996, p. 4), who refers to the criterion of 'nativeness' of a species to a predefined region: 'By invasion I mean the geographical expansion of a species into an area not previously occupied by that species.'

The assumption that a species must overcome a geographical barrier to become an invasive species seems evident, but does not address the issue of time: for instance, at what time a species was (or is) native to what environment. Furthermore, the definition does not pay attention to the natural process of land-cover change itself, but rather to the distinction between different, more or less stable environments in the world. For instance, a plant species could encroach in its region of origin but would be an invader in other regions in the world. It could be that the same process is then termed differently. Valéry et al. (2008) give the example of the European starling *Sturnus vulgaris L.* that was reported to be expanding in Europe but *invading* North America (with reference to Feare 1984).

Therefore, other authors try to overcome the shortcomings of the spatial definition and have focused on other aspects such as the impact of a species.

> We developed our proposed nomenclature on the explicit recognition that some new species 'have a negligible effect on the new environment, whereas some have [a] very large impact' (Davis & Thompson, 2000, p. 227).

> We proposed that usage of the word 'invasion' be confined to those circumstances in which the newcomers have a large impact on the community, ecosystem, or economy. (Davis & Thompson, 2002, p. 196)

According to this definition, a plant species with a high impact should be referenced as invasive. But, the impact of a species is difficult to access and highly interpretative. Therefore, it is an unstable criterion with which to describe invasive processes (Valéry et al., 2008). Although the impact of a species or its domination in an ecosystem plays an important role and is important to understand the ecological (invasive) processes, impact alone is not a sufficient condition. Therefore, I have chosen a third definition that considers not only the species itself as important but also the environmental conditions.

> From an ecological viewpoint, an invasive species is finally always alien to its novel environment as a result of either a change OF the environment (alien species) or a change IN the environment (native species or alien species that spread after a lag time). ... A biological invasion consists of a species acquiring a competitive advantage following the disappearance of natural obstacles to its proliferation, which allows it to spread rapidly and to conquer novel areas within recipient ecosystems in which it becomes a dominant population. (Valéry et al., 2008, pp. 1348–49, emphasis original)

The turning away from the species-centred definition of an ecological invasion is most interesting here.[8] Accordingly, an invasion can either take place if a plant succeeds in encroaching an area to a large extent (geographical definition) with a particular impact on the environment or local livelihoods (impact-driven definition). In contrast to other definitions, it can be either the plant that invades new territory or a change in the environment that triggers the invasive behaviour of a specific, even a native, plant species. Following this understanding of an invasion, not only *Prosopis juliflora* and *Opuntia* species, but also *Dodonaea viscosa* can be regarded as invasive species, because the land-use change that occurred in the highlands around Churo promoted its invasive behaviour.

However, this definition also has its limitations, and some characteristics of the spread of *Dodonaea viscosa* cannot be explained easily by changing land-use practices or land-cover changes. This has been exemplified in the last section on the expansion of *Dodonaea viscosa* in regions in which impacts

---

[8] Due to the numerous concepts of invasion biology (Enders et al., 2020; Falk-Petersen et al., 2006) and the diverging understandings of these concepts (Humair et al., 2014), I decided to focus on only a very limited number of invasion concepts. In the following, I do not concentrate primarily on which requirements have to be fulfilled for a plant to be classified as invasive *per definitionem*, but on recognising that rapid changes in the ecosystem can be caused by either alien species or changes in the environment that enable native plant species to spread more than previously. The latter can be considered to be the case with the apophyte species as *Dodonaea viscosa* that has only been able to expand due to changes in the environment.

of human action (at least visible human impacts on the land surface) are not detectable. It appears that *Dodonaea viscosa* invades not only human-influenced environments but also mountain sites in East Pokot where farming or fire management are absent.

The second limitation is more general and refers to the timescale of the invasion processes. This is a question that will have to be left unanswered here, despite its importance. The term 'rapid' does not adequately describe the time span of a plant invasion, although it seems reasonable to differentiate between incremental bush encroachment (over some centuries, e.g. in the case of the acacia expansion in East Pokot) and rapid invasion (over some decades, as observable in the case of *Dodonaea viscosa* in the Pokot highlands). The distinction that can be made here is also based on the ability of pastoralists to respond to the changes. Whereas the slow bush encroachment has allowed pastoralists to respond by, for example, adapting herd structures, the invasion of *Dodonaea viscosa* in the highlands has been met merely by avoiding the encroached regions.

The concepts of 'alien' or 'invasive' have also been adopted in the humanities, and Comaroff (2017) illustrates the controversies about new species and their dispersal in the context of politics, South African immigration discourses, the receding relevance of national borders, and the increasing emphasis on new demarcations along the idea of place, and belonging in the multi-species arena. The debate about what a 'natural' environment actually might resemble and which 'invaders' are considered disruptive gained traction especially in the context of conservation activities in southern Africa with special attention being paid to the issue of alien invaders (Comaroff & Comaroff, 2001). Certainly, this is a highly political topic, which, in many aspects, also reverts to public debates about migration, tradition, identity, and belonging. The Cartesian division of nature and culture is just as prominent in these debates as the question of what actually is 'natural' in a specific ecosystem. That environments change over time – partly due to changes in climate such as the desiccation of Lake Baringo in the eighteenth century, and partly due to anthropogenic influences such as the massive hunting of big game in the Baringo region and the defaunation – appears obvious in retrospect. However, the public discourses dealing with transformation processes in the present are much more intense, because they also involve the struggle for a desirable landscape image that is contested by numerous parties. What landscapes actually must resemble and what is harmful to them is assessed entirely differently by conservationists, farmers, or pastoralists, because they may 'be one person's livelihood and another's apocalypse' (Comaroff & Comaroff, 2001, p. 650).

Land invasion processes and its variations

This also holds true for the invasive processes that are described here; and their impact, although spatially limited, is huge. For the pastoral Pokot, this impact perspective holds true only for the case of *Dodonaea viscosa* that is spreading in the highlands, and in recent years, also in some mountain sites in East Pokot, while *Prosopis juliflora* and *Opunita spp.* exert a strong impact on the lake dwelling populations. The spatial dimension of pastoral landscape transition is as complex as its temporal dimension. The East Pokot pastoral landscapes range from the escarpment area in the west, to the lake site in the south, to the escarpment area in the east and the arid lands in the north. The acacia bush encroachment is observable all over the lowlands up to the highland areas, whereas the invasions of the plant species mentioned above are limited to small areas and will probably not expand all over the pastoral landscapes.

The process of 'invasion' – with its rapid temporal but limited spatial dimension – can also be conceived beyond its application to plant species, as other rapid processes also influence land-cover changes. As mentioned before, the Turkana–Pokot war (1969–84) had a strong impact on spatially limited areas, especially the border zones, due to the subsequent under-utilisation of the pasture land. The conflict between the two groups has a long history, and each group has invaded the territory of the other from time to time. Raids happen regularly, and livestock is raided to create wealth and gain prestige. In the past, these raids involved hundreds of warriors who invaded the enemy's land. Furthermore, Pokot often narrate stories about the time when Turkana started to arm themselves and conquered Pokot territory during the Turkana–Pokot war. During this time, Pokot pastoralists were pushed towards the south, unable to reconquer their land until they too became armed. After the end of the Pokot–Turkana war in the 1980s, Pokot pastoralists expanded their territory far into the north and occupied land that was formerly inhabited by Turkana people. The fluctuations of land occupation and the raids into enemy land by both groups can also be viewed as an invasion process. Because these conflicts then also left the border zones unoccupied, the evasion of pastoralists from these areas also had an effect on the land cover. As Conant (1982) shows, bush encroachment increased in areas with under-management.

The same logic of invasiveness holds true for the outbreaks of not only livestock diseases such as trypanosomiasis, East Coast Fever, rinderpest or contagious caprine pleuropneumonia but also human diseases such as smallpox that affected the Pokot in the late twentieth century. Over time, the outbreak of a disease can have tremendous negative effects on livestock populations, and herders do not tire of stressing the impact of any outbreak of an animal disease. Once contagious caprine pleuropneumonia (*lowkoi*) starts to affect goats, the danger of losing a large share of the herd is high. Therefore, the diversification of the herd structure is important to minimise risks to livelihoods, but the rapid spread of a disease among livestock and the subsequent loss of a large share of a household's herd can also be called an invasive process.

Perhaps even the development projects planned for East Pokot could be referred to as an invasive process because they initiate a rapid change, and pastoral people engage in heated debates over their consequences. Since 2014, this has been the case through the construction of roads and geothermal energy infrastructure in the rural areas of East Pokot. This opening of the region to external influences and how elders evaluate their effects is the topic of the following chapter in which I discuss the future of pastoral landscape.

9

Ecological Challenges and Social Transformations

The history of the pastoral Pokot, their formation in the eighteenth century, their specialisation in the nineteenth century and their diversification in the twentieth century demonstrate their capacity to deal with and respond to changing circumstances in several ways. Contrary to the often assumed resistance to change (Schneider, 1959), Oesterle describes the profound and rapid changes of pastoralism in East Pokot that 'transformed from specialised, highly mobile and subsistence-oriented cattle herding to largely sedentary and market-oriented keeping of small-stock' (Oesterle, 2008, p. 81) in the first decade of the twenty-first century. He illustrates the trend towards economic diversification of livelihoods, sedentarisation of former mobile households and a social stratification of Pokot communities. Oesterle highlights two important trends: first, the shifting focus from a cattle-oriented mobile pastoralism to a more sedentary form of small stock husbandry; second, the implementation of farming techniques in a formerly specialised pastoral group.

A trend Oesterle was not yet able to observe is the emergence of massive external interventions through development projects that have led to fundamental changes to the situation of the pastoral Pokot over a short period of time. Again, enormous landscape-level changes are looming on the horizon. Conservation projects aim to protect newly designated areas particularly at the fringes of Pokot territory (Greiner, 2016a), and large-scale geothermal energy production has the potential to revolutionise pastoral landscapes in the Pokot heartlands (Wetang'ula, 2017). The same is potentially true for other projects in the making in recent years, such as the discovery of oil in Turkana County (Johannes et al., 2014). Ferguson (2005) rightfully questions which characteristics such engagement by governmental and non-governmental actors in rural areas of the African continent might bring. The engagement of private companies in extracting minerals, or, as in this case, the development of a geothermal infrastructure and the generation of electricity by state actors, raises the question of whose interests are being pursued here and to what extent the interests of the local population can actually be represented and respected.

'Development' in East Pokot

From a government perspective, East Pokot was long treated marginally, and very few external influences were deployed in the region, as was also demonstrated in Chapter 3 describing the involvement of the churches in East Pokot, in terms of formal education, water infrastructure and agricultural measures, which were not supported by the state until the 1980s. By that time, the status of East Pokot was measured primarily in terms of its economic capacity and the land potential of East Pokot was listed as 'rangeland' (on a scale ranging from 'high' to 'medium' and 'low', followed by 'rangeland' at the bottom) (UNESCO, 1987, p. 14). In the 1990s, from an official report listing cash crops and food crops, East Pokot was still reported as having 'none' (Republic of Kenya, 1994a).

As stated in the project completion report of the Baringo Pilot Semi-Arid Areas Project, 'in the past, most economic development activity had been in the higher potential areas; arid and semi-arid areas had not benefitted from the relatively rapid growth experienced elsewhere in Kenya' (World Bank, 1990, p. 67). The first external interventions came from non-state actors, especially the churches; other stakeholders, including state institutions, joined in only later. However, since the onset of the external interventions, for instance the Freedom from Hunger Council and German Agro Action in the agro-pastoral highlands in the late 1970s, it has been evident that most efforts were made along the existing roads and in their vicinity. Thus, the focus was on both the region along the B4 to Nginyang, Chemolingot and the adjacent Kositei, as well as on the highland region along the Maralal road where agricultural development has been particularly successful and shaped the highland region for the long term. This can be seen in particular in the activities of the Baringo Pilot Semi-Arid Areas Project in the 1980s, which were concentrated along the roads (e.g. Chemolingot, Barbello, Chepkalacha, Churo and Tangulbei) and conducted water harvesting projects, or in a few cases established irrigation farming plots (World Bank, 1990). This focus on the development along the roads, can be ascertained for all project measures; not only agriculture and education but also for the establishment of water infrastructures (Republic of Kenya, 1994a).

This becomes particularly interesting when looking at the infrastructure recently built up during project implementation of the Geothermal Development Company. As Map 7 shows, a network of roads has recently been built throughout the rural area connecting previously remote regions with the centres in East Pokot and beyond to the rest of Kenya. Currently, the GDC project is also the strongest promoter of infrastructural development in East Pokot. Although there are some projects besides this mega-project for geothermal

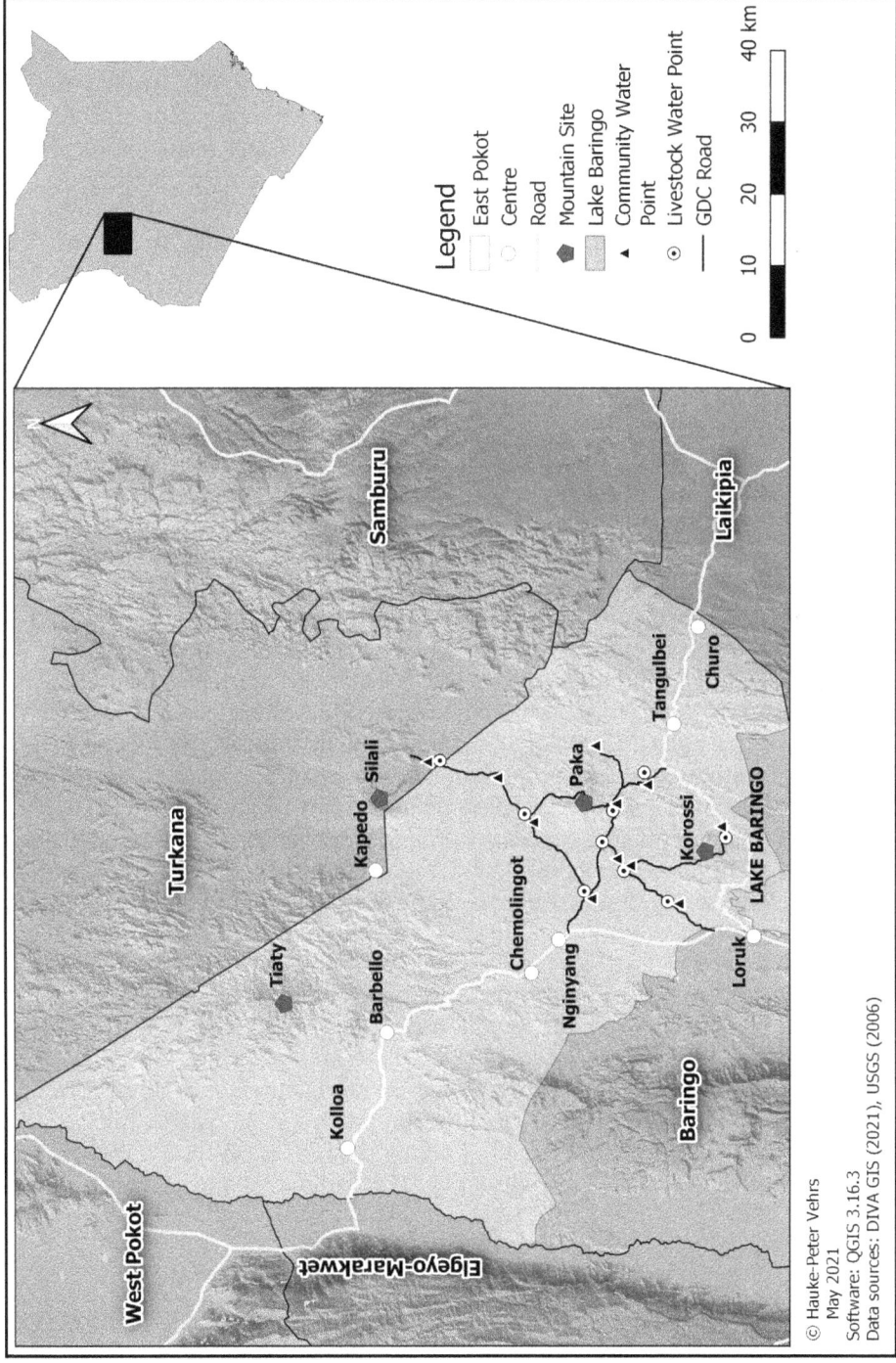

Map 7. The GDC road and water infrastructure, 2019 (Hauke-Peter Vehrs; spatial data on roads and water points provided by David Greven).

energy production that also pursue a similar development idea, these are all small compared to the efforts of GDC.[1]

The Geothermal Development Company Limited (GDC) started to implement its development project in East Pokot since the early 2010s (GDC, 2017), and it has established drilling sites in the four larger mountain areas of Korossi, Chepchok, Paka and Silali. The Kenya Electricity Generating Company (KenGen) and, since 2008, especially the GDC are responsible for promoting the expansion of geothermal infrastructure in Kenya. The first explorations outside of the Pokot context took place in Olkaria in the 1970s and 1980s, but the industry has experienced its biggest push since the 2000s, especially after the establishment of the GDC. So far, several geothermal units have been established in Kenya – for instance at Olkaria and Oserian as well as in Eburru and Menengai – and many more are planned. The main target is to 'develop green energy for Kenya from geothermal resources' (GDC, 2020) and therefore create a progressive and environmentally friendly energy future for East Africa. But the implementation of such a massive project may also exert a negative influence for local residents, as observed in the case of Olkaria where approximately 2,000 people were forcefully evicted in the course of setting up the geothermal projects in 2013 (Schade, 2017).

In East Pokot, plans are in place to construct a total of 15 to 20 geothermal wells over the next few years with an estimated potential of 3,000 MW (GDC, 2017). Furthermore, murram roads have been constructed to the mountain sites, and pipelines transport water to the well sites along with the community and livestock water points (see Map 7). Additionally, the project provides some job opportunities to the local communities, for instance as security guards. In general, it can be said that this development project represents the largest state intervention ever in the region with a prospect of long-term economic investment. Previous development or aid projects such as the Baringo Pilot Semi-Arid Areas Project or those of the Kenya Freedom from Hunger Council were always limited in time and money and therefore had a much smaller impact on local livelihoods. An important aspect of the implementation of the geothermal plants is the long-term time perspective and the extensive infra-structural reconstruction of the region. As can be seen in Map 7, the entire remote area is being made accessible, and these massive structural changes in the region are also being accompanied by the facilitation of many new opportunities such as increased mobility (internally for the pastoral Pokot, goods or livestock, but also externally for actors such as the military). There is little doubt that the changes introduced by GDC will have a profound impact

---

[1]   This includes recent projects that also still focus on water supply such as the Kenyan Red Cross Society's (KRCS) establishment of the 2013 Chesimirion Dam and the Rehabilitation of Arid Environments project that aims to restore grasslands in Baringo so that they will be useful for livestock herding (Mureithi et al. 2016).

on local livelihoods. If the development projects are expanded further, the abandoning of pastoralism is yet another option for some pastoralists. Perhaps the generation of revenues from the geothermal energy project, or other project connected with oil drilling or conservation, could be a viable option providing alternative livelihood approaches in the future. State-led development initiatives that are increasingly gaining in importance (Mosley & Watson, 2016) expedite change in the region both in terms of infrastructure, visible in the construction of roads or water pipelines (Greiner et al., 2021; Klagge et al., 2020), and in the way Pokot engage with development projects, the promises they represent for the future, and their own expectations towards, in this case, the GDC company also in terms of benefits it is expected to create.

In the following, I discuss alternative perspectives of possible future livelihoods besides cattle husbandry. Today's younger generation focuses on adapting to the new situation and the implementation of the GDC development project in East Pokot, emphasising the opportunities it offers. In this sense, the logic of cyclical succession of generation sets is used to justify and legitimise current changes. The initiation of the new generation set named Merkutwö in 2016 therefore offers the opportunity to anchor change and make it compatible with conventional pastoral perspectives.

Afterwards, I return to the bush encroachment debate and outline the possibilities of external interventions from a scientific perspective, and consider to what extent the restoration of the environment is possible or desirable. This would also bring about changes on the ground that do not fit into the pastoralist's land management. For this reason, I then discuss the future of pastoral livelihoods in the Kenyan context and the possibilities for pastoralists to adjust and adapt to rapid changes. One possible path for the future is therefore also exiting the pastoral way of life and turning towards completely different livelihood strategies.

Visions of the future beyond pastoralism

As has been described earlier, Pokot elders consider a renewal of pastoral structures possible, even if current trends may challenge existing configurations and the gerontocratic political system. It seems obvious to most pastoralists that their own future and that of the succeeding generation will clearly be shaped by a pastoral perspective. This does not seem surprising when one considers that, in the past, the alternatives to pastoral livelihoods were limited and that only a few children from pastoral families have so far experienced a different lifestyle or have taken a different path, for instance as is offered through formal education. Therefore, in the following, I do not focus on the pastoral visions of the future, but on visions that differ from them. It quickly becomes apparent that pastoral elements continue to have an important role in these visions about alternative future livelihood systems, so that one is inclined to speak not of a change in livelihoods, but rather of a shift in priorities and a reconfiguration of pastoral practices.

How the future is envisaged is first described through the eyes of a progressive member of the Paka community. Yuka is a pastoralist who finished grade seven of primary school some years ago and was hit by difficult circumstances in the recent past after most of his cattle were raided, leaving him in an uncertain situation. He decided to engage in several businesses as well as farming, and he keeps different kinds of livestock. He prefers to diversify his livelihood rather than follow one direction, and he points out that many members of the community have no choice but to focus on pastoralism, because they do not have the basic schooling and the command of Kiswahili language skills that give him access to fields that remain closed to them.

> Anybody who never went to school has no other work than herding. Their business is to compete with other [men] in numbers of wives and numbers of livestock. ... I tried a lot of businesses, selling and buying sugar and maize flour, and now I am riding a motorbike [motor-cycle taxi service]. This seems to be the best of all businesses so far. It brings more profit compared to other businesses I have done. You can get a profit of 1,000 [KSh] in a single Monday [market day] by riding motorbike. I am also a farmer, I grow maize. This [referring to his current job with the GDC] is the first casual work now. The biggest problem for me is the drought. When the drought comes, I close my businesses and move my animals to look for pastures. Another problem a businessmen faces is the money, since many people ask for a credit. Furthermore, I bring a lot of foodstuff to this place and use a lot of money for the transport. Only during rainy season, the business can bring in a small profit. ... I will not stop keeping my animals as well. Since I have a job, my animals will multiply in numbers because I have money and can buy food for my family. (Yuka, 12 June 2015)

Yuka is engaging in many different activities to generate income. Although he will not cease practising livestock husbandry, he identifies several constraints on future herding such as the regular sickness of animals, expensive drug treatments, the fluctuation of prices for livestock, the constant search for water and pasture, the problem of theft and raiding,[2] the risk of complete livelihood failure and the ongoing conflicts in the border zones.

However, the diversification of livelihood assets or the transition towards another livelihood approach is itself uncertain, and incentives are constrained. Oesterle recalls a lack of the 'power of the pen' in East Pokot, and relates it to

---

[2]   Pastoral Pokot distinguish between raiding and theft. In a raid, people steal livestock from another ethnic group, whereas theft is perceived as something happening within Pokot society that has to be judged by the council of elders in the *kokwö*.

Hodgson's description of the transformation of Maasais' masculine identities during the course of modernisation in Tanzania (Hodgson, 1999). He compares the difficult position of new livelihood approaches with very successful and uneducated pastoral Pokot who show that education does not necessarily correlate with a good life (Oesterle, 2007). Therefore, being a pastoralist is not only a viable but also a preferred strategy in the pastoral lowlands. This may also be true for future generations who find it difficult to break new ground and succeed with previously unknown strategies. In order to promote the gradual transition of pastoral livelihoods and to find support for it in the community, local politicians are trying to advocate development projects (e.g. GDC) within the pastoral community.

The former Member of County Assembly for the Paka region, Kibet Cheretei, frequently visited the Paka community during my fieldwork to discuss current developments with local people and build up acceptance for the new developments. Along with the recent development plans of the GDC, roads were built into East Pokot, providing easier mobility and wage labour but also access to the hinterland for the Kenyan army. As a local politician, Cheretei tried to explain the rapid changes to the community, emphasising the positive developments, discussing negative effects and persuading people not to hinder the construction workers. Along with the construction of roads, a water pipeline was built that feeds the geothermal wells with water as well as providing water to the local communities. Cheretei therefore argues as follows:

> When the water will come to this mountain, even the pasture is going to disappear. Because the availability of water everywhere means the concentration of people, [and the concentration] of animals is going to be high ... So, we need to turn the livelihood of the people from depending on animals to also going to this farming. (Kibet Cheretei, 1 July 2015)

In his future view of changing livelihoods, he argues for purposeful change and the support of pastoral people. He anticipates negative effects, such as overgrazing on Mt Paka – which is supposed to be a dry-season forage store – and the need to engage more intensively in farming. During his visits to Mt Paka, he also had to deal with the perceptions of people and mediate between the conflicting views of community members – for instance between elderly people and the younger generations. One way to convince people is to point out the possibilities of profiting from the opportunities provided by wage labour.

> I realised that people are willing to embrace change. Losirwule yesterday said: 'I have seen development and today I wear trousers because of GDC. If the people of GDC did not come to this place, I would not be having trousers.' Then, what he was saying is that they [Paka people] are willing to embrace development because the [strategy] of selling one goat at 2,000 KSh and surviving with that 2,000 KSh, and then selling

another goat – it is like a waste. And they are now seeing that if you can have a casual job to do, you can earn more money and you will [remain with] your goats, you will not sell your goats for food. (Kibet Cheretei, 1 July 2015)

Mediating these changes between Kenyan politics and local realities is a difficult task, and different perceptions of the world clash. On the one hand, the modernisation narrative guides the development plans of the GDC; on the other hand, pastoral people emphasise their views on the world and the recurrence of former generation sets that will return in future.

By having a generation that is going to come, like Merkutwö,[3] they [people of Mt Paka] believe that it was a rich generation [in the past]. It is a rich regeneration in terms of resources, pastures and many cows. People could get milk, and water was available in every river. And this mentality is also going to be adopted for the development that is going to come. When the GDC will come now, in this area will be many opportunities. There will be people doing *plumbering* [referring to the installation of machines], they are going to do their businesses, they are going to sell eggs, even to the people [from outside], who are doing the job [of the GDC]. There will be immense opportunities and these opportunities – in one way or another – are related to the generation of other [referring to past Pokot generations]. In the time of Merkutwö the opportunities were many. And in this order of the coming Merkutwö the opportunities are coming. (Kibet Cheretei, 1 July 2015)

Cheretei describes the future of the pastoral Pokot as being open to the developments and opportunities that will come, without neglecting the challenges that will accompany the changes. He uses the idea of the cyclical reinvention of generations to explain current changes to the Paka people. Therefore, Cheretei, who focuses on development and the representation of Pokot interests in the County Assembly, operates towards a transformation of the pastoral life as people know it, mediating between different cosmologies – the modernisation narrative and the perspectives of pastoral realities.

Both Yuka and Cheretei argue for a changing pastoral life due to changes in the pastoral landscape. Water provision by the GDC and the creation of job opportunities will impact on the way pastoralists arrange their livelihoods in the future. The visions are connected to revenue generation to sustain the household economy. In turn, the household herd does not need to be used to feed the family, and livestock wealth can be established. Furthermore, provision with fresh water along the GDC pipeline offers opportunities to grow vegetables in ways that are independent of the erratic and scarce precipitation

---

3   The Merkutwö generation set was initiated one year later in 2016.

in East Pokot. The visions of the future – at least from the perspective of Cheretei and many other politicians who emphasise economic development – include prosperity for the Pokot and provide many new opportunities.

However, by 2015, recent developments in the remote areas of East Pokot had only started to unfold their local impact, with pastoralism still the dominant way of living. To be a successful herder is still a great aspiration for many Pokot, although the conditions for establishing a wealthy pastoral household are challenging and are open to many risks. The pastoral livelihoods have reached a limit in terms of production and territorial expansion that is also informed by an increasing fragmentation of East Pokot pastoral landscapes.[4] The agro-pastoral and agricultural proportion of the population in East Pokot has increased steadily since the mid-twentieth century and forms a valuable alternative to pastoral livelihoods.

Environmental challenges and the contestation of pastoral landscapes

Pastoral people are currently exposed to many changes that have also taken place before in other pastoral landscapes. These changes confront them with an unprecedented environmental challenge that will shape the future of pastoral livelihoods in East Pokot. These challenges encompass not only the aforementioned bush encroachment and ecological invasion processes along with the increasing landscape fragmentation and conversion of former rangelands, but also diverging perspectives on rangeland management and restoration, and the strained relationship with the Kenyan state. Perhaps, the contestation of land use and the need to collaborate with state agents over the question about the future of pastoral livelihoods – rather than being marginalised and declared as bandits – is most important when it comes to responding to current changes. This includes the need for mutual understanding between pastoralists and state agents and their respective perspectives, and the open negotiation over land use and the identification of possible ways for pastoralists to participate in decision making. What makes this highly difficult, however, is the long history of mutual distrust. As a result, the relationship has continued to deteriorate in recent years. What is necessary is a convergence between the pastoral Pokot and the state, the recognition of state authority, and the need to cease illegal

---

[4]   The conflicts between pastoral groups and other actors escalate continuously during the dry season when herders migrate towards the border zones. During this time, herders and locals frequently clash in disputes over access to resources and private land, and the government intervenes in the interests of the people of the 'invaded' regions, as the following news reports show: 'Anarchy fears as Samburu, Pokot gunmen surround Laikipia farms' (Mwangi, 2017); 'Hundreds of cattle killed in police operation in Laikipia' (Munyeki, 2017).

practices including raiding, killing of enemies, and female circumcision – and for the pastoral Pokot to adopt state regulations into their own cosmology.

But also land-use and land-cover transformations will have a particularly important impact on the landscape configurations and therefore the possibilities for implementing pastoral livelihood strategies. In the case of the pastoral Pokot, negotiation processes about land access and recourse use are furthermore visible when, for instance, communal land use is gradually replaced by a variety of other land-use strategies. This process is observable in the cultivation of crops in the agro-pastoral highlands, the establishment of small enclosures in the pastoral areas and the construction of the geothermal power plants on the Paka, Korossi and Silali mountains. Among the Pokot, the negotiation of the enclosures in the pastoral areas is done *inter pares* and determines the temporary use of a limited resource: land. In contrast, the establishment of agricultural fields in the agro-pastoral areas is de facto a long-term appropriation of land that is mediated through the local authorities and perpetuates sedentary livelihoods. As has been shown, changes in pastoral landscapes are triggered by these increasing fragmentation processes that can also lead to habitat modifications and conversion. One of the major challenges in the management of rangelands in the pastoral landscape in East Pokot, and perhaps for other pastoral landscapes as well, is the incorporation of and dispute with new agents of change, and conflicting aspirations for these landscapes and land-use strategies being applied.

These internal fragmentation processes and external interventions of national actors, such as the GDC, will have a huge influence on how and where pastoralists can be situated. The construction of roads and geothermal wells, the establishment of community and livestock water points, the decrease in pasture land and the increase in conservation efforts will also shape the future pastoral landscape and people's livelihoods in East Pokot. These are being accompanied by the introduction of new technologies (e.g. mobile phones), the opportunities to engage in business and wage labour, the success of young men in acquiring wealth and therefore also challenging the gerontocratic social system, the advance of formal education and religion along with many other changes. For sure, successful herders will remain pastoralists in one way or the other. But others will follow alternative ways, either while continuing with a reduced livestock husbandry or without it altogether.

Furthermore, the construction of the geothermal wells is taking place on yet another level. The GDC represents national interests that also correspond to Kenya's Vision 2030. The appropriation of land is often communicated to the pastoral people, but the extent of the projects and their implications are often disregarded. The energy sector will be further expanded and is supposed to provide up to 5,000 MW by the year 2030 (Ngugi, 2012). The goal of such a project is to develop the country's economy, build infrastructure, improve living conditions for local communities and raise the standard of living in Kenya in general.

I want to argue that such development projects represent a certain idea that is steered by national or international actors. The same holds true for conservation projects established in the region (Ruko Conservancy, Kaptuya Community Conservancy, Ltungai Conservancy and the Laikipia Nature Conservancy; see Greiner 2012) that, on the one hand, seek to preserve or restore a desired state, but, on the other hand, also advocate a travelling idea that comes from outside the pastoral system. The conservation efforts of the past years have already led to a fragmentation of the open-property regimes in East Pokot, and they aimed to allocate land areas for conservation measures at the expense of the pastoral Pokot's access to and use of resources. The privatisation of land in the agro-pastoral highlands in Churo has informed the same trend of pastoral landscape fragmentation.

The issue of rapid changes initiated through development projects does not just affect pastoral Pokot but sometimes also raises the question of relations between different ethnic groups, as observable in the implementation of development projects in the border zones between Baringo, West Pokot and Turkana Counties. In the cases of oil drilling in Turkana County (Lind, 2017a) and the construction of a geothermal well at Mt Silali, both Turkana and Pokot people are claiming their territorial right to benefit from the exploitation of resources.

However, not all perspectives on change in East Pokot indicate that pastoralists will abstain from focusing on livestock husbandry. Rather, there exist the views – both from a pastoral and a scientific perspective – that rangeland capacity can be restored and that pastoral life can likewise be well positioned for the future.

The restoration of rangelands

Apart from the land management involved in dry-season pasture storage, pastoral Pokot do not shape their environments proactively. The idea of cutting trees and bushes to counteract the processes of bush encroachment and create space for grasses seems absurd, because in the view of many elderly pastoralists, the people and the environment will inevitably change with the initiation of the next generation set. Because the current bush-encroached environment is associated with the Kaplelach generation set, the forecast is that another environment with probably better conditions for grazing will commence with the following generations – a rejuvenated pastoral landscape will emerge. These two worldviews – we might call them the building and the dwelling perspectives (Ingold, 2000) – do not adapt to each other smoothly.

The ecological invasion processes described before confront the pastoral Pokot with new challenges that can arise rapidly. With reference to the biological control of invasion processes, scientists are discussing the possibilities of restoring ecosystems so as to absorb the negative effects of alien species and effectively control ecosystem development. The following quote demonstrates the considerations made when it comes to applying restoration techniques.

> We argue that management decisions to retain novel ecosystems are certain when goods and services provided by the system far outweigh the costs of restoration, for example in the case of intensively managed *Cenchrus* pastures. Decisions to return novel ecosystems to natural systems are also certain when the value of the system is low and restoration is easy and inexpensive as in the case of biocontrol of *Opuntia* infestations. In contrast, decisions whether to retain or restore novel ecosystems become complex and uncertain in cases where benefits are low and costs of control are high as, for example, in the case of stopping the expansion of *Prosopis* and *Juniperus* into semiarid rangelands. (Belnap et al., 2012, p. 569)

The notions of 'novel' and 'natural' ecosystems illustrate the difficulties that the restoration approach entails. The implicit idea of an ecosystem balance resonates here, and implicitly excludes the possibility of (necessary) changes to an ecosystem over time. This is not just essential in the context of climate change and the sometimes-rapid climatic variations involved. As the reconstruction of the transformations of pastoral landscapes in East Pokot over the last two hundred years has shown, ecosystems change through a large variety of different factors. At the same time, it becomes increasingly difficult for pastoral groups to respond to changing environments and landscape fragmentation in order to find ways to maintain their pastoral life. An active role in shaping the environment could therefore be a way to successfully respond to current environmental challenges and maintain a pastoral mode of living.

From a science perspective, however, implementing ecosystem interventions depends on their costs and benefits as well as on the associated perceived risks. For instance, introducing a natural enemy of an invasive species bears the risk that the newly introduced species will have unintended consequences for its new habitat, and this, in turn, might have negative effects on the environment and the local people. Many scientists have already analysed pastoral landscapes worldwide and suggest various solutions to restore degraded rangeland (Ombega et al., 2017). These include combatting biological invasions into pastureland (Ilukor et al., 2016), improving land-management systems and countervailing desertification (Weber & Horst, 2011). Furthermore, the control of bush encroachment processes for forage regeneration and tick control is evoked (Negasa et al., 2014) in which the branches can be used as barriers for the restoration of plant communities on bare ground (Kimiti et al., 2016). Furthermore, both formal and local knowledge can be used to fight animal diseases by not only educating pastoralists and increasing information dissemination through extension officers (Gustafson et al., 2015), but also applying local ecological knowledge for grassland restoration (Hudak, 1999). Moreover, the cultivation of grass species as fodder plants for a regular supply to the livestock (Lugusa et al., 2016) as well as the growth of other plant species as drought feed (Kagunyu & Wanjohi, 2015) can contribute to future pastoral livelihoods. From a scientific perspective, the rehabilitation of grasses is related to the reduction of grazing pressure and could occur relatively speedily. As Boonman states, 'one year of effective protection following bush clearance is enough to change this type of denuded land into a reasonable grass cover', but 'if rehabilitated land is not protected against overstocking, no effort is worthwhile' (1993, p. 56). Even the trade in carbon stocks for storing CO_2 in above-ground biomass is thought to be a way to integrate the pastoral livelihoods of the future into the global world (Dabasso et al., 2014).

But the gap between pastoral life and science is immense, and the question remains as to how pastoral landscapes will change in the future and how pastoral Pokot will both deal with changes and contribute to them. In contrast to the science-based future-making approaches to restoring and building pastoral landscapes (or other landscapes such as conservation or industrial landscapes), the pastoralist's reaction to interventions might sometimes also be negative.

Pastoralism and changing pastoral landscapes in eastern Africa

Looking beyond the case described here, pastoral groups in East Africa and across the African continent (and worldwide) are constantly having to deal with change. Similar cases of environmental changes and livelihood trans-formations are reported from several regions in East Africa[5] and beyond,[6] and most pastoral groups have dealt successfully with a broad variety of changes. For many pastoral groups in general, social and environmental conditions have changed over time, and bush encroachment and pasture land degradation have been described as pertinent hallmarks of these changes. As mentioned before, new challenges arise that exclude pastoralists from access to pasture resources, such as the fragmentation of the landscape due to privatisation processes and the designation of conservation areas. The question, therefore, has to be changed from one asking whether pastoral groups can manage their land sustainably to one asking how pastoral people can maintain access to key resources and sustain their livelihood against or in collaboration with new agents emerging in their lands. In the following, I

---

[5]   See for example Homewood and Rodgers (1991); for the case of Ethiopia, see Angassa and Oba (2008); for the case of the Greater Mara ecosystem, see Jandreau and Berkes (2016); and for the case of Uganda, see Byakagaba et al. (2018).

[6]   For the case of Mali, see Brottem (2016); for the case of Nigeria, see Majekodunmi et al. (2017); and for the case of Benin, see Tamou et al. (2018).

revisit examples from various African pastoral groups in order to understand the differences and similarities of the situations that challenge pastoralists in the twenty-first century.

The prospects for pastoralism in East Africa point in different directions. As Catley et al. (2016) show for the cases of Somali and Afar pastoral groups, successful herders might maintain their focus on livestock husbandry while unsuccessful or poor households are likely to exit pastoralism or adapt other strategies to generate income. Homewood (1999) also states with reference to African rangelands that wealthier households can benefit from using common pasture under normal conditions while retreating to privately owned land under extreme conditions such as drought, whereas poorer households might not have the access to private land or the resources to gain access to it. Moreover, the establishment of enclosed areas for grazing or for the cultivation of crops points to a trend that is observable across East Africa in which open-access land and commons are fragmented, resulting in a de facto privatisation of land and resources.[7] Sometimes, the privatisation of communal land has even resulted in the emergence of inheritance rules that are internalised to the pastoral group organisation, as described in the case of Samburu pastoralists in Kenya (Lesorogol, 2010).

The discussion over pastoral land tenure systems and privatisation processes is not new (Galaty, 1994), but developments in the past do not suggest that pastoral groups can reclaim their land-use rights easily; they suggest that national politics seem to continually marginalise pastoralists' interests and needs (Kantai, 2007). With the fragmentation and exclusion processes in pastoral regions over the past decades, the actual territory for livestock husbandry often shrinks, or access to restricted resources is subordinated to group-external regulations (e.g. in conservancies).

As Nyberg et al. (2015) identify for the case of West Pokot agro-pastoralists, the appropriation of enclosed pieces of land becomes more important and plays a key role in the process of diversifying livelihoods. Kibet et al. (2016), evaluate another model that proposes the innovative element of group ranches in Laikipia (Kenya), and they discuss their prospects for livelihood diversification and income generation in terms of forage supply and wildlife conservation.

Niamir-Fuller et al. (2012) also argue in favour of the positive effects of pastoral land use, for instance the potential to incorporate it with conservation efforts and the protection of wildlife. In some cases, relations between conservation areas and pastoral land use are productive and beneficial. Yurco (2017, p. 9) shows such a development in the 'remaking of pastoral livelihoods in Laikipia, Kenya', and Bedelian and Ogutu (2017) describe the case of the

---

7   As described in the case of Ethiopia by Beyene (2009); in the case of Kenya, by Greiner (2016b); or in the case of Niger, by Snorek et al. (2017).

Maasai Mara where some pastoralists profit in terms of access to pasture land and revenues from tourism while simultaneously protecting wildlife. However, the co-existence of both wildlife and livestock also depends on the population numbers, and a 'moderate grazing' (Riginos et al., 2012) of the livestock populations is essential in successful conservation management. Of course, negotiating access to these lands and the profits of using the limited resources is a difficult process that includes some people and excludes others. Homewood et al. (2012) argue that the benefits of wildlife and tourism do not reach the majority of people, and this, in turn, results in neither an overall sustainable management of the conservation area nor any improvement in local livelihoods. However, co-existence with wildlife is possible for pastoral groups, whereas the attitude towards wildlife can change with the adoption of cultivation (McCabe, 2003). Therefore, Lankester and Davis (2016) suggest that pastoral livelihoods must be supported in various ways to ensure a co-existence between wildlife and pastoralists.

In my view, the old debates about land degradation and pastoral overexploitation from the 1970 and 1980s have been overcome – at least in the humanities – and current debates are less concerned about unsustainable land-use practices and more concerned about the future use of pastoral landscapes. Apart from the scientific community, a change in perspectives on pastoral groups and their environmental impact is generally not discernible. As Homewood et al. argue 'policy among East African governments is still rooted in the view that pastoralism is an inefficient and destructive use of land' (2009, p. v).

Therefore, the role of pastoralists in the future visions of East African landscapes remains ambivalent. On the one hand, their role in conservation efforts is viewed suspiciously, as is their role in many violent land disputes. On the other hand, their livelihoods can be maintained under extreme conditions, and their contribution to the maintenance of the savannah ecosystems and biodiversity is often highlighted. Homewood et al. (2001), for instance, investigated the decrease of wildebeest populations in the Serengeti–Mara ecosystem and found that the increased population of smallholders and their agro-pastoral activities did not lead to declining wildlife numbers. In contrast, the large-scale conversion of rangeland for mechanised farming in the Kenyan part of the national park had a strong negative influence on the calving of the wildebeest (Homewood et al., 2001). Also from an ecological view, the (worldwide) degradation of rangelands can be linked more to the fragmentation of the landscapes than to overgrazing (Hobbs et al., 2008). The responses of pastoral people to dealing with fragmented landscapes are also diverse.

However, Jandreau and Berkes raise the most important issue when it comes to pastoral landscapes in general – in their case, the Greater Mara ecosystem: 'how knowledge is shared, by whom, for whom and at whose cost' (Jandreau & Berkes, 2016, p. 12). Therefore, the success or failure of pastoral livelihoods might lie in access to key resources and the management of the pastoral landscapes, including all the new agents involved.

If we look beyond the current trends, some developments have not (yet) taken place in East Pokot. For instance, due to defaunation, wildlife tourism has so far not acquired any important role in the imagination of Pokot futures, in contrast to other regions (Thompson & Homewood, 2002). The same holds true for extensive formal education and political participation that Homewood (2008) identifies as two factors influencing the trajectories of change in her outlook on the future of African pastoralism.

As for the engagement with issues of indigeneity, this has little prominence in East Pokot. In the context of pastoral Maasai, Hodgson (2011) describes the invocation by Maasai activists of the notions of indigenous and later pastoral identity in the context of international networks of donor funding, activism and their struggle for recognition in national politics. As Spear and Waller (1993) show with clarity in the edited volume 'Being Maasai', an unambiguous definition of pastoral identity is not possible, but instead is characterised above all by its variability and its capacity to change. The attribution of identity along ethnic lines is subject to continual negotiation and contention.

In East Pokot, this development towards the establishment of a more 'indigenous' identity by no means corresponds to other pastoral contexts. This may be due to the former marginalisation of the region both in the development context and in terms of its integration into national politics. However, a heated debate is noticeable, at least in social media, about Pokot identity and about the portrayal of pastoral Pokot as bandits. This public controversy seeks to criticise military interventions that aim to disarm the Pokot 'bandits' and mitigate the persistent conflicts in the border regions. However, this debate is less focused on a positive connotation of pastoral identity and indigeneity, but more on the delineation of ethnic lines that are generalised on the national level to legitimise interventions, and are furthermore deployed by Pokot activists (e.g. on Facebook) both to draw attention to intra-Pokot differences in terms of identity and livelihoods and to criticise rights violations during the military interventions.

It must be noted that externally driven development does not necessarily have to benefit 'the community'. On the one hand, it is often not clear who exactly this 'community' is, who belongs to it, who should benefit and to what extent (Lind et al., 2020b). In addition, there are also varying interests within the local groups that influence the distribution of revenues or the communication with the agents of the development project. Lind exemplifies this in the case of oil production in Turkana County, where external intervention not only generates benefits but also fails to meet expectations, thereby forming the basis for intensifying intra-ethnic conflict as well as inter-ethnic conflict with the Pokot (Lind, 2017b).

The future of pastoral landscapes in East Africa

In this last section, I want illustrate some visions of the future pastoral landscapes in East Pokot and outline possible different paths into the future. I revisit the ecological challenges and social transformations – the incremental bush encroachment; the livelihood adaptations and transformations; and the rapid changes, invasions and defaunations – and discuss differing imaginations of the future. It should be noted, however, that there are a wide range of different future orientations that also depend on which possibilities and limitations emerge locally.

The pastoral life of the Pokot has undergone extreme changes in recent decades from the rearing of cattle to a diversification of herd composition (towards browsing species) and the establishment of slowly but steadily increasing agricultural practices. In particular, developments in agriculture have led to the establishment of agricultural production beyond the subsistence level in favoured regions that forms the basis of agro-pastoral livelihoods. However, these livelihoods are not shaped exclusively by the transformation of livelihoods towards agriculture, but, above all, by a sedentary way of life, an orientation towards school education and ecclesiastical values and a decline of certain practices that are of great importance in the pastoral context. These include, above all, ceremonies based on the exchange of livestock, which also constitute the social network of the pastoral community. Similarly, the intra- and intergenerational relations in Pokot society are no longer marked by being initiated into society through certain rites of passage (although especially the male circumcision and *sapana* initiation are to some extent still part of agro-pastoral life). As described before, the number of ceremonies in the agro-pastoral context is decreasing, and the strict rules of marriage are no longer as strong as they continue to be in the pastoral context. The social organisation and the intergenerational construction of the community is slowly changing in the agro-pastoral context, and is being replaced by other institutions such as churches. Moreover, the pastoral social organisation is being questioned and young Pokot no longer depend entirely on the older generation sets in terms of livestock ownership, marriage possibilities or income opportunities. It could be argued that agro-pastoral Pokot are undergoing a change that is oriented towards their integration into Kenyan society, and one that includes both pastoral elements and new influences. This change, however, is accompanied by a detachment from the conventional values of the pastoral community and a change in land use that is difficult to reconcile with the hitherto ascribed pastoral ways of life.

The pastoralists, however, continue to strive for a life based on a large acquisition of livestock that determines to a large extent their position in the community. However, the strategies for achieving this have changed over time, and contrary to earlier assumptions that the pastoral Pokot would resist any kind of change, it can be observed that especially the two younger generation sets are exploring new sources of income. In contrast to the agro-pastoral context, however, this reorientation has not yet been accompanied by a fundamental change in livelihoods, but has instead been used to enlarge existing herds. Today, there is not much to be seen of the once-reported specialisation in cattle. On the contrary, the subsequent phase of diversification of livelihoods – from cattle to goats, and from cattle to corn – has continued and is including domains that were previously not accessible for pastoralists. This applies in particular to the domains of wage labour and business activities created by the development of the region for the production of geothermal energy.

I would like to highlight again the different types of change and their correlations mentioned in this book. Contrary to earlier, often unilineal arguments about pasture management, degradation or social transformation, I would like to offer an explanation within the framework of historical ecology. In this sense, the different social and ecological processes are viewed from a historical perspective, and transformational processes are addressed on a systemic level and triangulated with local perspectives. Both levels – the Pokot and the abstract scientific system perspective – provide different explanatory approaches to understanding and evaluating the situation of today's pastoralists.

McPeak et al. (2012) also discuss the changing opportunities in rural contexts and come to the conclusion that pastoral livelihoods are also able to respond to today's conditions of uncertainty.

> While we note this uncertainty about the future, we would stress that our findings indicate that the livestock-based economy has proven to be resilient despite the many changes it has confronted over time. Simply put, livestock and livestock products have been and will continue to be the basis of the economy in these regions. (McPeak et al., 2012, p. 169)

Homewood (2018) also discusses the future possibilities of pastoral groups in terms of the availability of livestock and other income assets. She identifies four different pathways along which pastoralists with low-livestock and low-income assets may be left behind, whereas those with high-income but low-livestock assets may be motivated to move out of pastoralism. Furthermore, those pastoralists who have high livestock assets but low-income assets might remain pastoralists, whereas those with both high livestock and high-income assets might also combine their assets to increase herd sizes.

Spencer (1997) also recalls the changes colonial rule brought to East Africa and anticipates new, huge challenges for pastoralists with possibly irreversible consequences for their livelihoods. He differentiates between three different 'career paths' for pastoralists: the two extreme types involving either abandoning pastoralism or subscribing completely to the pastoral life (Spencer, 1997). Only 'career path B' deals with the possibility of pastoralists retaining their mode of life with temporary engagement in other activities, such as farming, wage labour and honey production. This 'career path' is also observable at Mt Paka where pastoral people are diversifying their livelihood assets. In a few decades, Paka people will neither be 'pure' pastoralists nor a 'post-pastoralist' community. Confining the change of pastoral people in terms of these categories implies a linear development from a pastoral to a 'post-pastoral' society, but, as described above, the categories of pastoral and agro-pastoral Pokot cannot be separated and must always be considered in relation to each other.

If I were to assess the prospects for pastoralism in East Pokot, I would argue that the hitherto successful pastoralists who have acquired large flocks and established themselves as pastoralists will continue to focus on a pastoral path, even though other sources of income will be added to their regular activities. Nonetheless, the focus will remain on livestock husbandry and not on other activities. Those pastoralists who do not manage to make a living from livestock will have to consider other options such as farming or wage labour.

Moreover, the Pokot who engage in agro-pastoralism, with a focus on maize cultivation, will continue to expand locally. This faction will continue to consolidate, and maize cultivation has become as much a part of the landscape in East Pokot – at least in certain regions – as livestock husbandry. However, the prospects for an expansion from existing farming areas to the entire East Pokot region seem rather unlikely, because especially the highlands with better climatic and soil conditions provide good conditions for agro-pastoral liveli-hoods. The continuation of already existing differences between pastoral liveli-hoods in the lowlands and agro-pastoral livelihoods in the highlands will thus prevail, because both land-use systems are well adapted to local conditions. However, sedentary agro-pastoralists have one advantage over pastoralists in that they can secure exclusive access to land both through the enclosure of arable land and, in the future, through the recognition of land rights. This shift towards private land rights in an otherwise open-property regime restricts the pastoralists, because access to resources is gradually reduced, forcing them to seek these resources elsewhere. Existing conflicts of the pastoral Pokot in the border regions may be exacerbated, and one of the most important challenges in the coming years will be to negotiate access to resources with government representatives. A business-as-usual scenario, in which violent access to resources outside one's own territory is considered a viable option, seems rather unlikely in view of the fact that the Kenyan government's reactions to these acts of violence are also becoming increasingly restrictive, and all Pokot in the region are struggling with the negative effects.

In responding to past and present environmental changes, both pastoralists and agro-pastoralists are capable of adapting – again taking into account the specific circumstances of environmental change. The pastoral Pokot have shown that they can respond to the fragmentation of the pastoral landscape and the decline of pastures for cattle by accessing resources in other regions as well as by fundamentally changing the herd structure. One major problem is that the ongoing fragmentation processes – that are also informed by ecological invasions – and the resulting reduction in grazing land cannot simply be compensated through territorial expansion, because the margins of the Pokot territory are already occupied. Agro-pastoral livelihoods are also affected by environmental change, but less by encroachment and invasion processes than by rainfall variations and climate change.

Clearly, major challenges include the negotiation of the social transformations initiated with both the GDC project and the devolution process as well as the organisation of land rights in East Pokot – both between those who follow different livelihoods (pastoral, agro-pastoral, wage and formal labour) and between the generations who have different perspectives on their individual futures as well as on the community's future. This also includes negotiating the reorganisation of power that is still in the hands of the elders but shifting increasingly into the hands of Pokot politicians, with gerontocratic structures being challenged by economically successful Pokot who did not follow a pastoral path, but who nevertheless occupy an important position in society through their personal achievements. The tension between the generations is tangible in the context of these rapid changes and the economic opportunities they create.

However, the attempt to predict or anticipate the future of pastoralism in East Africa more generally remains difficult. Nevertheless, I have identified many fundamental points here that might be important for the future of pastoral livelihoods. These include future livestock management such as changing livestock husbandry strategies (Niamir-Fuller, 2016), the export trade of livestock and income generation (Catley et al., 2016), local breeding concepts and breed performance (Kaufmann et al., 2016) or innovative market strategies (Köhler-Rollefson, 2016). The organisation of land ownership and access to land and essential resources is another key point, including the coming community land tenure, but also issues of land grabbing and conflicts over access to land and resources (Haller et al., 2016), and the role of indigenous knowledge for the management of rangelands (Seid et al., 2016a). Obviously, climate change and flexible pastoral response strategies are crucial components in this regard that will determine the future of pastoral groups (Herrero et al., 2016) and the relations between their livelihoods, wildlife populations and environmental changes (Lankester & Davis, 2016).

Yet the possibilities to address new challenges will also have a profound influence on the success of pastoral groups. This includes internal reflection and the response to new circumstances such as formal education (Dyer, 2016), the reorganisation of labour in pastoral routines (Butt, 2016), dealing with new forms of communication, modernisation and capacity building (Seid et al., 2016b) and health improvement for both humans and livestock (Schelling et al., 2016). Furthermore, external actors, their narratives and goals must be assessed and evaluated within the pastoral community in order to deal with them. This also involves improving local institutions and integrating them into regional and national politics (Bonfoh et al., 2016), responding to the intervention of state programmes (Janzen et al., 2016) and developing a sustainable land use through collaborative learning and claiming the right to stewardship over land and resources (Ouedraogo & Davies, 2016).

The question of what character pastoralism will take in the future remains vague, but as Galaty and Bonte outlined three decades ago,

> the future of Africa's arid lands and their human populations will continue to rest on a pastoral base. The major questions of today concern the means by which the livelihood and the social existence of pastoral peoples can be secured and enhanced, given the myths and predicaments of their past and current realities. (Galaty & Bonte, 1991, p. 291)

I share their opinion, with the reservation that the pastoral ways of life that we experience today will continue to shift in the future and result in new forms of pastoral life.

More recently, Catley et al. (2016) portray the outlook for future pastoral livelihoods in two directions: on the one hand, the growth of regional meat supply by pastoralists in East Africa[8] with the development of 'robust and responsive livestock production and marketing in pastoralist areas' will remain highly important, whereas, on the other hand, more pastoralists will exit pastoralism due to impoverished livelihoods and a lack of prospects for individual households. Little (2013) highlights political participation, population growth, rural-urban migration, education and other ways of exiting pastoralism as key issues to recent pastoralists. Non-pastoral activities will increase, he contends, also competing with pastoral land uses, implying the necessity for pastoral communities to employ or sustain a large number of non-pastoralists. Little also predicts an increase in cultivation activities for pastoral communities that will particularly affect 'poor' pastoralists and lead to tensions and conflict over water and access to land between cultivators and herders.

The role of pastoralists in Kenya and in other African countries remains ambivalent. On the one hand, many pastoral groups are marginalised and viewed critically by non-pastoral people due to their way of living or their involvement in intra- and inter-ethnic conflicts. On the other hand, the pastoral

---

[8] Behnke and Muthami (2011) report that more than 80 per cent of the beef consumed in Kenya is produced by pastoralists from East Africa, with 72 per cent of the cattle raised within the country. For small stock, the numbers for nationally produced animals (sheep and goats) are even higher, with 94 per cent being raised in Kenya.

groups in Kenya provide a great share of livestock products to both national and regional markets. Their role in the national economies is important, though their way of life and their opportunistic livelihoods do not always fit into an economy that anticipates the future based on prediction rather than prophecy. The modern state, including Kenya, constructs the future, restores landscapes and builds the environments according to the needs and aspirations of the majority of its citizens. Today's pastoral Pokot, however, do not intentionally anticipate the future or construct their environment.

The long-term changes in the environment play an important role in this respect. On the one hand, it was climatic changes in the eighteenth century that made pastoral life in the Rift Valley possible, because Lake Baringo filled up with water again after its desiccation. On the other hand, this specialisation in cattle husbandry has also come to an end with the transformation of the grass savannah to bush savannah. It was not the pastoralists of the region who were mainly responsible for this, but the circumstances in which the wildlife populations were exterminated by colonial hunters and local people. These processes of defaunation have triggered the landscape change that was intensified at a later stage by the growing inability of the Pokot to manage pastures through the use of fire.

I would like to stress again that these two processes have been identified as being immanently important for long-term change; but that in the end, far more factors have had an impact on change. I have listed these in Chapter 7, including the climate, population dynamics, pastoralist mobility and the slow commercialisation of pastoral livelihoods. In particular, the strong increase of the population and the rapidly decreasing TLU/capita ratio are challenges that a pastoral society must face with innovations. The most important challenge of recent times, however, is the temporal dimension of change that makes it difficult to adapt to rapid changes or has a strong impact on the social organisation of pastoral communities.

The ecological 'invasion' processes confront the pastoralists with unexpected challenges, even if they are often not directly seen as such. But the rapid expansion of *Dodonaea viscosa*, for example, hits the pastoralists particularly hard, though not the agro-pastoralists. This is because the former have to constantly open up new grazing grounds and, in this respect, migrate far beyond their own territory during the dry season and become involved in conflicts with the local population there. Hence, the pastoralists are forced to recognise the limits of their own way of life and to explore new possibilities. Nevertheless, the pastoral life remains the desired one, and possibilities for diversification of livelihoods are used to strengthen the fading pastoral structures.[9] It is the task of the elders who are able to draw on their experiences

---

[9] It is assumed that for most ecosystems, the relevance of invasive species will increase in the future, because of the estimated high potential for their further

to find solutions and who rely on the support of long-trusted institutions such as the prophet to organise pastoral communities. Furthermore, local politicians try to steer change and adapt the elders' explanatory patterns to the challenges of the future. It would therefore be completely wrong to speak of an end to pastoralism.

Instead, all pastoral groups in East Africa and beyond must respond to the current challenges. These include, on the one hand, the rapid changes to the environment that are undermining the existing possibilities for adaptation and require the development of new strategies to meet these challenges. On the other hand, pastoral groups, which, in their history, have also often not had a very close relationship with the colonial and post-colonial states, depend on collaboration with their respective governments or associated partners if they are to find solutions to the major problems such as climate change. Confrontation and interaction with the new actors in the pastoral landscapes will therefore be crucial in determining the future orientation of pastoralists and whether it will be possible to maintain important pastoral elements over time.

---

distribution (Seebens et al., 2020). How far the further distribution of certain species in other ecosystems will be perceived as a threat (in the sense of a negative evaluation of invasive species on the local ecosystem) or as a necessary adaptation (e.g. in forestry to rapidly changing ecological conditions due to climate change) still has to be assessed in each individual case. In the case of the pastoral Pokot, this is a particular problem, because actively shaping the landscape has not played an important role to date. How far this might continue to be the case in the future is not certain. Nonetheless, it can be assumed that the spread of other alien species will also pose new challenges for pastoralists.

APPENDIX: LISTS OF PLANT NAMES
(POKOT–SCIENTIFIC AND SCIENTIFIC–POKOT)[1]

Table A1. List of plant names: Pokot–scientific.

Vernacular	Scientific names	Family
Abrute (also called *purteyon*)	*Brachiaria deflexa, Setaria homonyma*	Poaceae
Adomeyon	*Cordia sinensis*	Boraginaceae
Adwarian (*Puresongolion*)	*Aristida mutabilis*	Poaceae
Akelkelayan	*Cyathula orthocantha*	Amaranthaceae
Aletelete	*Gisekia pharnaceoides, Trianthema triquetra, Portulaca oleracea*	Gisekiaceae; Aizoaceae; Portulacaceae
Amekunyan	*Indigofera cliffordiana, I. Hochstetteri, I. spicata*	Fabaceae
Amerkwoyon; Amakwaratian	*Cenchrus ciliaris, Pennisetum setaceum, Setaria pumila, S. verticillata*	Poaceae
Angoleyekion	*Tetrapogon cenchriformis, T. tenellus*	Poaceae
Anyua	*Vachellia reficiens*	Fabaceae
Aporpotoyon	*Aneilema johnstonii, A. petersii, Commelina benghalensis, C. bracteosa, C. forskalaei, C. latifolia, C. petersii, Cyanotis lanata*	Commelinaceae
Arengreng	*Tragus berteronianus*	Poaceae
Areronyon	*Cadaba farinosa*	Capparaceae
Ashokonyon	*Salvadora persica*	Salvadoraceae

---

[1] With reference to Timberlake, 1987; Reckers, 1990; UNESCO, 2013.

Vernacular	Scientific names	Family
Asukuruyon	*Tribulus cistoides,* *T. terrestris*	Zygophyllaceae
Atat	*Vachellia elatior*	Fabaceae
Atulayan	*Indigofera tinctoria,* *Phyllanthus rotundifolius*	Fabaceae; Phyllanthaceae
Awawatian	*Saccharum spontaneum*	Poaceae
Cactus	*Opuntia stricta*	Cactaceae
Chaya	*Sehima nervosum*	Poaceae
Cheluwowes	*Aristida adscensionis*	Poaceae
Chemangayan	*Senegalia senegal*	Fabaceae
Chemwania (also called Kowontö)	*Cymbopogon caesius,* *C. giganteus, Pennisetum* *setaceum*	Poaceae
Chepkamatian	not specified (assumed: *Hypoestes forskaolii* ssp. *hildebrandtii)*	
Chepkaneroi	*Cleome hanburyana*	Capparaceae
Chepkratian	not specified	
Cheptuya	*Euclea divinorum,* *E. racemosa*	Ebenaceae
Chepuluswo	*Maerus subcordata*	Capparaceae
Chesotim	*Ormocarpum keniense;* *Turraea parvifolia*	Fabaceae; Meliaceae
Chesowoyö	*Cymbopogon spp.*	Poaceae
Churukechir	*Eragrostis superba*	Poaceae
Chuwuw	*Vachellia hockii*	Fabaceae
Kacheptilil	*Justicia exigua,* *J. uncinulata*	Acanthaceae
Kamaran	*Ormocarpum keniense,* *O. kirkii, O. trichocarpum*	Fabaceae
Kapengayan	not specified	
Kapul	not specified	
Katang	*Commiphora africana,* *C. madagascariensis*	Burseraceae
Kella	not specified	
Kembirwo	*Acalypha volkensii,* *Phyllanthus cf. Guineensis*	Euphorbiaceae; Phyllanthaceae
Kericheyan	not specified	

Table A1 continued.

Vernacular	Scientific names	Family
Kipaupau	*Enteropogon macrostachys*	Poaceae
Kokochwo	*Premna resinosa*	Verbenaceae
Koloswo	*Terminalia brownie*	Combretaceae
Koserinyan	*Triumfetta rhomboidea*	Malvaceae
Kowontö (also called *Chemwania*)	*Cymbopogon caesius, C. giganteus, Pennisetum setaceum*	Poaceae
Kram	*Ozoroa reticulata*	Anacardiaceae
Lopara	*Justicia odora; Leucas jamesii*	Acanthaceae; Lamiaceae
Losikiria	*Seriococomopsis hildebrandtii*	Amaranthaceae
Lotal	*Ruellia patula*	Acanthaceae
Makäny	*Ficus sycomorus*	Moraceae
Makau	*Grewia villosa*	Malvaceae
Malumtich	*Bothriochloa insculpta*	Poaceae
Manampelion	*Teclea pilosa, Vepris glomerata*	Rutaceae
Mintarotwo	*Commiphora Africana*	Burseraceae
Moikut	*Cyperus articulatus, C. rotundus, C. tuberosus*	Cyperaceae
Mukun	*Dactyloctenium aegyptium*	Poaceae
Ngawian	not specified	
Ngilet	*Eragrostris namaquensis, Sporobolus cordofanus, S. ioclados*	Poaceae
Ngurumenwo	*Digera muricata; Talinum portulacifolium*	Amaranthaceae; Portulacaceae
Nyuswo	*Loudetia spp.*	Poaceae
Okopko	*Vachellia nilotica*	Fabaceae
Panyarit	Umbrella term for several acacia species, such as *V. etbaica, S. mellifera, V. reficiens* and *S. senegal*	Fabaceae
Parasunta	*Combretum molle*	Combretaceae
Pekonion	*Chloris virgata, Heteropogon contortus*	Poaceae

Vernacular	Scientific names	Family
Pelesian	*Sporobolus festivus*	Poaceae
Pelil	*Vachellia nubica*	Fabaceae
Pkapu	*Abutilon fruticosum, A. hirtum, A. mauritianum, Hibiscus calyphyllus, H. vitifolius*	Malvaceae
Pkata	*Lycium europaeum*	Solanaceae
Poto	*Tarenna graveolens*	Rubiaceae
Prosopis	*Prosopis juliflora*	Fabaceae
Ptaru	*Senegalia brevispica*	Fabaceae
*Puresongolion (*also called *Adwarian)*	*Aristida mutabilis*	Poaceae
Purteyon (also called *Abrute*)	*Brachiaria deflexa, Setaria homonyma*	Poaceae
Puyun	*Eragrostis cilianensis*	Poaceae
Renoi	*Vachellia xanthophloea*	Fabaceae
Rikoyo	*Combretum aculeatum; Seddera latifolia*	Combretaceae; Convolvulaceae
Ririon	*Delonix elata*	Fabaceae
Sangak	Small bushes of *Vachellia tortilis*	Fabaceae
Seretion	*Cynodon niemfuensis*	Poaceae
Ses	*Vachellia tortilis*	Fabaceae
Sitat	*Grewia bicolor*	Malvaceae
Sorich	*Boscia coriacea*	Capparaceae
Talamogh	*Senegalia mellifera*	Fabaceae
Tapoyo	*Lannea triphylla*	Anacardiaceae
Taran	*Grewia tenax*	Malvaceae
Tikit	*Terminalia spinosa*	Combretaceae
Tirok	*Ziziphus mucronata*	Rhamnaceae
Tuwio	*Maerua crassifolia*	Capparaceae
Tuwot	*Diospyros acabra*	Ebenaceae
Tuyunwo	*Balanites aegyptiaca*	Zygophyllaceae

Table A2. List of plant names: Scientific–Pokot.

Scientific names	Family	Vernacular
Abutilon fruticosum, A. hirtum, A. mauritianum, Hibiscus calyphyllus, H. vitifolius	Malvaceae	*Pkapu*
Acalypha volkensii, Phyllanthus cf. Guineensis	Euphorbiaceae; Phyllanthaceae	*Kembirwo*
Aneilema johnstonii, A. petersii, Commelina benghalensis, C. bracteosa, C. forskalaei, C. latifolia, C. petersii, Cyanotis lanata	Commelinaceae	*Aporpotoyon*
Aristida adscensionis	Poaceae	*Cheluwowes*
Aristida mutabilis	Poaceae	*Adwarian; Puresongolion*
Balanites aegyptiaca	Zygophyllaceae	*Tuyunwo*
Boscia coriacea	Capparaceae	*Sorich*
Bothriochloa insculpta	Poaceae	*Malumtich*
Brachiaria deflexa, Setaria homonyma	Poaceae	*Abrute* (also called *Purteyon*)
Cadaba farinosa	Capparaceae	*Areronyon*
Cenchrus ciliaris, Pennisetum setaceum, Setaria pumila, S. verticillata	Poaceae	*Amerkwoyon; Amakwaratian*
Chloris virgata, Heteropogon contortus	Poaceae	*Pekonion*
Cleome hanburyana	Capparaceae	*Chepkaneroi*
Combretum aculeatum; Seddera latifolia	Combretaceae; Convolvulaceae	*Rikoyo*
Combretum molle	Combretaceae	*Parasunta*
Commiphora Africana	Burseraceae	*Mintarotwo*
Commiphora africana, C. madagascariensis	Burseraceae	*Katang*
Cordia sinensis	Boraginaceae	*Adomeyon*
Cyathula orthocantha	Amaranthaceae	*Akelkelayan*
Cymbopogon caesius, C. giganteus, Pennisetum setaceum	Poaceae	*Kowontö*
Cymbopogon spp.	Poaceae	*Chesowoyö*
Cynodon niemfuensis	Poaceae	*Seretion*
Cyperus articulatus, C. rotundus, C. tuberosus	Cyperaceae	*Moikut*
Dactyloctenium aegyptium	Poaceae	*Mukun*

Scientific names	Family	Vernacular
Delonix elata	Fabaceae	*Ririon*
Digera muricata; Talinum portulacifolium	Amaranthaceae; Portulacaceae	*Ngurumenwo*
Diospyros acabra	Ebenaceae	*Tuwot*
Enteropogon macrostachys	Poaceae	*Kipaupau*
Eragrostis cilianensis	Poaceae	*Puyun*
Eragrostis superba	Poaceae	*Churukechir*
Eragrostris namaquensis, Sporobolus cordofanus, S. ioclados	Poaceae	*Ngilet*
Euclea divinorum, E. racemosa	Ebenaceae	*Cheptuya*
Ficus sycomorus	Moraceae	*Makäny*
Gisekia pharnaceoides, Trianthema triquetra, Portulaca oleracea	Gisekiaceae; Aizoaceae; Portulacaceae	*Aletelete*
Grewia bicolor	Malvaceae	*Sitat*
Grewia tenax	Malvaceae	*Taran*
Grewia villosa	Malvaceae	*Makau*
Indigofera cliffordiana, I. Hochstetteri, I. spicata	Fabaceae	*Amekunyan*
Indigofera tinctoria, Phyllanthus rotundifolius	Fabaceae; Phyllanthaceae	*Atulayan*
Justicia exigua, J. uncinulata	Acanthaceae	*Kacheptilil*
Justicia odora; Leucas jamesii	Acanthaceae; Lamiaceae	*Lopara*
Lannea triphylla	Anacardiaceae	*Tapoyo*
Loudetia spp.	Poaceae	*Nyuswo*
Lycium europaeum	Solanaceae	*Pkata*
Maerua crassifolia	Capparaceae	*Tuwio*
Maerus subcordata	Capparaceae	*Chepuluswo*
Opuntia stricta	Cactaceae	*Cactus*
Ormocarpum keniense; Turraea parvifolia	Fabaceae; Meliaceae	*Chesotim*
Ormocarpum keniense, O. kirkii, O. trichocarpum	Fabaceae	*Kamaran*
Ozoroa reticulata	Anacardiaceae	*Kram*
Premna resinosa	Verbenaceae	*Kokochwo*
Prosopis juliflora	Fabaceae	*Prosopis*
Ruellia patula	Acanthaceae	*Lotal*

Table A2 continued.

Scientific names	Family	Vernacular
Saccharum spontaneum	Poaceae	*Awawatian*
Salvadora persica	Salvadoraceae	*Ashokonyon*
Sehima nervosum	Poaceae	*Chaya*
Senegalia brevispica	Fabaceae	*Ptaru*
Senegalia mellifera	Fabaceae	*Talamogh*
Senegalia senegal	Fabaceae	*Chemangayan*
Seriococomopsis hildebrandtii	Amaranthaceae	*Losikiria*
Small bushes of Vachellia tortilis	Fabaceae	*Sangak*
Sporobolus festivus	Poaceae	*Pelesian*
Tarenna graveolens	Rubiaceae	*Poto*
Teclea pilosa, Vepris glomerata	Rutaceae	*Manampelion*
Terminalia brownie	Combretaceae	*Koloswo*
Terminalia spinosa	Combretaceae	*Tikit*
Tetrapogon cenchriformis, T. tenellus	Poaceae	*Angoleyekion*
Tragus berteronianus	Poaceae	*Arengreng*
Tribulus cistoides, T. terrestris	Zygophyllaceae	*Asukuruyon*
Triumfetta rhomboidea	Malvaceae	*Koserinyan*
Vachellia elatior	Fabaceae	*Atat*
Vachellia hockii	Fabaceae	*Chuwuw*
Vachellia nilotica	Fabaceae	*Okopko*
Vachellia nubica	Fabaceae	*Pelil*
Vachellia reficiens	Fabaceae	*Anyua*
Vachellia tortilis	Fabaceae	*Ses*
Vachellia xanthophloea	Fabaceae	*Renoi*
Ziziphus mucronata	Rhamnaceae	*Tirok*

BIBLIOGRAPHY

Note: The bibliography is divided into multiple categories so authors may appear in more than one section.

Monographs and edited collections

Anderson, D.M. (2002). *Eroding the Commons: The Politics of Ecology in Baringo, Kenya, 1890–1963* (Oxford: James Currey).

Anderson, D.M. & Broch-Due, V. (eds) (1999). *The Poor are Not Us: Poverty and Pastoralism in Eastern Africa* (Oxford: James Currey).

Beech, M.W.H. (1911). *The Suk: Their Language and Folklore* (Oxford: Clarendon Press).

Blaikie, P. (1985). *The Political Economy of Soil Erosion in Developing Countries* (London: Longman).

Blaikie, P. & Brookfield, H.C. (1987). *Land Degradation and Society* (London, New York: Methuen).

Bollig, M. (2006). *Risk Management in a Hazardous Environment: A Comparative Study of Two Pastoral Societies* (Boston: Springer).

Bollig, M., Schnegg, M. & Wotzka, H.-P. (2013). *Pastoralism in Africa: Past, Present and Future* (New York: Berghahn).

Boonman, G. (1993). *East Africa's Grasses and Fodders: Their Ecology and Husbandry* (Dordrecht: Springer).

Bovey, R.W. (2016). *Mesquite: History, Growth, Biology, Uses, and Management* (College Station: Texas A&M University Press).

Catley, A., Scoones, I. & Lind, J. (2013). *Pastoralism and Development in Africa: Dynamic Change at the Margins* (New York, London: Routledge).

Chapman, A. (1908). *On Safari: Big-game Hunting in British East Africa – With Studies in Bird-Life* (London: Edward Arnold).

Clewell, A.F. & Aronson, J. (2007). *Ecological Restoration: Principles, Values and Structure of an Emerging Profession* (Washington: Island Press).

Crumley, C.L. (1994). *Historical Ecology: Cultural Knowledge and Changing Landscapes* (Santa Fe: School of American Research Press).

Coy, M.W. (1989). *Apprenticeship: From Theory to Method and Back Again* (New York: State University of New York Press).

Dickinson, F.A. (1908). *Big Game Shooting on the Equator* (London, New York: J. Lane).

Dietz, T. (1987). *Pastoralists in Dire Straits: Survival Strategies and External Interventions in a Semi-Arid Region at the Kenya/Uganda Border: Western Pokot, 1900–1986* (Amsterdam: Koninklijk Nederlands Aandrijkskundig Genootschap).

Dyson-Hudson, N. (1966). *Karimojong Politics* (Oxford: University Press).

Elton, C.S. (1958). *The Ecology of invasions by Animals and Plants* (London: Springer Science & Business Media).

Fairhead, J. & Leach, M. (1996). *Misreading the African Landscape: Society and Ecology in a Forest-Savanna Mosaic* (Cambridge: University Press).

Feare, C. (1984). *The Starling* (Oxford: University Press).

Fratkin, E., Galvin, K.A. & Roth, E.A. (1994). *African Pastoralist Systems: An Integrated Approach* (Boulder: L. Rienner Publishers).

Fratkin, E.M. & Roth, E.A. (2005). *As Pastoralists Settle: Social, Health, and Economic Consequences of the Pastoral Sedentarization in Marsabit District, Kenya* (New York: Kluwer Academic Publishers).

Galaty, J.G. (1990). *The World of Pastoralism: Herding Systems in Comparative Perspective* (New York: Guilford Press).

Galvin, K.A., Hobbs, N.T., Behnke, R.H. & Reid, R.S. (2008). *Fragmentation in Semi-Arid and Arid Landscapes: Consequences for Human and Natural Systems* (Dordrecht: Springer).

Gissibl, B. (2016). *The nature of German Imperialism: Conservation and the Politics of Wildlife in Colonial East Africa* (New York: Berghahn).

Gravesen, M.L. (2021). *The Contested Lands of Laikipia: Histories of Claims and Conflict in a Kenyan Landscape* (Leiden, Boston: Brill).

Gregory, J.W. (1896). *The Great Rift Valley: Being the Narrative of a Journey to Mount Kenya and Lake Baringo: With some Account of the Geology, Natural History, Anthropology and Future Prospects of British East Africa* (London: J. Murray).

Guerrant, E.O., Havens, K. & Maunder, M. (2004). *Ex Situ Plant Conservation: Supporting Species Survival in the Wild* (Washington: Island Press).

Hennings, R.O. (1951). *African Morning* (London: Chatto Windus).

Hodgson, D.L. (2000). *Rethinking Pastoralism in Africa: Gender, Culture & the Myth of the Patriarchal Pastoralist* (Oxford: James Currey).

—— (2011). *Being Maasai, Becoming Indigenous: Postcolonial Politics in a Neoliberal World* (Bloomington: Indiana University Press).

Homewood, K. (2008). *Ecology of African Pastoralist Societies* (Oxford: James Currey).

Homewood, K. & Rodgers, W.A. (1991). *Maasailand Ecology: Pastoralist Development and Wildlife Conservation in Ngorongoro, Tanzania* (Cambridge: University Press).

Homewood, K., Kristjanson, P. & Trench, P. (2009). *Staying Maasai? Livelihoods, Conservation, and Development in East African Rangelands* (New York: Springer).

Howell, E.A., Egan, D.J. & Meine, C. (2005). *The Historical Ecology Handbook: A Restorationist's Guide to Reference Ecosystems* (Washington: Island Press).

Huntingford, G. (1953). *The Southern Nilo-Hamites* (London: International African Institute).

Ingold, T. (2000). *The Perception of the Environment: Essays on Livelihood, Dwelling and Skill* (London, New York: Routledge).

—— (2013). *Making: Anthropology, Archaeology, Art and Architecture* (London: Routledge).

Johnston, K. (1884). *Africa: Stanford's Compendium of Geography and Travel Based on Hellwald's 'Die Erde und ihre Völker'* (London: Edward Stanford).

Kuiper, G. (2019). *Agro-industrial Labour in Kenya: Cut Flower Farms and Migrant Workers' Settlements* (Cham: Palgrave Macmillan).

Kull, C.A. (2004). *Isle of Fire: The Political Ecology of Landscape Burning in Madagascar* (Chicago: University of Chicago Press).

Leach, M. & Mearns, R. (1996). *The Lie of the Land: Challenging Received Wisdom on the African Environment* (Oxford: James Currey).

Lind, J., Okenwa, D. & Scoones, I. (2020a). *Land, Investment & Politics: Reconfiguring Eastern Africa's Pastoral Drylands* (Woodbridge: James Currey).

Lugard, F.J.D. (1893). *The Rise of our East African Empire: Early Efforts in Nyasaland and Uganda* (Edinburgh, London: W. Blackwood and Sons).

Mainguet, M. (1994). *Desertification: Natural Background and Human Mismanagement* (Berlin, Heidelberg: Springer).

Manji, A. (2020). *The Struggle for Land and Justice in Kenya* (Woodbridge: James Currey).

Mariner, J.C. & Paskin, R. (2000). *Manual on Participatory Epidemiology: Methods for the Collection of Action-Oriented Epidemiological Intelligence* (Food and Agriculture Organization, Rome).

McPeak, J.G., Little, P.D. & Doss, C.R. (2012). *Risk and Social Change in an African Rural Economy: Livelihoods in Pastoralist Communities* (London, New York: Routledge).

Meiu, G.P. (2017). *Ethno-Erotic Economies: Sexuality, Money, and Belonging in Kenya* (Chicago: University of Chicago Press).

Mieth, F. (2007). *Defying the Decline of Pastoralism: Pokot Perceptions of Violence, Disarmament, and Peacemaking in the Kenya/Uganda Border Region* (Amsterdam: Vrije Universiteit).

Morrison, M.L. (2002). *Wildlife Restoration: Techniques for Habitat Analysis and Animal Monitoring* (Washington: Island Press).

Nordstrom, C. & Robben, A.C.G.M. (1995). *Fieldwork under Fire: Contemporary Studies of Violence and Survival.* (University of California Press).

Packard, S., Mutel, C.F. & Jordan, W.R. (2005). *The Tallgrass Restoration Handbook: For Prairies, Savannas, and Woodlands* (Washington: Island Press).

Peters, C. (1891). *New Light on Dark Africa: Being the Narrative of the German Emin Pasha Expedition, its Journeyings and Adventures among the Native Tribes of Eastern Equatorial Africa, the Gallas, Massais, Wasukuma, etc., etc., on the Lake Baringo and the Victoria Nyanza* (London, New York, Melbourne: Ward, Lock, and Co).

Powell-Cotton, P. (1904d). *In Unknown Africa: A Narrative of Twenty Months Travel and Sport in Unknown Lands and Among New Tribes* (London: Hurst and Blackett, limited).

Reid, R.S. (2012). *Savannas of Our Birth: People, Wildlife, and Change in East Africa* (Berkeley: University of California Press).

Rosati, A., Tewolde, A., Mosconi, C. & Allan, M.F. (2009). *Animal Production and Animal Science Worldwide: WAAP Book of the Year 2007; A Review on Developments and Research in Livestock Systems* (Wageningen: Academic Publishers).

Schillings, C.G. (1907). *In Wildest Africa* (New York, London: Harper & Brothers).

Schneider, H.K. (1953). *The Pakot (Suk) of Kenya with Special Reference to the Role of Livestock in their Subsistence Economy* (Ann Arbor: UMI).

Schwartz, H.J., Shaabani, S. & Walther D. (1991). *Range Management Handbook of Kenya,* Volume II, 1: 'Marsabit District'. Gesellschaft für Technische Zusmmanarbeit (Berlin: Schonwald Druck).

Scoones, I. (1994). *Living with Uncertainty: New Directions in Pastoral Development in Africa* (London: Intermediate Technology Publications).

Shigesada, N. & Kawasaki, K. (1997). *Biological Invasions: Theory and Practice* (Oxford: University Press).

Somerville, K. (2016). *Ivory: Power and Poaching in Africa* (Hurst & Company, London).

Spear, T.T. & Waller, R.D. (eds) (1993). *Being Maasai: Ethnicity and Identity in East Africa* (London: James Currey).

Spencer, P. (1965). *The Samburu: A Study of Gerontocracy in a Nomadic Tribe* (London: Routledge & Kegan Paul).

—— (1997). *The Pastoral Continuum: The Marginalization of Tradition in East Africa* (Oxford: Clarendon Press).

Spinage, C.A. (2003). *Cattle Plague: A History* (New York: Kluwer).

—— (2012). *African Ecology: Benchmarks and Historical Perspectives* (Berlin, Heidelberg: Springer).

Stoller, P. (1989) *The Taste of Ethnographic Things: The Senses in Anthropology* (Philadelphia: University of Pennsylvania Press).

Tambiah, S.J. (1999). *Magic, Science, Religion, and the Scope of Rationality* (Cambridge: University Press).

Thomson, J. (1887). *Through Masai Land: A Journey of Exploration among the Snowclad Volcanic Mountains and Strange Tribes of Eastern Equatorial Africa. Being the Narrative of the Royal Geographical Society's Expedition to Mount Kenia and Lake Victoria Nyanza, 1883–1884* (London: Sampson Low, Marston, Searle & Rivington).

Timberlake, J. (1987). *Ethnobotany of the Pokot of Northern Kenya* (London: Royal Botanic Gardens).

van Gennep, A. (2010). *The Rites of Passage* (London, New York: Routledge).

von Hoehnel, L. (1894). *Discovery of Lakes Rudolf and Stefanie; A Narrative of Count Samuel Teleki's Exploring & Hunting Expedition in Eastern Equatorial Africa in 1887 & 1888* (London: Longmans, Green & Co.).

von Tiedemann, A. (1907). *Tana, Baringo, Nil: Mit Karl Peters zu Emin Pascha* (Berlin: C.A. Schwetschke und Sohn).

Chapters in edited collections

Balée, W. (1998). 'Historical Ecology: Premises and Postulates', in W. Balée (ed.), *Advances in Historical Ecology* (New York: Columbia University Press), 13–29.

Balée, W. & Erickson, C.L. (2006). 'Time, Complexity, and Historical Ecology', in W. Balée & C.L. Erickson (eds), *Time and Complexity in Historical Ecology* (New Work: Columbia University Press), 1–18.

Barrow, E.G. (1986). 'The Value of Traditional Knowledge in Present-Day

Soil-Conservation Practice: The Example of West Pokot and Turkana', in D.B. Thomas, E.K. Biamah & A.M. Kilewe (eds), *Soil and Water Conservation in Kenya: Proceedings of the Third National Workshop, Kabete, Nairobi, 16–19 September 1986*, 471–85.

Bollig, M. & Oesterle, M. (2013). 'The Political Ecology of Specialisation and Diversification: Long-Term Dynamics of Pastoralism in East Pokot District, Kenya', in M. Bollig, M. Schnegg & H.-P. Wotzka (eds), *Pastoralism in Africa: Past, Present and Future* (New York: Berghahn), 289–315.

Brockington, D. & Homewood, K. (1996). 'Debates Concerning Mkomazi Game Reserve Tanzania', in M. Leach and R. Mearns (eds), *The Lie of the Land: Challenging Received Wisdom on the African Environment* (Oxford: James Currey), 91–104.

Catley, A. & Aklilu, Y. (2013). 'Moving up or Moving out? Commercialization, Growth and Destitution in Pastoralist Areas', in A. Catley, I. Scoones & J. Lind (eds), *Pastoralism and Development in Africa: Dynamic Change at the Margins* (New York, London: Routledge), 85–97.

Conant, F.P. (1982). 'Thorns Paired, Sharply Recurved: Cultural Controls and Rangeland Quality in East Africa', in B. Spooner & H.S. Mann (eds), *Desertification and Development: Dryland Ecology in Social Perspective* (London: Academic Press), 111–22.

Crumley, C.L. (2018). 'Historical Ecology', in H. Callan (ed.), *The International Encyclopedia of Anthropology* (Hoboken: John Wiley & Sons Ltd), 1–5.

Egan, D. & Howell, E.A. (2001). 'Introduction', in D. Egan & E.A. Howell (eds), *The Historical Ecology Handbook: A Restorationist's Guide to Reference Ecosystems* (Washington: Island Press), 1–23.

Erickson, C. (2003). 'Historical Ecology and Future Explorations', in J. Lehmann, D.C. Kern, B. Glaser & W.I. Woods (eds), *Amazonian Dark Earths: Origin, Properties, Management* (Dordrecht: Kluwer Academic), 455–500.

Faas, A.J. & Jones, E.C. (2016). 'Social Network Analysis Focused on Individuals Facing Hazards and Disasters', in E.C. Jones & A.J. Faas (eds), *Social Network Analysis of Disaster Response, Recovery, and Adaptation* (Amsterdam: Butterworth-Heinemann), 11–23.

Fernández-Llamazares, Á., Díaz-Reviriego, I. & Reyes-García, V. (2016). 'Defaunation Through the Eyes of the Tsimane', in V. Reyes-García and A. Pyhälä (eds), *Hunter-gatherers in a Changing World* (Cham: Springer International Publishing), 77–90.

Fratkin, E. (2013). 'Seeking Alternative Livelihoods in Pastoral Areas', in A. Catley, I. Scoones & J. Lind (eds), *Pastoralism and Development in Africa: Dynamic Change at the Margins* (London, New York: Routledge), 197–205.

Fratkin, E. & Smith, K. (1994). 'Labor, Livestock, and Land: The Organization of Pastoral Production', in E. Fratkin, K.A. Galvin & E.A. Roth (eds), *African Pastoralist Systems: An Integrated Approach* (Boulder: L. Rienner Publishers), 91–112.

Galaty, J.G. (1994). 'Rangeland Tenure and Pastoralism in Africa', in E. Fratkin, K.A. Galvin & E.A. Roth (eds), *African Pastoralist Systems: An Integrated Approach* (Boulder: L. Rienner Publishers), 185–204.

—— (1996). 'Pastoralists', in A. Barnard & J. Spencer (eds), *Encyclopedia of Social and Cultural Anthropology* (London: Routledge), 415–16.

—— (2013). 'Land Grabbing in the Eastern African Rangelands', in A. Catley, I. Scoones & J. Lind (eds), *Pastoralism and Development in Africa: Dynamic Change at the Margins* (London, New York: Routledge), 143–53.

Galaty, J.G. & Bonte, P. (1991). 'The Current Realities of African Pastoralists', in J.G. Galaty & P. Bonte (eds), *Herders, Warriors, and Traders: Pastoralism in Africa* (Boulder: Westview Press), 267–92.

Galvin, K.A. & Little, M.A. (1999). 'Dietary Intake and Nutritional Status', in P.W. Leslie & M.A. Little (eds), *Turkana Herders of the Dry Savanna: Ecology and Biobehavioral Response of Nomads to an Uncertain Environment* (Oxford: University Press), 125–46.

Greiner, C. (2020). 'Negotiating Access to Land and Resources at the Geothermal Frontier in Baringo, Kenya', in J. Lind, D. Okenwa & I. Scoones (eds), *Land, Investment & Politics: Reconfiguring Eastern Africa's Pastoral Drylands* (Woodbridge: James Currey), 101–09.

Handwerker, W.P. & Borgatti, S.P. (2014). 'Reasoning with Numbers', in H.R. Bernard & C.C. Gravlee (eds), *Handbook of Methods in Cultural Anthropology* (Lanham: Rowman & Littlefield), 487–97.

Kusimba, C.M. (2011). 'The Human-Wildlife Conundrum: A View from East Africa', in C.T. Fisher, J.B. Hill & G.M. Feinman (eds), *The Archaeology of Environmental Change: Socionatural Legacies of Degradation and Resilience* (Tucson: University of Arizona Press), 135–59.

Lamprey, H. (1983). 'Pastoralism Yesterday and Today: The Overgrazing Problem', in F. Bourlière (ed.), *Tropical Savannas* (Amsterdam: Elsevier), 643–66.

Letai, J. & Lind, J. (2013). 'Squeezed from all Sides: Changing Recourse Tenure and Pastoralist Innovation on the Laikipia Plateau, Kenya', in A. Catley, I. Scoones & J. Lind (eds), *Pastoralism and Development in Africa: Dynamic Change at the Margins* (London, New York: Routledge), 164–76.

Lind, J., Okenwa, D. & Scoones, I. (2020b). 'The Politics of Land, Resources and Investment in Eastern Africa's Pastoral Drylands', in J. Lind, D. Okenwa & I. Scoones (eds), *Land, Investment & Politics: Reconfiguring Eastern Africa's Pastoral Drylands* (Woodbridge: James Currey), 1–32.

Little, M.A., Dyson-Hudson, R., Dyson-Hudson, N. & Winterbauer, N. (2007a). 'Environmental Variations in the South Turkana Ecosystem', in M.A. Little (ed.), *Turkana Herders of the Dry Savanna: Ecology and Biobehavioral Response of Nomads to an Uncertain Environment* (Oxford: University Press), 316–32.

Little, M.A., Dyson-Hudson, R. & McCabe, J.T. (2007b). 'Ecology of South Turkana', in M.A. Little (ed.), *Turkana Herders of the Dry Savanna: Ecology and Biobehavioral Response of Nomads to an Uncertain Environment* (Oxford: University Press), 43–65.

Little, P.D. (2013). 'Reflections on the Future of Pastoralism in the Horn of Africa', in A. Catley, I. Scoones & J. Lind (eds), *Pastoralism and Development in Africa: Dynamic Change at the Margins* (London, New York: Routledge), 243–49.

McCarty, C. & Molina, J.L. (2014). 'Social Network Analysis', in H.R. Bernard &

C.C. Gravlee (eds), *Handbook of Methods in Cultural Anthropology* (Lanham: Rowman & Littlefield), 631–57.

McPeak, J.G. & Little, P.D. (2006). 'Cursed If You Do, Cursed If You Don't: The Contradictory Processes of Sedentarization of Pastoralists in Northern Kenya', in E. Fratkin and E.A. Roth (eds), *As Pastoralists Settle: Social, Health, and Economic Consequences of the Pastoral Sedentarization in Marsabit District, Kenya* (London, New York: Kluwer), 87–104.

Muniappan, R., Reddy, G.V.P. & Raman, A. (2009). 'Biological Control of Weeds in the Tropics and Sustainability', in R. Muniappan, G.V.P. Reddy & A. Raman (eds), *Biological Control of Tropical Weeds Using Arthropods* (Cambridge: University Press), 1–16.

Ogutu, W.O., Mueller-Schaerer, H., Schaffner, U., Edwards, P.J. & Day, R. (2008). 'Is Prosopis Meeting its Match in Baringo?', in M.H. Julien, R. Sforza, M.C. Bon, H.C. Evans, P.E. Hatcher, H.L. Hinz & B.G. Rector (eds), *Proceedings of the XII International Symposium on Biological Control of Weeds, La Grande Motte, France, 22–27 April, 2007* (Wallingford: CABI), 360.

Peristiany, J.G. (1975). 'The Ideal and the Actual: The Role of Prophets in the Pokot Political System', in J. Beattie & G. Lienhardt (eds), *Studies in Social Anthropology: Essays in Memory of E.E. Evans-Pritchard by his former Oxford Colleagues* (Oxford: Clarendon Press), 167–212.

Pringle, R.M., Palmer, T.M., Goheen, J.R., McCauley, D.J. & Keesing, F. (2010). 'Ecological Importance of Large Herbivores in the Ewaso Ecosystem', in N.J. Georgiadis (ed.) *Conserving Wildlife in African Landscapes: Kenya's Ewaso Ecosystem*, Smithsonian Contributions to Zoology, 632 (Washington: Smithsonian Institution), 43–53.

Reid, R.S., Serneels, S., Nyabenge, M. & Hanson, J. (2005). 'The Changing Face of Pastoral Systems in Grass-Dominated Ecosystems of Eastern Africa', in J.M. Suttie & S.G. Reynolds (eds), *Grasslands of the World* (Rome: Food and Agriculture Organization of the United Nations), 19–76.

Reid, R.S., Galvin, K.A. & Kruska, R.S. (2008). 'Global Significance of Extensive Grazing Lands and Pastoral Societies: An Introduction', in K.A. Galvin, N.T. Hobbs, R.H. Behnke & R.S. Reid (eds), *Fragmentation in Semi-Arid and Arid Landscapes: Consequences for Human and Natural Systems* (Dordrecht: Springer), 1–24.

Richardson, L. & St. Pierre, E.A. (2005). 'Writing: A Method of Inquiry.', in N.K. Denzin & Y.S. Lincoln (eds), *The SAGE Handbook of Qualitative Research* (Thousand Oaks: Sage Publications), 959–78.

Roth, E.A., Fratkin, E. & Galvin, K.A. (1994). 'Future Directions in Pastoral Society and Research', in E. Fratkin, K.A. Galvin & E.A. Roth (eds), *African Pastoralist Systems: An Integrated Approach* (Boulder: L. Rienner Publishers), 231–36.

Schneider, H.K. (1959). 'Pakot Resistance to Change', in W.R. Bascom & M.J. Herskovits (eds), *Continuity and Change in African Cultures* (Chicago: University of Chicago Press), 144–67.

Spencer, P. (2018). 'Age Systems and Kinship', in H. Callan (ed.), *The International Encyclopedia of Anthropology* (Hoboken, Chichester: Wiley Blackwell), 1–2.

van Klinken, R.D., Hoffmann, J.H., Zimmermann, H.G. & Roberts, A.P. (2009). '*Prosopis* Species (Leguminosae)', in R. Muniappan, G.V.P. Reddy, & A. Raman (eds), *Biological Control of Tropical Weeds Using Arthropods* (Cambridge: University Press), 353–77.

Vergunst, J.L. & Ingold, T. (2006). 'Fieldwork on Foot: Perceiving, Routing, Socializing', in S. Coleman & P. Collins (eds), *Locating the Field: Space, Place and Context in Anthropology* (Oxford, New York: Berghahn), 67–85.

Waller, R. (1988). 'Emutai: Crisis and Response in Maasailand 1883–1902', in D.H. Johnson & D.M. Anderson (eds), *The Ecology of Survival: Case Studies from Northeast African History* (London, Boulder: L. Crook Academic Pub; Westview Press), 73–114.

Zimmermann, H., Moran, C. & Hoffmann, J. (2009). 'Invasive Cactus Species (Cactaceae)', in R. Muniappan, G.V.P. Reddy, & A. Raman (eds), *Biological Control of Tropical Weeds Using Arthropods* (Cambridge: University Press), 108–29.

Journal articles

Alden Wily, L. (2018). 'The Community Land Act in Kenya Opportunities and Challenges for Communities', *Land,* 7(1), 12.

Almagor, U. (1979). 'Raiders and Elders: A Confrontation among the Dassanetch of Generations', *Senri Ethnological Studies,* 3, 119–45.

Alvarez, M., Leparmarai, P., Heller, G. & Becker, M. (2016). 'Recovery and Germination of *Prosopis juliflora* (Sw.) DC Seeds after Ingestion by Goats and Cattle', *Arid Land Research and Management,* 31(1), 71–80.

Alvarez, M., Heller, G., Malombe, I., Matheka, K.W., Choge, S. & Becker, M. (2019) 'Classification of *Prosopis juliflora* Invasion in the Lake Baringo Basin and Environmental Correlations', *African Journal of Ecology,* 57(3), 296–303.

Anderson, D.M. (2004). 'Massacre at Ribo Post: Expansion and Expediency on the Colonial Frontier in East Africa', *The International Journal of African Historical Studies,* 37(1), 33–54.

—— (2016). 'The Beginning of Time? Evidence for Catastrophic Drought in Baringo in the Early Nineteenth Century', *Journal of Eastern African Studies,* 10(1), 45–66.

Angassa, A. & Oba, G. (2008). 'Herder Perceptions on Impacts of Range Enclosures, Crop Farming, Fire Ban and Bush Encroachment on the Rangelands of Borana, Southern Ethiopia', *Human Ecology,* 36(2), 201–15.

Balée, W. (2006). 'The Research Program of Historical Ecology', *Annual Review of Anthropology,* 35(1), 75–98.

Barton, J. (1921). 'Notes on the Suk Tribe of Kenia Colony', *The Journal of the Royal Anthropological Institute of Great Britain and Ireland,* 51, 82–99.

Baskin, J.M., Baskin, C.C. & Li, X. (2000). 'Taxonomy, Anatomy and Evolution of Physical Dormancy in Seeds', *Plant Species Biology,* 15(2), 139–52.

Bassett, E.M. (2017). 'The Challenge of Reforming Land Governance in Kenya under the 2010 Constitution', *The Journal of Modern African Studies,* 55(4), 537–66.

Beachey, R.W. (1967). 'The East African Ivory Trade in the Nineteenth Century', *The Journal of African History,* 8(2), 269–90.

Becker, M., Alvarez, M., Heller, G., Leparmarai, P., Maina, D., Malombe, I., Bollig, M. & Vehrs, H. (2016). 'Land-Use Changes and the Invasion Dynamics of Shrubs in Baringo', *Journal of Eastern African Studies,* 10(1), 111–29.

Bedelian, C. & Ogutu, J.O. (2017). 'Trade-Offs for Climate-Resilient Pastoral Livelihoods in Wildlife Conservancies in the Mara Ecosystem, Kenya', *Pastoralism: Research, Policy and Practice,* 7(1).

Belnap, J., Ludwig, J.A., Wilcox, B.P., Betancourt, J.L., Dean, W.R.J., Hoffmann, B.D., et al. (2012). 'Introduced and Invasive Species in Novel Rangeland Ecosystems: Friends or Foes?', *Rangeland Ecology & Management,* 65(6), 569–78.

Bessems, I., Verschuren, D., Russell, J.M., Hus, J., Mees, F. & Cumming, B.F. (2008). 'Palaeolimnological Evidence for Widespread Late 18th Century Drought across Equatorial East Africa', *Palaeogeography, Palaeoclimatology, Palaeoecology,* 259(2–3), 107–20.

Beyene, F. (2009). 'Exploring Incentives for Rangeland Enclosures among Pastoral and Agropastoral Households in Eastern Ethiopia', *Global Environmental Change,* 19(4), 494–502.

Bianco, B.A. (1991). 'Women and Things: Pokot Motherhood as Political Destiny', *American Ethnologist,* 18(4), 770–85.

—— (1996). 'Songs of Mobility in West Pokot', *American Ethnologist,* 23(1), 25–42.

Boles, O.J.C., Shoemaker, A., Courtney Mustaphi, C.J., Petek, N., Ekblom, A. & Lane, P.J. (2019). 'Historical Ecologies of Pastoralist Overgrazing in Kenya: Long-Term Perspectives on Cause and Effect', *Human Ecology,* 47(3), 419–34.

Bollig, M. (1990b). 'Ethnic Conflicts in North-West Kenya: Pokot-Turkana Raiding 1969–1984', *Zeitschrift für Ethnologie,* 115, 73–90.

—— (1992b). 'East Pokot Camel Husbandry', *Nomadic Peoples,* (31), 34–50.

—— (1995). 'The Veterinary System of the Pastoral Pokot', *Nomadic Peoples,* 36/37, 17–33.

—— (2016). 'Adaptive Cycles in the Savannah: Pastoral Specialization and Diversification in Northern Kenya', *Journal of Eastern African Studies,* 10(1), 21–44.

Bollig, M. & Lang, H. (1999). 'Demographic Growth and Resource Exploitation in Two Pastoral Communities', *Nomadic Peoples,* 3(2), 16–34.

Bollig, M. & Oesterle, M. (2008). 'Changing Communal Land Tenure in an East African Pastoral System: Institutions and Socio-Economic Transformations among the Pokot of NW Kenya', *Zeitschrift für Ethnologie,* 133, 301–22.

Bollig, M. & Schulte, A. (1999). 'Environmental Change and Pastoral Perceptions: Degradation and Indigenous Knowledge in Two African Pastoral Communities', *Human Ecology,* 27(3), 493–514.

Bonfoh, B., Fokou, G., Crump, L., Zinsstag, J. & Schelling, E. (2016). 'Institutional Development and Policy Frameworks for Pastoralism: From Local to Regional Perspectives', *Revue scientifique et technique (International Office of Epizootics),* 35(2), 499–509.

Boone, C., Dyzenhaus, Dyzenhaus, A., Manji, A., Gateri, C.W., Ouma, S., Owino, J.K., Gargule, A. & Klopp, J.M. (2019). 'Land Law Reform in Kenya:

Devolution, Veto Players, and the Limits of an Institutional Fix', *African Affairs,* 118(471), 215–37.

Bright, R. (1899). 'Our Adventures in Unknown Uganda', *The Wide World Magazine,* 4(20), 169–77.

Brooks, D.R. (1985). 'Historical Ecology: A New Approach to Studying the Evolution of Ecological Associations', *Annals of the Missouri Botanical Garden,* 72(4), 660–80.

Brottem, L.V. (2016). 'Environmental Change and Farmer-Herder Conflict in Agro-Pastoral West Africa', *Human Ecology,* 44(5), 547–63.

Bürgi, M. & Gimmi, U. (2007). 'Three Objectives of Historical Ecology: The Case of Litter Collecting in Central European Forests', *Landscape Ecology,* 22(1), 77–87.

Butt, B. (2016). 'Ecology, Mobility and Labour: Dynamic Pastoral Herd Management in an Uncertain World', *Revue scientifique et technique (International Office of Epizootics),* 35(2), 461–72.

Byakagaba, P., Egeru, A., Barasa, B. & Briske, D.D. (2018). 'Uganda's Rangeland Policy: Intentions, Consequences and Opportunities', *Pastoralism: Research, Policy and Practice,* 8(1).

Catley, A., Lind, J. & Scoones, I. (2016). 'The Futures of Pastoralism in the Horn of Africa: Pathways of Growth and Change', *Revue scientifique et technique (International Office of Epizootics),* 35(2), 389–403.

Choge, S.K., Pasiecznik, N.M., Harvey, M., Wright, J., Awan, S.Z. & Harris, P.J. (2009). '*Prosopis* Pods as Human Food, with Special Reference to Kenya', *Water SA,* 33(3).

Coast, E., Fanghanel, A., Lelièvre, E. & Randall, S. (2016). 'Counting the Population or Describing Society? A Comparison of English and Welsh and French Censuses', *European Journal of Population = Revue europeenne de demographie,* 32, 165–88.

Comaroff, J. (2017). 'Invasive Aliens: The Late-Modern Politics of Species Being', *Social Research: An International Quarterly,* 84(1), 29–52.

Comaroff, J. & Comaroff, J.L. (2001). 'Naturing the Nation: Aliens, Apocalypse and the Postcolonial State', *Journal of Southern African Studies,* 27(3), 627–51.

Dabasso, B.H. & Okomoli, M.O. (2015). 'Changing Pattern of Local Rainfall: Analysis of a 50-Year Record in Central Marsabit, Northern Kenya', *Weather,* 70(10), 285–89.

Dabasso, B.H., Taddese, Z. & Hoag, D. (2014). 'Carbon Stocks in Semi-Arid Pastoral Ecosystems of Northern Kenya', *Pastoralism: Research, Policy and Practice,* 4(1).

Davies, M.I.J. (2008). 'The Irrigation System of the Pokot, Northwest Kenya', *Azania: Archaeological Research in Africa,* 43(1), 50–76.

—— (2012). 'Some Thoughts on a "Useable" African Archaeology: Settlement, Population and Intensive Farming among the Pokot of Northwest Kenya', *The African Archaeological Review,* 29(4), 319–53.

Davies, M.I.J. & Moore, H.L. (2016). 'Landscape, Time and Cultural Resilience: A Brief History of Agriculture in Pokot and Marakwet, Kenya', *Journal of Eastern African Studies,* 10(1), 67–87.

Davis, M.A. & Thompson, K. (2000). 'Eight Ways to be a Colonizer; Two Ways to be an Invader: A Proposed Nomenclature Scheme for Invasion Ecology', *Bulletin of the Ecological Society of America,* 81, 226–30.

—— (2002). '"Newcomers" Invade the Field of Invasion Ecology: Question the Field's Future', *Bulletin of the Ecological Society of America,* 83(3), 196–97.

Denoth, M., Frid, L. & Myers, J.H. (2002). 'Multiple Agents in Biological Control: Improving the Odds?', *Biological Control,* 24, 20–30.

Dirzo, R., Young, H.S., Galetti, M., Ceballos, G., Isaac, N.J.B. & Collen, B. (2014). 'Defaunation in the Anthropocene', *Science,* 345(6195), 401–06.

Dublin, H.T., Sinclair, A. & McGlade, J. (1990). 'Elephants and Fire as Causes of Multiple Stable States in the Serengeti-Mara Woodlands', *The Journal of Animal Ecology,* 59(3), 1147–64.

Dundas, K. (1910). 'Notes on the Tribes Inhabiting the Baringo District, East Africa Protectorate', *The Journal of the Royal Anthropological Institute of Great Britain and Ireland,* 40, 49–72.

—— (1911). 'Notes on the Fauna of Baringo District', *Journal of The East Africa and Uganda Natural History Society,* 2(3), 63–67.

Dyer, C. (2016). 'Approaches to Education Provision for Mobile Pastoralists', *Revue scientifique et technique (International Office of Epizootics),* 35(2), 631–38.

Eastwood, B. (1903). 'A Battle with a Rhino', *The Wide World Magazine,* 11(65), 418–27.

Edgerton, R.B. (1964). 'Pokot Intersexuality: An East African Example of the Resolution of Sexual Incongruity', *American Anthropologist,* 66(6), 1288–99.

Enders, M., Havemann, F., Ruland, F., Bernard-Verdier, M., Catford, J.A., Gómez-Aparicio, L., et al. (2020). 'A Conceptual Map of Invasion Biology: Integrating Hypotheses into a Consensus Network', *Global Ecology and Biogeography,* 29(6), 978–91.

Falk-Petersen, J., Bøhn, T. & Sandlund, O.T. (2006). 'On the Numerous Concepts in Invasion Biology', *Biological Invasions,* 8(6), 1409–24.

Ferguson, J. (2005). 'Seeing Like an Oil Company: Space, Security, and Global Capital in Neoliberal Africa', *American Anthropologist,* 107(3), 377–82.

Foxcroft, L.C. & Hoffmann, J.H. (2000). 'Dispersal of *Dactylopius opuntiae* Cockerell (Homoptera Dactylopiidae), a Biological Control Agent of *Opuntia stricta* (Haworth.) Haworth. (Cactaceae) in the Kruger National Park', *Koedoe,* 43(2), 1–5.

Foxcroft, L.C., Rouget, M., Richardson, D.M. & Fadyen, S.M. (2004). 'Reconstructing 50 Years of *Opuntia stricta* Invasion in the Kruger National Park, South Africa: Environmental Determinants and Propagule Pressure', *Diversity and Distributions,* 10(5–6), 427–37.

Galaty, J.G. (2016). 'Reasserting the Commons: Pastoral Contestations of Private and State Lands in East Africa', *International Journal of the Commons,* 10(2), 709–27.

Galvin, K.A. (2009). 'Transitions: Pastoralists Living with Change', *Annual Review of Anthropology,* 38, 185–98.

Geertz, C. (1972). 'Deep Play: Notes on the Balinese Cockfight', *Daedalus,* 101(1), 1–37.

—— (1974). '"From the Native's Point of View": On the Nature of Anthropological

Understanding', *Bulletin of the American Academy of Arts and Sciences,* 28(1), 26–45.

Goheen, J.R., Palmer, T.M., Keesing, F., Riginos, C. & Young, T.P. (2010). 'Large Herbivores Facilitate Savanna Tree Establishment via Diverse and Indirect Pathways', *The Journal of Animal Ecology,* 79(2), 372–82.

Gravesen, M.L. & Kioko, E.M. (2019). 'Cooperation in the Midst of Violence: Land Deals and Cattle Raids in Narok and Laikipia, Kenya', *Africa,* 89(3), 562–85.

Greiner, C. (2012). 'Unexpected Consequences: Wildlife Conservation and Territorial Conflict in Northern Kenya', *Human Ecology,* 40(3), 415–25.

—— (2016a). 'Land-Use Change, Territorial Restructuring, and Economies of Anticipation in Dryland Kenya', *Journal of Eastern African Studies,* 10(3), 530–47.

—— (2016b). 'Pastoralism and Land-Tenure Change in Kenya: The Failure of Customary Institutions', *Development and Change,* 48(1), 78–98

Greiner, C. & Mwaka, I. (2016). 'Agricultural Change at the Margins: Adaptation and Intensification in a Kenyan Dryland', *Journal of Eastern African Studies,* 10(1), 130–49.

Greiner, C., Alvarez, M. & Becker, M. (2013). 'From Cattle to Corn: Attributes of Emerging Farming Systems of Former Pastoral Nomads in East Pokot, Kenya', *Society & Natural Resources,* 26(12), 1478–90.

Greiner, C., Greven, D. & Klagge, B. (2021). 'Roads to Change: Livelihoods, Land Disputes, and Anticipation of Future Developments in Rural Kenya', *The European Journal of Development Research,* 33, 1044–68.

Guldemond, R. & van Aarde, R. (2008). 'A Meta-Analysis of the Impact of African Elephants on Savanna Vegetation', *The Journal of Wildlife Management,* 72(4), 892–99.

Gulliver, P.H. (1958). 'The Turkana Age Organization', *American Anthropologist,* 60(5), 900–22.

Gustafson, C.R., VanWormer, E., Kazwala, R., Makweta, A., Paul, G., Smith, W. & Mazet J.A.K. (2015). 'Educating Pastoralists and Extension Officers on Diverse Livestock Diseases in a Changing Environment in Tanzania', *Pastoralism: Research, Policy and Practice,* 5(1).

Guyer, J.I. (1981). 'Household and Community in African Studies', *African Studies Review,* 24(2/3), 87.

Guyer, J.I. & Peters, P.E. (1987). 'Introduction', *Development and Change,* 18(2), 197–214.

Hakansson, N.T. (2004). 'The Human Ecology of World Systems in East Africa: The Impact of the Ivory Trade', *Human Ecology,* 32(5), 561–91.

Haller, T., van Dijk, H., Bollig, M., Greiner, C., Schareika, N. & Gabbert, C. (2016). 'Conflicts, Security and Marginalisation: Institutional Change of the Pastoral Commons in a "Glocal" World', *Revue scientifique et technique (International Office of Epizootics),* 35(2), 405–16.

Hare, F.K., Kates, R.W. & Warren, A. (1977). 'The Making of Deserts: Climate, Ecology, and Society', *Economic Geography,* 53(4), 332–46.

Hardin, G. (1968). 'The Tragedy of the Commons', *Science,* 162 (3859), 1243–48.

Heine, C. (2015). 'Pastoralists as Stewards of the Environment', *D+C International Journal*, 38–39.

Hempson, G.P., Archibald, S. & Bond, W.J. (2017). 'The Consequences of Replacing Wildlife with Livestock in Africa', *Scientific Reports,* 7(1).

Herrero, M., Addison, J., Bedelian, C., Carabine, E., Havlík, P. & Henderson, B., van der Steeg, J. & Thornton, P.K. (2016) 'Climate Change and Pastoralism: Impacts, Consequences and Adaptation', *Revue scientifique et technique (International Office of Epizootics),* 35(2), 417–33.

Hobbs, N.T., Galvin, K.A., Stokes, C.J., Lackett, J.M., Ash, A.J. & Boone, R.B., N., Reid, R. & Thornton, P.K. (2008). 'Fragmentation of Rangelands: Implications for Humans, Animals, and Landscapes', *Global Environmental Change,* 18(4), 776–85.

Hobley, C.W. (1906). 'Notes on the Geography and People of the Baringo District of the East Africa Protectorate', *The Geographical Journal,* 28(5), 471–81.

Hodgson, D.L. (1999). '"Once Intrepid Warriors": Modernity and the Production of Maasai Masculinities', *Ethnology,* 38(2), 121–50.

Homewood, K. (1999). 'Comments' in L.M. Ruttan and M. Borgerhoff Mulder, 'Are East African Pastoralists Truly Conservationists?', *Current Anthropology,* 40(5), 621–52.

—— (2004). 'Policy, Environment and Development in African Rangelands', *Environmental Science & Policy,* 7(3), 125–43.

Homewood, K., Lambin, E.F., Coast, E., Kariuki, A., Kikula, I. & Kivelia, J., Said, M., Serneels, S. & Thompson, M. (2001). 'Long-Term Changes in Serengeti-Mara Wildebeest and Land Cover: Pastoralism, Population, or Policies?', *Proceedings of the National Academy of Sciences of the United States of America,* 98(22), 12544–49.

Homewood, K., Trench, P.C. & Brockington, D. (2012). 'Pastoralist Livelihoods and Wildlife Revenues in East Africa: A Case for Coexistence?', *Pastoralism: Research, Policy and Practice,* 2(19).

Hudak, A.T. (1999). 'Rangeland Mismanagement in South Africa: Failure to Apply Ecological Knowledge', *Human Ecology,* 27(1), 55–78.

Humair, F., Edwards, P.J., Siegrist, M. & Kueffer, C. (2014). 'Understanding Misunderstandings in Invasion Science: Why Experts don't Agree on Common Concepts and Risk Assessments', *NeoBiota,* 20, 1–30.

Ilukor, J., Rettberg, S., Treydte, A. & Birner, R. (2016). 'To Eradicate or not to Eradicate? Recommendations on *Prosopis juliflora* Management in Afar, Ethiopia, from an Interdisciplinary Perspective', *Pastoralism: Research, Policy and Practice,* 6(1).

Jandreau, C. & Berkes, F. (2016). 'Continuity and Change within the Social-Ecological and Political Landscape of the Maasai Mara, Kenya', *Pastoralism: Research, Policy and Practice,* 6(1).

Janzen, S.A., Jensen, N.D. & Mude, A.G. (2016). 'Targeted Social Protection in a Pastoralist Economy: Case Study from Kenya', *Revue scientifique et technique (International Office of Epizootics),* 35(2), 587–96.

Johannes, E.M., Zulu, L.C. & Kalipeni, E. (2014). 'Oil Discovery in Turkana County, Kenya: A Source of Conflict or Development?', *African Geographical Review,* 34(2), 142–64.

Johnstone, I.M. (1986). 'Plant Invasion Windows: A Time-Based Classification of Invasion Potential', *Biological Reviews,* 61(4), 369–94.

Kagunyu, A.F. & Wanjohi, J.G. (2015). 'The Emergency of Euphorbia Tirucalli as Drought Feeds for Camels in Northern Kenya', *Pastoralism: Research, Policy and Practice,* 5(1).

Kantai, P. (2007). 'In the Grip of the Vampire State: Maasai Land Struggles in Kenyan Politics', *Journal of Eastern African Studies,* 1(1), 107–22.

Kaufmann, B.A., Lelea, M.A. & Hulsebusch, C.G. (2016). 'Diversity in Livestock Resources in Pastoral Systems in Africa', *Revue scientifique et technique (International Office of Epizootics),* 35(2), 445–59.

Kiage, L.M. & Liu, K. (2009). 'Palynological Evidence of Climate Change and Land Degradation in the Lake Baringo Area, Kenya, East Africa, since AD 1650', *Palaeogeography, Palaeoclimatology, Palaeoecology,* 279(1–2), 60–72.

Kibet, S., Nyangito, M., MacOpiyo, L. & Kenfack, D. (2016). 'Tracing Innovation Pathways in the Management of Natural and Social Capital on Laikipia Maasai Group Ranches, Kenya', *Pastoralism: Research, Policy and Practice,* 6(1).

Kimiti, D.W., Riginos, C. & Belnap, J. (2016). 'Low-Cost Grass Restoration Using Erosion Barriers in a Degraded African Rangeland', *Restoration Ecology,* 25(3), 376–84.

Kimuyu, D.M., Veblen, K.E., Riginos, C., Chira, R.M., Githaiga, J.M. & Young, T.P. (2017). 'Influence of Cattle on Browsing and Grazing Wildlife Varies with Rainfall and Presence of Megaherbivores', *Ecological Applications: A Publication of the Ecological Society of America,* 27(3), 786–98.

Klagge, B., Greiner, C., Greven, D. & Nweke-Eze, C. (2020). 'Cross-Scale Linkages of Centralized Electricity Generation: Geothermal Development and Investor-Community Relations in Kenya', *Politics and Governance,* 8(3), 211–22.

Klopp, J.M. & Lumumba, O. (2017). 'Reform and Counter-Reform in Kenya's Land Governance', *Review of African Political Economy,* 44(154), 577–94.

Köhler-Rollefson, I. (2016). 'Innovations and Diverse Livelihood Pathways: Alternative Livelihoods, Livelihood Diversification and Societal Transformation in Pastoral Communities', *Revue scientifique et technique (International Office of Epizootics),* 35(2), 611–18.

Lankester, F. & Davis, A. (2016). 'Pastoralism and Wildlife: Historical and Current Perspectives in the East African Rangelands of Kenya and Tanzania', *Revue scientifique et technique (International Office of Epizootics),* 35(2), 473–84.

Leslie, P. & McCabe, J.T. (2013). 'Response Diversity and Resilience in Social-Ecological Systems', *Current Anthropology,* 54(2), 114–43.

Lesorogol, C.K. (2010). 'The Impact of Privatization on Land Inheritance among Samburu Pastoralists in Kenya', *Development and Change,* 41(6), 1091–116.

Levick, S.R., Baldeck, C.A. & Asner, G.P. (2015). 'Demographic Legacies of Fire History in an African Savanna', *Functional Ecology,* 29(1), 131–39.

Lind, J. (2018). 'Devolution, Shifting Centre-Periphery Relationships and Conflict in Northern Kenya', *Political Geography,* 63, 135–47.

Little, P.D. (1996). 'Pastoralism, Biodiversity, and the Shaping of Savanna Landscapes in East Africa', *Africa: Journal of the International African Institute,* 66(1), 37–51.

—— (2016). 'A Victory in Theory, Loss in Practice: Struggles for Political Representation in the Lake Baringo-Bogoria Basin, Kenya', *Journal of Eastern African Studies,* 10(1), 189–207.

—— (2019). 'When "Green" Equals Thorny and Mean: The Politics and Costs of an Environmental Experiment in East Africa', *African Studies Review,* 62(3), 132–63.

Little, P.D., Aboud, A.A. & Lenachuru, C. (2009). 'Can Formal Education Reduce Risks for Drought-Prone Pastoralists? A Case Study from Baringo District, Kenya', *Human Organization,* 68(2), 154–65.

Little, P.D., Smith, K., Cellarius, B.A., Coppock, D.L. & Barrett, C.B. (2001). 'Avoiding Disaster: Diversification and Risk Management among East African Herders', *Development and Change,* 32, 401–33.

Lugusa, K.O., Wasonga, O.V., Elhadi, Y.A. & Crane, T.A. (2016). 'Value Chain Analysis of Grass Seeds in the Drylands of Baringo County, Kenya: A Producers' Perspective', *Pastoralism: Research, Policy and Practice,* 6(1).

Majekodunmi, A.O., Dongkum, C., Langs, T., Shaw, A.P.M. & Welburn, S.C. (2017). 'Shifting Livelihood Strategies in Northern Nigeria: Extensified Production and Livelihood Diversification amongst Fulani Pastoralists', *Pastoralism: Research, Policy and Practice,* 7(1).

Manji, A. (2012). 'The Grabbed State: Lawyers, Politics and Public Land in Kenya', *The Journal of Modern African Studies,* 50(3), 467–92.

—— (2014). 'The Politics of Land Reform in Kenya 2012', *African Studies Review,* 57(1), 115–30.

Marchant, R. (2010). 'Understanding Complexity in Savannas: Climate, Biodiversity and People', *Current Opinion in Environmental Sustainability,* 2(1–2), 101–08.

Marchant, R., Richer, S., Boles, O., Capitani, C., Courtney-Mustaphi, C.J., Lane, P., et al. (2018). 'Drivers and Trajectories of Land Cover Change in East Africa: Human and Environmental Interactions from 6000 Years ago to Present', *Earth-Science Reviews,* 178, 322–78.

Mathevet, R., Peluso, N.L., Couespel, A. & Robbins, P. (2015). 'Using Historical Political Ecology to Understand the Present: Water, Reeds, and Biodiversity in the Camargue Biosphere Reserve, Southern France', *Ecology and Society,* 20(4).

Maundu, P., Kibet, S., Morimoto, Y., Imbumi, M. & Adeka, R. (2009). 'Impact of *Prosopis juliflora* on Kenya's Semi-Arid and Arid Ecosystems and Local Livelihoods', *Biodiversity,* 10(2–3), 33–50.

McCabe, J.T. (2003). 'Disequilibrial Ecosystems and Livelihood Diversification among the Maasai of Northern Tanzania: Implications for Conservation Policy in Eastern Africa', *Nomadic Peoples,* 7(1), 74–91.

McCabe, J.T., Leslie, P.W. & Deluca, L. (2010). 'Adopting Cultivation to Remain Pastoralists: The Diversification of Maasai Livelihoods in Northern Tanzania', *Human Ecology,* 38(3), 321–34.

McCabe, J.T., Smith, N.M., Leslie, P.W. & Telligman, A.L. (2014). 'Livelihood Diversification through Migration among a Pastoral People: Contrasting Case Studies of Maasai in Northern Tanzania', *Human Organization,* 73(4), 389–400.

Meiu, G.P. (2015). '"Beach-Boy Elders" and "Young Big-Men": Subverting the

Temporalities of Ageing in Kenya's Ethno-Erotic Economies', *Ethnos,* 80(4), 472–96.

Midgley, J.J. & Bond, W.J. (2001). 'A Synthesis of the Demography of African Acacias', *Journal of Tropical Ecology,* 17(06).

Moritz, M. (2016). 'Open Property Regimes', *International Journal of the Commons,* 10(2), 688.

Mosley, J. & Watson, E.E. (2016). 'Frontier Transformations: Development Visions, Spaces and Processes in Northern Kenya and Southern Ethiopia', *Journal of Eastern African Studies,* 10(3), 452–75.

Müller-Dempf, H. (1991). 'Generation-Sets: Stability and Change, with Special Reference to Toposa and Turkana Societies', *Bulletin of the School of Oriental and African Studies, University of London,* 54(3), 554–67.

—— (2009). 'The Ngibokoi Dilemma: Generation-sets and Social System Engineering in Times of Stress – an Example from the Toposa of Southern Sudan', *Zeitschrift für Ethnologie,* 134(2), 189–211.

—— (2017). 'Ateker Generation-Set Systems Revisited: Field Facts and Findings, and a Systematisation', *Max Planck Institute for Social Anthropology Working Papers,* 183.

Mureithi, S.M., Verdoodt, A., Njoka, J.T., Gachene, C.K.K. & van Ranst, E. (2016). 'Benefits Derived from Rehabilitating a Degraded Semi-Arid Rangeland in Communal Enclosures, Kenya', *Land Degradation & Development,* 27(8), 1853–62.

Mutsotso, M., Kimaiyo, D. & Gaciuki, P. (2014). 'The Centrality of Cattle in the Social Organization of the East Pokot Pastoralists of North Western Kenya', *European Scientific Journal,* 10(8), 491–507.

Mwangi, E. & Swallow, B. (2008). '*Prosopis juliflora* Invasion and Rural Livelihoods in the Lake Baringo Area of Kenya', *Conservation and Society,* 6(2), 130–40.

Mworia, J.K., Kinyamario, J.I., Omari, J.K. & Wambua, J.K. (2011). 'Patterns of Seed Dispersal and Establishment of the Invader *Prosopis juliflora* in the Upper Floodplain of Tana River, Kenya', *African Journal of Range & Forage Science,* 28(1), 35–41.

Ndhlovu, T., Milton-Dean, S.J. & Esler, K.J. (2011). 'Impact of *Prosopis* (Mesquite) Invasion and Clearing on the Grazing Capacity of Semiarid Nama Karoo Rangeland, South Africa', *African Journal of Range & Forage Science,* 28(3), 129–37.

Negasa, B., Eba, B., Tuffa, S., Bayissa, B., Doyo, J. & Husen, N. (2014). 'Control of Bush Encroachment in Borana Zone of Southern Ethiopia: Effects of Different Control Techniques on Rangeland Vegetation and Tick Populations', *Pastoralism: Research, Policy and Practice,* 4(18).

Niamir-Fuller, M. (2016).'Towards Sustainability in the Extensive and Intensive Livestock Sectors', *Revue scientifique et technique (International Office of Epizootics),* 35(2), 371–87.

Niamir-Fuller, M., Kerven, C., Reid, R. & Milner-Gulland, E. (2012). 'Co-Existence of Wildlife and Pastoralism on Extensive Rangelands: Competition or Compatibility?', *Pastoralism: Research, Policy and Practice,* 2(8).

Nyberg, G., Knutsson, P., Ostwald, M., Öborn, I., Wredle, E., Otieno, D.J., et al.

(2015). 'Enclosures in West Pokot, Kenya: Transforming Land, Livestock and Livelihoods in Drylands', *Pastoralism: Research, Policy and Practice,* 5(1).

Oba, G., Stenseth, N.C. & Lusigi, W.J. (2000). 'New Perspectives on Sustainable Grazing Management in Arid Zones of Sub-Saharan Africa', *BioScience,* 50(1), 35–51.

Oesterle, M. (2008). 'From Cattle to Goats: The Transformation of East Pokot Pastoralism in Kenya', *Nomadic Peoples,* 12(1), 81–91.

Offen, K.H. (2004). 'Historical Political Ecology: An Introduction', *Historical Geography,* 32, 19–42.

Ombega, N.J., Mureithi, S.M., Koech, O.K., Karuma, A.N. & Gachene, C.K.K. (2017). 'Effect of Rangeland Rehabilitation on the Herbaceous Species Composition and Diversity in Suswa Catchment, Narok County, Kenya', *Ecological Processes,* 6(1).

Orr, D.W. (2019). 'Renegotiating the Periphery: Oil Discovery, Devolution, and Political Contestation in Kenya', *The Extractive Industries and Society,* 6(1), 136–44.

Ouedraogo, R. & Davies, J. (2016). 'Enabling Sustainable Pastoralism: Policies and Investments that Optimise Livestock Production and Rangeland Stewardship', *Revue scientifique et technique (International Office of Epizootics),* 35(2), 619–30.

Peristiany, J.G. (1951). 'The Age-Set System of the Pastoral Pokot: The "Sapana" Initiation Ceremony', *Journal of the International African Institute,* 21(3), 188–206.

Powell-Cotton, P. (1904a). 'A Lonely Trans-African Tramp: From the East Coast to Lake Baringo', *The Wide World Magazine,* 12(71), 372–78.

—— (1904b). 'A Lonely Trans-African Tramp: Around Baringo and Mount Elgon', *The Wide World Magazine,* 12(71), 457–62.

—— (1904c). 'In Search of the Five-Horned Giraffe', *The Wide World Magazine,* 14(80), 115–21.

Pyšek, P., Davis, M.A., Daehler, C.C. & Thompson, K. (2004). 'Plant Invasions and Vegetation Succession: Closing the Gap', *Bulletin of the Ecological Society of America,* 85(3), 105–09.

Randall, S. (2015). 'Where Have all the Nomads Gone? Fifty Years of Statistical and Demographic Invisibilities of African Mobile Pastoralists', *Pastoralism: Research, Policy and Practice,* 5(1).

Randall, S. & Coast, E. (2015). 'Poverty in African Households: The Limits of Survey and Census Representations', *The Journal of Development Studies,* 51(2), 162–77.

Randall, S., Coast, E., Antoine, P., Compaore, N., Dial, F.-B., Fanghanel, A., et al. (2015). 'UN Census "Households" and Local Interpretations in Africa Since Independence', *SAGE Open,* 5(2).

Rani, M.S., Pippalla, R.S. & Mohan, K. (2009). 'Dodonaea viscosa Linn. – An Overview', *Asian Journal of Pharmaceutical Research and Health Care,* 1(1), 97–112.

Reid, R.S., Thornton, P.K. & Kruska, R.L. (2004). 'Loss and Fragmentation of Habitat for Pastoral People and Wildlife in East Africa: Concepts and Issues', *African Journal of Range & Forage Science,* 21(3), 171–81.

Riginos, C., Porensky, L.M., Veblen, K.E., Odadi, W.O., Sensenig, R.L. & Kimuyu, D., Keesing, F., Wilkerson, M.L. & Young, T.P. (2012). 'Lessons on the Relationship between Livestock Husbandry and Biodiversity from the Kenya Long-Term Exclosure Experiment (KLEE)', *Pastoralism: Research, Policy and Practice,* 2(1).

Roba, Hassan, G. & Oba, G. (2009). 'Efficacy of Intregrating Herder Knowledge and Ecological Methods for Monitoring Rangeland Degradation in Northern Kenya', *Human Ecology,* 37(5), 589–612.

Roques, K.G., O'Connor, T.G. & Watkinson, A.R. (2001). 'Dynamics of Shrub Encroachment in an African Savanna: Relative Influences of Fire, Herbivory, Rainfall and Density Dependence', *Journal of Applied Ecology,* 38(2), 268–80.

Rowe, J.A. (1994). 'Rinderpest in the Sudan 1888–1890: The Mystery of the Missing Panzootic', *Sudanic Africa,* 5, 149–78.

Sassoon, J.B. (1994). 'A Pokot Marriage', *Kenya Past and Present,* 1994, 49–54.

Schelling, E., Greter, H., Kessely, H., Abakar, M.F., Ngandolo, B.N., Crump, L., et al. (2016). 'Human and Animal Health Surveys among Pastoralists', *Revue scientifique et technique (International Office of Epizootics),* 35(2), 659–71.

Schneider, H.K. (1957). 'The Subsistence Role of Cattle among the Pakot in East Africa', *American Anthropologist,* 59(2), 278–300.

Seddon, P.J., Griffiths, C.J., Soorae, P.S. & Armstrong, D.P. (2014). 'Reversing Defaunation: Restoring Species in a Changing World', *Science,* 345(6195), 406–12.

Seebens, H., Bacher, S., Blackburn, T.M., Capinha, C., Dawson, W., Dullinger, S., et al. (2020). 'Projecting the Continental Accumulation of Alien Species through to 2050', *Global Change Biology,* 27, 970–82.

Seid, M.A., Kuhn, N.J. & Fikre, T.Z. (2016a). 'The Role of Pastoralism in Regulating Ecosystem Services', *Revue scientifique et technique (International Office of Epizootics),* 35(2), 435–44.

Seid, M.A., Yoseph, L.W., Befekadu, U.W., Muhammed, A. & Fikre, T.Z. (2016b). 'Communication for the Development of Pastoralism', *Revue scientifique et technique (International Office of Epizootics),* 35(2), 639–48.

Shackleton, R.T., Witt, A.B.R., Piroris, F.M. & van Wilgen, B.W. (2017). 'Distribution and Socio-Ecological Impacts of the Invasive Alien Cactus *Opuntia stricta* in Eastern Africa', *Biological Invasions,* 19(8), 2427–41.

Singh, A.B. & Kumar, P. (2002). 'Common Environmental Allergens Causing Respiratory Allergy in India', *The Indian Journal of Pediatrics,* 69(3), 245–50.

Smit, I.P.J., Asner, G.P., Govender, N., Kennedy-Bowdoin, T., Knapp, D.E. & Jacobson, J. (2010). 'Effects of Fire on Woody Vegetation Structure in African Savanna', *Ecological Applications: A Publication of the Ecological Society of America,* 20(7), 1865–75.

Smith, L.L. & Ueckert, D.N. (1974). 'Influence of Insects on Mesquite Seed Production', *Journal of Range Management,* 27(1), 61.

Snorek, J., Moser, L. & Renaud, F.G. (2017). 'The Production of Contested Landscapes: Enclosing the Pastoral Commons in Niger', *Journal of Rural Studies,* 51, 125–40.

Spencer, P. (1976). 'Opposing Streams and the Gerontocratic Ladder: Two Models of Age Organisation in East Africa', *Man,* 11(2), 153–75.

Strum, S.C., Stirling, G. & Mutunga, S.K. (2015). 'The Perfect Storm: Land Use Change Promotes *Opuntia stricta*'s Invasion of Pastoral Rangelands in Kenya', *Journal of Arid Environments,* 118, 37–47.

Swetnam, T.W., Allen, C.D. & Betancourt, J.L. (1999). 'Applied Historical Ecology: Using the Past to Manage for the Future', *Historical Variability,* 9(4), 1189–206.

Szabó, P. (2015). 'Historical Ecology: Past, Present and Future', *Biological Reviews of the Cambridge Philosophical Society,* 90(4), 997–1014.

Szabó, P. & Hédl, R. (2011). 'Advancing the Integration of History and Ecology for Conservation', *Conservation Biology: The Journal of the Society for Conservation Biology,* 25(4), 680–87.

Talbot, L.M. (1986). 'Demographic Factors in Resource Depletion and Environmental Degradation in East African Rangeland', *Population and Development Review,* 12(3), 441.

Tamou, C., Ripoll-Bosch, R., de Boer, I.J.M. & Oosting, S.J. (2018). 'Pastoralists in a Changing Environment: The Competition for Grazing Land in and around the W Biosphere Reserve, Benin Republic', *Ambio,* 47(3), 340–54.

Tarits, C., Renaut, R.W., Tiercelin, J.-J., Le Hérissé, A., Cotten, J. & Cabon, J.-Y. (2006). 'Geochemical Evidence of Hydrothermal Recharge in Lake Baringo, Central Kenya Rift Valley', *Hydrological Processes,* 20(9), 2027–55.

Thompson, M. & Homewood, K. (2002). 'Entrepreneurs, Elites, and Exclusion in Maasailand: Trends in Wildlife Conservation and Pastoralist Development', *Human Ecology,* 30(1), 107–38.

Tregidgo, D.J., Barlow, J., Pompeu, P.S., de Almeida Rocha, M. & Parry, L. (2017). 'Rainforest Metropolis Casts 1,000-km Defaunation Shadow', *Proceedings of the National Academy of Sciences of the United States of America,* 114(32), 8655–59.

Valéry, L., Fritz, H., Lefeuvre, J.-C. & Simberloff, D. (2008). 'In Search of a Real Definition of the Biological Invasion Phenomenon Itself', *Biological Invasions,* 10(8), 1345–51.

Vehrs, H.-P. (2016). 'Changes in Landscape Vegetation, Forage Plant Composition and Herding Structure in the Pastoralist Livelihoods of East Pokot, Kenya', *Journal of Eastern African Studies,* 10(1), 88–110.

Vehrs, H.-P.& Heller, G.R. (2017). 'Fauna, Fire and Farming: Landscape Formation over the Past 200 Years in Pastoral East Pokot, Kenya', *Human Ecology,* 45, 613–25.

Veldhuis, M.P., Ritchie, M.E., Ogutu, J.O., Morrison, T.A., Beale, C.M., Estes, A.B. et al. (2019). 'Cross-Boundary Human Impacts Compromise the Serengeti-Mara Ecosystem', *Science,* 363(6434), 1424–28.

Vermeij, G.J. (1996). 'An Agenda for Invasion Biology', *Biological Conservation,* 78, 3–9.

Vries, D. de, Leslie, P.W. & McCabe, J.T. (2006). 'Livestock Acquisitions Dynamics in Nomadic Pastoralist Herd Demography: A Case Study Among Ngisonyoka Herders of South Turkana, Kenya', *Human Ecology,* 34, 1–25.

Warren, A. (1995). 'Changing Understandings of African Pastoralism and the Nature of Environmental Paradigms', *Transactions of the Institute of British Geographers,* 20(2), 193–203.

——— (2002). 'Land Degradation is Contextual', *Land Degradation & Development,* 13(6), 449–59.

Weber, K.T. & Horst, S. (2011). 'Desertification and Livestock Grazing: The Roles of Sedentarization, Mobility and Rest', *Pastoralism: Research, Policy and Practice,* 1(19).

Weitzberg, K. (2015). 'The Unaccountable Census: Colonial Enumeration and its Implications for the Somali People of Kenya', *The Journal of African History,* 56(3), 409–28.

Western, D. (1989). The Ecological Role of Elephants in Africa, *Pachyderm,* 12, 42–45.

Western, D. & Maitumo, D. (2004). 'Woodland Loss and Restoration in a Savanna Park: A 20-Year Experiment', *African Journal of Ecology,* 42, 111–21.

Wikan, U. (1992). 'Beyond the Words: The Power of Resonance', *American Ethnologist,* 19(3), 460–82.

Yadeta, T., Veenendaal, E., Sykora, K., Tessema, Z.K. & Asefa, A. (2018). 'Effect of *Vachellia tortilis* on Understory Vegetation, Herbaceous Biomass and Soil Nutrients along a Grazing Gradient in a Semi-Arid African Savanna', *Journal of Forestry Research,* 29(6), 1601–09.

Young, H.S., McCauley, D.J., Galetti, M. & Dirzo, R. (2016). 'Patterns, Causes, and Consequences of Anthropocene Defaunation', *Annual Review of Ecology, Evolution, and Systematics,* 47(1), 333–58.

Yurco, K. (2017). 'Herders and Herdsmen: The Remaking of Pastoral Livelihoods in Laikipia, Kenya', *Pastoralism: Research, Policy and Practice,* 7(1).

Zimov, S.A. (2005). 'Essays on Science and Society. Pleistocene Park: Return of the Mammoth's Ecosystem', *Science,* 308(5723), 796–98.

Government papers and statutes

Edmondson, R.N. (1965a). *Quarterly Report for September 1965.* Baringo District Range Office. Nakuru National Archives: EV 6/1.

——— (1965b). *Safari Report 5th to 9th January, 1965: Safari to Pokot Land.* Baringo District Range Office. Nakuru National Archives: RGE/3/34.

——— (1966). *Quarterly Report for January, February, March, 1966.* Baringo District Range Office. Nakuru National Archives: EV 6/1.

KNBS and ICF International (2016). *2014 Kenya Demographic and Health Survey Atlas of County-level Health Indicators.* Available at: www.dhsprogram.com/pubs/pdf/ATR16/ATR16.pdf [Accessed 27 April 2021].

Nasieku, D.O. (1975). *Stock Raids/Tribal Clashes,* The Provincial Commissioner, Rift Valley Province. Kenya National Archives, Nakuru, KNA/NKU/C.12/IV/131.

Ndung'u Commission (2004). *Report of the Commission of Inquiry into the Illegal/Irregular Allocation of Public Land.* Available at: http://kenyalaw.org/kl/fileadmin/CommissionReports/A_Report_of_the_Land_Commission_of_Inquiry_into_the_Illegal_or_Irregular_Allocation_of_Land_2004.pdf [Accessed 30 April 2021].

Republic of Kenya (1972). 'Grass Fires Act, Chapter 327', revised Edition 2012 (National Council for Law Reporting). Available at: http://kenyalaw.org/kl/fileadmin/pdfdownloads/Acts/GrassFiresAct__Cap327.pdf [Accessed 19 May 2021].

—— (1975). *Baringo District Development Plan 1974–1978.*

—— (1977). *Baringo District Annual Report: For Year Ending 31st December 1976.*

—— (1981). *Kenya Population Census, 1979: Volume I.* Available at: www.knbs. or.ke/index.php?option=com_phocadownload&view=category&download=43 6:population-census-report-volume-i&id=103:population-and-housing-census-1979&Itemid=599 [Accessed 28 June 2016].

—— (1982). *Baringo District Annual Report for the Year 1981.*

—— (1994a). *Baringo District Development Plan 1994–96.*

—— (1994b). *Kenya Population Census, 1989: Volume I* (Nairobi: Central Bureau of Statistics. Ministry of Planning and National Development).

—— (1998). *Baringo District Development Plan 1997–2001.*

—— (2001). *Kenya Population Census, 1999: Volume I* (Nairobi: Central Bureau of Statistics, Ministry of Planning and National Development).

—— (2008). *East Pokot Development Plan 2008–2012.*

—— (2009). *Census vol. II Q 11: Livestock Population by Type and District – 2009.* Available at: www.opendata.go.ke/datasets/7acafcec6b2d41e990c200db b045768b [Accessed 18 September 2014].

—— (2010). *The 2009 Kenya Population and Housing Census. Vol. I* (Kenya National Bureau of Statistics. Ministry of State for Planning, National Development and Vision 2030)

—— (2011). *Annual Report 2011. East Pokot District.*

—— (2012a). *Land Registration Act.* Available at: http://extwprlegs1.fao.org/docs/ pdf/ken112133a.pdf [Accessed 30 April 2021].

—— (2012b). *The Land Act.* Available at: http://www.parliament.go.ke/sites/ default/files/2017-05/LandAct2012.pdf [Accessed 30 April 2021].

—— (2016). *The Community Land Act.* Available at: http://kenyalaw.org/kl/ fileadmin/pdfdownloads/Acts/CommunityLandAct_27of2016.pdf [Accessed 6 May 2021].

—— (2019). *2019 Kenya Population and Housing Census: Volume II: Distribution of Population by Administrative Units.* Available at: http://housingfinanceafrica. org/app/uploads/VOLUME-II-KPHC-2019.pdf [Accessed 19 May 2021].

—— (2020a). *Distribution of Livestock Population by Type, Fish Ponds and Fish Cages by County and Sub County 2019 Census Volume IV.*

—— (2020b). 'Gazette Notice No. 4571', The Kenya Gazette, 3 July. Available at: https://gazettes.africa/archive/ke/2020/ke-government-gazette-dated-2020-07-03-no-128.pdf [Accessed 5 May 2020].

Other reports and manuscript sources

Bollig, M. (1988). *Paka Besteigung: Eindrücke vom Weg. November 29th, 1988,* unpublished manuscript (Fieldnotes. Mat 5).

Catholic Diocese of Nakuru (1980). *East Pokot Agricultural Project: Progress Report, 1978–1980.*

—— (1994). *Baringo Community Development Programme: Phase One (1986–1989) Final Report.*

Full Gospel Churches of Kenya (1991). *Kapeddo Health Care and School Projects 1964–1991.*

Reckers, U. (1989). *Land Potential in Nginyang Division: The Interface between Land Use Pattern and Ecology* (Kositei: Kenya Freedom from Hunger Council Report).

—— (1990). *The Potential of Nginyang division. Second report* (Bonn: Deutsche Welthungerhilfe).

SALTLICK (1991). *A Report on a Baseline Data Survey in the Nginyang and Tangulbei Divisions of Baringo District Kenya*, Food Security Programme (Isiolo: Kenya Freedom from Hunger Council).

UNESCO (1987). *Kenya Rural Press Extension Project. District Cultural and Socio-Economic Profiles: Baringo District.*

—— (2013). *Safeguarding Intangible Cultural Heritage: Traditional Foodways of the East Pokot Community of Kenya* (Nairobi: Digital Process Works).

World Bank (1990).*Project Completion Report. Kenya. Baringo Pilot Semi-Arid Areas Project.*

Newspapers

Kagwanja, P. (2014). 'Cutting Bullet Supply Key to Draining Swamps in the North Rift of Lawlessness' (Nairobi: *Daily Nation*, 11 September 2014).

Kariuki, N. (2015). 'Baringo County Conflicts. Why Peace Remains a Pipe Dream: The Government has Abandoned us, so we Resort to Self-Defence' (Nairobi: *Daily Nation*, 8 November 2015).

Kipsang, W. (2015). 'Bandit Raids Push 10,000 out of School in Baringo' (Nairobi: *Daily Nation*, 18 March 2015).

Koech, F. (2017a). 'Police Investigating Killing of MCA, Parliamentary Aspirant' (Nairobi: *Daily Nation*, 18 February).

—— (2017b). 'Bandit Attacks Force Hundreds to Flee Homes in Baringo' (Nairobi: *Daily Nation*, 22 February).

—— (2017c). 'William Ruto Orders Police to Shoot, Kill Bandits on Sight' (Nairobi: *Daily Nation*, 24 February).

—— (2017d). 'Missing Baringo MCA Thomas Minito Killed' (Nairobi: *Daily Nation*, 19 May).

Lomorita, J. (2017). 'Police Seem Overwhelmed by Insecurity in Baringo' (Nairobi: *Daily Nation*, 16 March).

Macharia, L. (2021). 'North Rift Faces Lockdown in Harsh Security Crackdown: Dusk-to-Dawn Curfew in Iron-Fisted Security Operation after Kapedo Failed to Wipe out Criminal Gangs, Bandits' (Nairobi: *The Star*, 2021). Available at: www.the-star.co.ke/counties/rift-valley/2021-04-06-north-rift-faces-lockdown-in-harsh-security-crackdown [Accessed 6 May 2021].

Munyeki, J. (2017). 'Hundreds of Cattle Killed in Police Operation in Laikipia' (Nairobi: *The Standard*). Available at: www.standardmedia.co.ke/article/2001259299/hundreds-of-cattle-killed-in-police-operation-in-laikipia [Accessed 23 May 2018].

Mwangi, W. (2017). 'Anarchy Fears as Samburu, Pokot Gunmen Surround Laikipia Farms' (Nairobi: *The Star*, 14 January).

Theses

Du Plessis, L. (2005). *The Culture and Environmental Ethic of the Pokot People of Laikipia, Kenya* (University of Stellenbosch). Available at: http://scholar.sun.ac.za/bitstream/handle/10019.1/2392/duplessis_culture_2005.pdf [Accessed 23 May 2018].

Mwaka, I. (2014). *Bee-Keeping and Honey Production as Alternative Livelihood Strategies among the Pokot of Baringo County, Kenya* (Cologne: Culture and Environment in Africa Series), 4.

Conference proceedings

Becker, A. (2014). 'The Vicious Circle of Brewing: Transitioning Livelihoods and the Emergence of New Gender Relations in East Pokot', Workshop paper: *Social-Ecological Transitions, Exchange and Emergence: Resilience and Vulnerability in the Wider Baringo Basin and Adjoining Highlands*, 1 September 2014.

Westley, S.B. (1977). *East African Pastoralism: Anthropological Perspectives and Development Needs: Papers Presented at the Conference, Nairobi, Kenya, 22–26 August 1977*, International Livestock Centre for Africa.

Online sources

Ansoms, A. (2010). 'The Story Behind the Findings: Ethical and Emotional Challenges of Field Research in Conflict-Prone Environments', University of Antwerp. Available at: http://conflictfieldresearch.colgate.edu/wp-content/uploads/2015/02/Ethical_Emotional_Challenges.pdf [Accessed 18 May 2021].

Barrow, E.G. (1988). 'Trees and Pastoralists: The Case of the Pokot and Turkana', Social Forestry Network. Available at: www.odi.org/sites/odi.org.uk/files/odi-assets/publications-opinion-files/936.pdf [Accessed 14 August 2020].

Basukala, A.K., Vehrs, H.-P., Bollig, M., Greiner, C. & Thonfeld, F. (2019a). 'Dataset: Spatial-Temporal Analysis of Land-Use and Land-Cover Change in East Pokot, Kenya'. CRC/TRR228 Database (TRR228DB), DOI: 10.5880/TRR228DB.1

—— (2019b). 'Spatial-Temporal Analysis of Land-Use and Land-Cover Change in East Pokot, Kenya'. Documentation, CRC/TRR228 Database (TRR228DB), DOI: 10.5880/TRR228DB.2

Behnke, R. & Muthami, D. (2011). 'The Contribution of Livestock to the Kenyan Economy', IGAD LPI Working Paper. Available at: https://cgspace.cgiar.org/bitstream/handle/10568/24972/IGAD_LPI_WP_03-11.pdf [Accessed 21 May 2018].

Crumley, C.L. (2003). 'Historical Ecology: Integrated Thinking at Multiple Temporal and Spatial Scales' (Lund University). Available at: http://citeseerx.ist.psu.edu/viewdoc/download?doi=10.1.1.554.2791&rep=rep1&type=pdf [Accessed 23 April 2021].

Desert Rose Ministries (2018a). 'East Pokot Project'. Available at: http://desertroseministries.com/pokot [Accessed 23 March 2018].

—— (2018b). 'Latest News'. Available at: http://desertroseministries.com/news [Accessed 23 March 2018].

Drew, J. (2018). 'Pastoralism in the Shadow of a Windfarm: An Ethnography of People, Places and Belonging in Northern Kenya' (University of Sussex). Available at: http://sro.sussex.ac.uk/id/eprint/74127 [Accessed 23 May 2018].

GDC – Geothermal Development Company Limited (2017). 'Baringo-Silali Project'. Available at: www.gdc.co.ke/baringo.php [Accessed 5 August 2018].

—— (2020). 'Who We Are'. Available at: www.gdc.co.ke/about_us.php [Accessed 13 October 2020].

Klein, H. (2002). 'Biological Control of Legumes (Family Fabaceae) of American Origin: Prosopis Seed Beetles (*Algarobius prosopis* and *Neltumius arizonensis*)'. ARC-Plant Protection Research Institute. Available at: www.arc.agric. za/arc-ppri/Leaflets%20Library/Prosopis%20seed%20beetles.pdf [Accessed 18 May 2021].

Lind, J. (2017a). 'Building Peace in the New Oil Frontiers of Northern Kenya'. Available at: https://opendocs.ids.ac.uk/opendocs/bitstream/ handle/123456789/13644/ResearchImpact_OilKenya_Online.pdf [Accessed 17 May 2018].

—— (2017b). 'Governing Black Gold: Lessons from Oil Finds in Turkana, Kenya', IDS and Saferworld. Available at: https://opendocs.ids.ac.uk/opendocs/ handle/20.500.12413/13279 [Accessed 16 October 2020].

Manji, A. (2015). 'Whose Land Is It Anyway? The Failure of Land Law Reform in Kenya', Africa Research Institute. Available at: www.africaresearchinstitute. org/newsite/publications/whose-land-is-it-anyway [Accessed 30 April 2021].

Matwetwe, H. (2017). 'A Study of the Pokot Cultural Worldview: Missiological Implications for Seventh-Day Adventist Witness Among the Pastoral Nomads of Kenya', Dissertation. Available at: https://digitalcommons.andrews.edu/ dissertations/1643 [Accessed 4 August 2020].

Mwangi, E. & Swallow, B. (2005). 'Invasion of *Prosopis juliflora* and Local Livelihoods: Case Study from the Lake Baringo Area of Kenya', World Agroforestry Centre. Available at: www.worldagroforestry.org/downloads/ Publications/PDFS/WP13657.pdf [Accessed 18 May 2021].

Ngugi, P.K. (2012). 'Kenya's Plans for Geothermal Development – A Giant Step Forward for Geothermal', Nairobi. Available at: https://orkustofnun.is/gogn/ unu-gtp-sc/UNU-GTP-SC-14-03.pdf [Accessed 20 April 2018].

Nshakira-Rukundo, E., Greven, D., Tabe-Ojong, M.P., JR., Bollig, M., Börner, J., Dannenberg, P., Greiner, C. & Heckelei, T. (2021). 'Collaborative Research Centre 228: Future Rural Africa: Baseline Household Survey (2019) – Kenya'. CRC/TRR228. Available at: www.trr228db.uni-koeln.de/DOI/doi.php?doiID=7 [Accessed 24 December 2021].

Pleistocene Park (2018). 'Pleistocene Park: Restoration of the Mammoth Steppe Ecosystem – Scientific Background'. Available at: www.pleistocenepark.ru/ en/background [Accessed 19 April 2018].

Schade, J. (2017). 'Kenya "Olkaria IV" Case Study Report: Human Rights Analysis of the Resettlement Process'. Available at: www.unibielefeld.de/fakultaeten/soziologie/fakultaet/arbeitsbereiche/ab6/ag_faist/downloads/WP_151.pdf [Accessed 14 December 2020].

Sitole, D. (2016). 'Kenya: Innovation Solves Pastoralists' Problem after 70 Years'. Available at: www.africanewsagency.fr/2016/12/12/kenya-innovation-solves-pastoralists-problem-after-70-years/?lang=en [Accessed 30 April 2018].

Smith, K. & Little, P.D. (2002). 'Understanding Community Perceptions of Livelihoods, Assets, and Recovery Strategies: Preliminary Findings from Northern Kenya'. Available at: http://pdf.usaid.gov/pdf_docs/Pnade754.pdf [Accessed 21 August 2017].

Sortland, T.E. (2017). 'Samburu Youth Navigating Violent Terrains: Reconfiguring Samburu Masculinity in Northern Kenya'. Available at: https://bora.uib.no/bora-xmlui/handle/1956/16125 [Accessed 15 December 2021].

Wetang'ula, G. (2017). 'Environmental and Socioeconomic Baseline Studies for Geothermal Development – with Example from Silali Geothermal Prospect'. Available at: http://theargeo.org/agid/reports/0108A%20EnvironmentalBaselineStudiesGW1701.pdf [Accessed 19 May 2021].

World Bank (2020). 'Population Growth (annual %)'. Available at: http://api.worldbank.org/v2/en/indicator/SP.POP.GROW?downloadformat=excel [Accessed 19 May 2021].

—— (2021). 'Fertility Rate, Total (Births per Woman) – Kenya'. Available at: https://data.worldbank.org/indicator/SP.DYN.TFRT.IN?locations=KE [Accessed 27 April 2021].

Multimedia

Davidson, B. (1984). 'Africa: A Voyage of Discovery with Basil Davidson: Episode 2: Mastering a Continent', film directed by B. Davidson.

DIVA-GIS (2020). 'Free Spatial Data'. Available at: www.diva-gis.org/gdata [Accessed 7 October 2020].

QGIS (2021). Geographic Information System, Open Source Geospatial Foundation Project. Computer software. Available at: http://qgis.osgeo.org [Accessed 7 October 2020].

USGS (2006). Earth Explorer. Available at: https://earthexplorer.usgs.gov [Accessed 19 May 2021].

Foreign-language works

Bollig, M. (1990a). 'Der Kampf um Federn und Farben – Promotion von Altersgruppen bei den Pokot Ost-Kenias', in G. Völger and K.v. Welck (eds), *Männerbande, Männerbünde - zur Rolle des Mannes im Kulturvergleich* (Cologne: Rautenstrauch-Joest-Museum), 259–66.

—— (1992a). *Die Krieger der gelben Gewehre: Intra- und interethnische Konfliktaustragung bei den Pokot Nordwestkenias* (Muenster: Lit).

—— (1996). 'Krieger und Waffenschieber in der ostafrikanischen Savanne', in E. Orywal, A. Rao & M. Bollig (eds), *Krieg und Kampf: Die Gewalt in unseren Köpfen* (Berlin: Reimer) 147–56.

Girel, J. (2006). 'Quand le passé éclaire le présent: Écologie et histoire du paysage', *Géocarrefour,* 81(4), 249–64.

Gissibl, B. (2011). 'Das kolonisierte Tier: Zur Ökologie der Kontaktzonen des deutschen Kolonialismus', *WERKSTATTGeschichte,* 56, 7–28.

Klingspor, P. (1909). *Britisch-Ostafrika, nach seiner Geschichte Natur und*

Entwickelung unter englischer Herrschaft (Bonn: Kunstdruckerei Broch & Schwarzinger).

Ludwig, C. (1985). *Zur Chemie und Pharmakologie der Saponine aus* Dodonaea viscosa *(L.) Jacq. und* Schefflera venulosa *(Wight et Arn.) Harms* (München: Dissertation).

Oesterle, M. (2007). *Innovation und Transformation bei den pastoralnomadischen Pokot (East Pokot, Kenia)*. Dissertation. Available at: http://kups.ub.uni-koeln.de/2327 [Accessed 23 March 2016].

Seidler, A. (2016). 'Sámuel Teleki und Ludwig Höhnel in Ostafrika: Analyse eines Reiseberichtes', in J. Nyerges, A. Verók & E. Zvara (eds), *MONOKgraphia. Tanulmányok Monok István 60. születésnapjára* (Budapest: Kossuth kiadó), 620–29.

Spittler, G. (2001). 'Teilnehmende Beobachtung als dichte Teilnahme', *Zeitschrift für Ethnologie*, 126, 1–25.

INDEX

Page numbers in **bold** refer to pages containing illustrations or tables.

Future Rural Africa

* Forthcoming

www.ingramcontent.com/pod-product-compliance
Lightning Source LLC
Chambersburg PA
CBHW051959270326
41929CB00015B/2709